MW00697707

SUFISM
AS THERAPY

Omar
Ali-Shah

TRACTUS BOOKS

Edited by Augy Hayter from tape recordings

Copyright ©1995 by Tractus and Omar Ali-Shah

All rights reserved. No part of this book may be repro-
duced or utilized in any form or by any means, electronic
or mechanical including photocopying, recording, or by
any information storage and retrieval system, without
permission in writing from the the author or publisher.

*"La loi du 11 mars 1957 n'autorisant, aux termes des alinéas
2 et 3 de l'article 41, d'une part, que les "copies ou reproduc-
tions strictement reservées à l'usage privée du copiste et non
destinées a une utilisation collective" et, d'autre part, que les
analyses et les courtes citations dans un but d'exemple et
d'illustration," toute representation ou reproduction intégrale
ou partielle fait sans le consentement et l'auteur ou de ses
ayants droits ou ayant cause, est illicite" (alinéa ler de l'article
40). "Cette représentation ou reproduction, par quelque procédé
que ce soit, constituerait une contrefaçon sanctionnée par les
articles 425 et suivants du Code Pénal."*

Front cover by Graphics Group / France

ISBN 2 - 909347 - 03 - X

Tractus
P.O. Box 6777
Reno, Nevada 89513 USA
Tel/Fax: (702) 345-7585
and
Tractus Books
43, rue de la Gaîté
75014 Paris, France
Tel: (33-1) 40 47 63 63
Fax: (33-1) 44 07 12 07

SUFISM AS THERAPY

5. THT Congress, Mexico City October 1986

6. THT Congress, Serra Negra, Brazil March 31 to April 8, 1990

INTRODUCTION

To understand this book, I think it would be useful to state the context in which these talks were given to therapists of different nationalities and specializations by Agha, the Sayed Omar Ali-Shah, Naqshband Ibn Hashemi. As a common bond, these therapists, who embrace all of the medical, paramedical and therapeutic professions, are students of the Sufi Tradition in which Agha is our teacher.

Agha began delivering formal talks to therapists and doctors in Segovia, Spain in 1985, following questions which had been put to him in Turkey in 1982 by a number of mostly psychological therapists who, having a healthy modesty about the quality of their therapeutic performance, wanted to know if the Sufi Tradition could provide some technical input for its improvement.

Our Teacher therefore convened us in various congresses to meet with each other and share our knowledge, techniques and therapeutic abilities with our colleagues from different countries, so that eventually we might develop a common therapeutic ground based on the Sufi Tradition.

Most of us began by preparing impressive articles and papers modelled on our own past experience of international meetings in our professions. We were more interested in competing with and impressing each other, and in developing a power structure amongst ourselves (so common a trait with health-care givers) than in sharing our knowledge.

Our first session was tense. Representatives of different countries were named to coordinate work and a president elected of what was to become the International Association of Traditional Holistic Therapies (THT) that would develop and promote the "Granada Therapy", a working name which was proposed by Agha, using the pomegranate as symbol. The seeds of this fruit are part of the totality, yet each sac is separate and capable of generating other fruits.

The other symbolic significance of Granada for Sufis is that, historically, the city of Granada showed us what was possible when the Christian, Jewish and Islamic cultures, so different and so alike, lived and shared with each other. Together they developed one of the high points in the history of human civilizations, as well as also showing us what can happen later when one part forces itself upon the other. None of us had this in mind when we met, and had it not been for Agha's pointing this out, our Association would probably have declined in much the same way that science and culture did in Spain in the time of Ferdinand and Isabella.

Fortunately, Agha had taken this (and much more) into account, and some of his first interventions led us to look for a common ground between the different therapeutic approaches instead of emphasizing differences which can only generate competitiveness. Thus, his idea was that we focus on looking for those elements that are part of a patient's healing process, regardless of the techniques used.

It took us over four years to put this idea into practice. The second THT meeting took place in Mexico after a year. During the preceding year we had been working on the theme of stress management and how it affects different illnesses. Once again we had a series of papers, but this time they were all related to stress, from preventing it to its therapeutic management. At this point there was a greater feeling of collaboration, a greater desire to learn and much less competition between ourselves. We also started working in small groups, in which we would discuss the papers, share experiences and demonstrate our different therapeutic approaches and suggest alternative methods to lower stress.

As time went by, Agha increased his input to these sessions. At the meeting in Mexico, Agha's talks more and more suggested the direction in which the Granada Therapy would develop. He slowly introduced themes for us to reflect on and refine, such as clarifying our therapeutic intention each time we meet with the patient.

Our next meeting was in Agaete, Canary Islands. Perhaps because of geographical distance, fewer therapists were present. Agha, as is his way, surprised us all by introducing a very "unscientific" subject we had all systematically avoided dealing with, which was that of the "inner being", its meaning and its relationship to mental and physical health. Our understanding of this concept was that the inner being is a part of a person's makeup that defines us as humans and remains constantly unchanged.

This was a quantum leap for us, and in a way, our own minds were starting to work along some of the lines which the Granada Therapy was indicating. Our stumbling block was getting rid of our limited "scientific" frameworks in order to benefit from wider frameworks being proposed instead of being blinkered by them. It is rational frameworks like these that separate us from each other and prevent us from using other realities or dimensions we are aware of, but that we are forced to deny in academic circles because they are not measurable in conventional terms.

We felt liberated in this meeting, and we also felt more free to discuss our "non-objective" experiences between ourselves. We could talk of our subjective perceptions that can either aid or block the patient-therapist relationship, in spite of the technique utilized. We talked about various other aids such as ionization of the surrounding air, music, colours, artifacts and objects of the Tradition and the effects they might produce.

Between ourselves, we began to relate with each other on a more personal basis, rather than as technicians or as narrow therapeutic specialists. Our experiences led us to identify the common ground we had not realized we shared, and this brought us closer together.

The impact of this meeting was not just on a personal level, because the later transmission of information we had received to our colleagues that had been unable to attend had an amplifying effect. Even our offices started changing their aspect; various artifacts were added which reflected many of the ideas we had been discussing. We started discreetly adding calligraphies, diagrams and colours, which, aside from their own function vis-à-vis our clients, served as constant reminders to us of themes we had been working on such as stress, intention, inner being, and energy; thus preventing us from falling into the kind of automatic routines that can beset our profession.

The last two formal meetings of this therapeutic group took place place in Serra Negra, Brazil and at Montefiascone, in southern Italy. Here, Agha gave us more specific information about the Sufic concept of what might constitute the essence of the Granada Therapy. In these meetings, the efforts of the therapists were directed, in small discussion groups, towards assimilating and trying to find a way to apply and practice the body of intuition-based knowledge that Agha was communicating and that we were communicating as therapists, both for our own use as therapists and in order to communicate it onwards to our colleagues.

This book transcribes Agha's talks to us, during meetings that brought together anything between a dozen and hundreds of persons. It condenses several centuries of Sufi knowledge into a form that has been updated and adapted to the context of present-day medical knowledge and the circumstances of modern life. The clear and precise information and instruction contained in this book deals with what is at the core of all therapy, in its widest and purest sense.

The intention of these talks and this book is to complement common scientific knowledge, not to replace it. It is important to note that using these concepts contributes to already existing therapeutic techniques and knowledge without trying to replace modern medical technologies in any way, shape or form. They add to them a dimension of contact and energy which activates the individual's power to heal himself.

It is in this sense that the therapist, regardless of his specialty, works as a catalyst of the person's vital forces, which may have stopped working properly due to a lack of balance and contact with their own inner harmony.

This is not a new concept, but in modern times it has been to a great extent ignored by the medical professions. We have given ourselves divine attributes and have forgotten that our only power is that of awakening the healing qualities that the patient or client already possesses. The concept expressed here is that, due to the person's separating himself from a natural order (which some people may or may not call God), he or she has displaced a natural healing quality and has left the door open for illness to take them over.

The healing function described here consists in bringing a rational scientific training together with one's own more personal therapeutic ability when these are in harmony with the energy of the Tradition.

These talks are now available to the general public for the first time in book form. They are not like cooking recipes, but rather invite a deep and personal exercise of thought about oneself, and about the meaning of this body of information within the spiritual context of the Sufi Tradition. Nevertheless, we are also talking about its therapeutic use outside of the Sufi context, because the universal appeal of this book is the way in which one is invited to consider the human being's health and development as something which is wider and more complex than the pure physiology of the human body.

This book presents the human being as a totality within a larger and more complex totality that often escapes us due to our personal limitations and conditioning. Nevertheless, our intuition can recognize the various dimensions of this totality, develop a "feel" for it, and make contact with it in many ways.

We would hope that this book be helpful both in the diffusion of the Sufi teaching, and that these suggestions may begin to be used at the medical, curative and psychological level in all areas relating to health and human development.

As health professionals, we hope that the approach represented in these talks can contribute to an evaluation by the scientific community of its own limitations, and to a new openness when researching aspects of the human being and body that defy narrow measurement.

Anatolio Friedberg, Ph.D.

Mexico City, 1994

Founder and former President of the
Mexican Association of Family Therapists

Sufism as Therapy

DIALOGUE BETWEEN AGHA AND BRAZILIAN THERAPISTS
KILYOS, TURKEY - AUGUST 1982

QUESTIONS AND ANSWERS

Q : I have been working with the Fischer-Hoffmann system of therapy for five years. At first it was very strong and powerful for me, but now I feel myself losing interest, mainly because I have doubts about the importance of this technique. I ask myself: what am I doing with the persons? I feel that they open themselves to me very much after going through the initial therapy, but after some time they close themselves again. I feel the need of finding some guidelines for the future, and I feel I cannot do this by myself.

Since I am in the Tradition, what can I do to combine the two things, the Tradition and the therapy? Are there some guidelines you could give us for people who have done this therapy? That is my main question, other people can have others.

A : There are many techniques, but none of these techniques are completely successful. They can produce a temporary improvement, but after that, the person needs another orientation.

It is clear that there is no single technique for a psychologically disturbed person that can be used for every nature of psychosis, because it depends on the kind of psychosis involved, how deep it is, what its basis is, and other factors you know about already.

Why is this so? This happens, because in the West, even with all the modern technological advances, people don't really know what the brain is. So if you are working with something you don't know one hundred percent, your efforts will always be hesitant.

Personally, I think the most important way to treat a patient is to get to know him gradually and completely. It is not enough for people just to talk to you to help you to establish a picture of their problems or psychological condition, because obviously, if they are disturbed, they will hide one thing or exaggerate others.

At that point the picture you get is out of focus. If you then work on that picture or focus, on what basis are you working? On this or on that? You have to begin by saying: "I want to make a picture of this person." And then you ask yourself "In order to make it, what do I need? Let's say that I need "the colour of the eyes, the hair, the lips, the angle of the nose, the shape of the bones" in order to make this picture.

The patient or client doesn't have to tell you: "My hair is red" because you can already see its colour. If he wants to say "It is red" when it is black, you say "Okay, it's red" while still placing the right colour in your own mind's picture. So little by little, you come to know the person completely.

You get to know him with some detachment. You have to be able to look at him with a certain objectivity, because it might even be dangerous to get yourself too much involved with his or her problems. You simply get to know the person.

There is one thing you have to extract from the Tradition that doesn't exist in western psychotherapy, and you have to introduce it very carefully into your therapy, at the right moment and in the right quantity.

What is that magic ingredient? Does it exist in Freud, Jung, Adler, Reich or any other therapy? It doesn't, maybe because these people thought it wasn't important enough. They couldn't perceive any usefulness for this thing. Maybe they didn't know how to use it or perhaps they were afraid of it. It's a simple thing which is actually the difference between life and death: it's a quality called love.

In none of the therapies in the West do you ever find some indication of the how and why or use of love. I don't know why such an important component was left aside. I think it's due to the fact that it can't be scientifically controlled: they cannot turn it into their slave. Since you cannot use it incorrectly, people would have to use it correctly or not use it at all. So they decided not to use it.

I think the basis of any therapy at all is 50% love and 50% understanding of the person. If you put those two ingredients together, you will automatically develop a sound attitude and technique towards the person and towards his or her problems. For me, this love is the absent factor in western psychological thought.

If you include it, you will be able to make it work for you and for the client. By this, I mean that you can in fact use it, by saying to yourself "Yes I can do it"; if only because I am saying to you that you can.

Since the Tradition is not a democracy, I am able to say this. Love is something that either works or doesn't.

Q : How can we get to know a person?

A : You begin by using the classical kind of psychological or psychiatric interview, in other words the semi-medical situation. The person is lying there, someone is taking notes, and the questions you need to put should be changed in their shape so they can be accepted by the person as conversation. This means you can meet your clients in a restaurant, a coffee shop, or in a night-club. You can walk with them by the river and talk. It is a good idea to begin by breaking the classical situation of white jacket, stethoscope and writing pad.

Secondly, after talking with them, find some topics about which you can both talk; it may be hunting, fishing, books, travel or anything at all. Let them talk about those subjects.

Afterwards, enhance your own enthusiasm about the subject, talking a lot about it, taking them to whatever point you want, in order to fill in the gaps in your picture. Part of your ability must be how you do this, how you lead them. By those means, you get at their picture and complete it.

Then you think: "This or that area is still blank"; you then mobilize the enthusiasm of your client for fishing or whatever else you are talking about, leading him towards the gaps.

It may take you several different efforts to fill in those gaps, so do not expect to arrive there suddenly, by a jump. A restraint or shutting down on the part of the person may occur, and if he notices you are taking him to that area, it may produce a negative effect. He may then retract himself, and if you notice any symptom of closing on his part, leave the subject aside and try it again later, in some other place or in a different context.

Again, that is the only way to do it. There is no fast way of filling in this picture. But I repeat, this picture is drawn objectively, by keeping a distance, and not subjectively.

Q : Knowing how to carry out our therapy technique is very important. We were trained to do it and we have been successful, because the technique is very powerful, but my problem now is to carry the therapy forward with the person after they have successfully finished the initial part of their therapy. They have newly-open hearts and want something more: what can one do with them?

A : You can't decide 100% that this person has finished the therapy.

Q : As far as the technique goes?

A : As far as the technique goes, you can apply something new. If you conclude that the technique has reached a point where you can stop, obviously you will not simply abandon the person. What you have to do is keep in touch. Then you have to give them something else.

Q : That's the point.

A : Well, I know what I would give them, it would be the Sufi Tradition, but sometimes it's hard to do because their various conditionings make it difficult. The religious, social, sexual, political, economical or any other conditionings make it difficult for them to begin studies in the Tradition at the point from which they should be starting. I would tell them this in any way I can.

Actually, I don't know of any better thing to help them. Which means this: if I apply a little thought, I can change a fuse, fix a tyre, command an army division or teach the Tradition. So my abilities are limited.

What I would suggest is the following: as Miguel did in Argentina, perhaps you can translate a book of the Tradition into Portuguese and give it to be read by people. You can also, as some people do in the West, place them in the hands of the Church. If that produces a deep and constant effect on them, why not?

Q : I am going to ask you a wide personal question. I have been trying for three years to write you a letter to get an answer to a question I will put to you now. I am a psychiatrist and I do my work in an efficient way, but I don't find happiness inside myself doing my work. That is my only question, and I would like to have your help.

A : Well, my help is always available, and if you couldn't write to me for three years, I can give you a stamp if you want, as long as the letter is not written in Portuguese.

I think that any dissatisfaction you have in your work is understandable. This is perhaps because you criticize yourself, and from your own critical point of view, your work is not good enough.

So I suggest to you that you introduce some things from the Tradition into your work and, as far as possible, into your treatment, and I believe you'll get more satisfaction because you will have better action and a bigger percentage of success than is the case now.

But don't wait three years to write me, because remember, a letter takes less than three weeks to arrive, so it will take three years and three weeks for each letter to get to me, and I can become neurotic waiting for it.

Q : You know Agha, one thing. I myself have solved my own problem about working with my therapy and being in the Tradition, but I am sure that sometimes there have been delicate situations involving using elements of the Tradition in our work. From what you say, I think one can wrongly use elements of the Tradition in what we do. How can they be introduced?

A : You introduce them through publications, through old stories of the Tradition such as the Nasrudin tales, and through other people. Or else you use what you have learnt from the Tradition in your work.

I can't tell you to do things you don't know how to do. If you know a subject well, you change it into a familiar and useful tool, and you can use it as you feel, gently or sternly. I repeat again, you have to evaluate the person and you have to judge his capacity to use the information you are giving him, so that there is a feedback to you. If I want to tell you something, I can tell you, but you have to understand it first before passing it on, otherwise it is lack of responsibility.

Q : I'm coming to the conclusion that my work and my development in the Tradition are the same thing.

Q : When I use my own connection with the Tradition with a patient, could the fact that I am taking into consideration my own expectations be damaging for the patient?

A : It depends on your intention. If your intention is really and truly to help the patient and, through this help, to learn a little bit more for yourself, by no means will this be damaging to the patient.

As I have said, you cannot damage a patient by misusing something from the Tradition, but you can certainly make him confused when you use something from the Tradition that is not really familiar to you. Nevertheless, you still do not damage him.

Q : Is there any specific knowledge in the Tradition we could think about and use with the patient? I received one indication, which was to work with sounds and colours with my patients, but I don't know where to look for that kind of material, neither with whom. How does one look for material of the Tradition that is not part of the general information we all receive?

A : There are no specific works designed for this purpose. Masters of the Tradition who studied questions concerning psychological disturbances and illness used, and still use, music, colours and zikrs.

I will send you some colour patterns and some music that can be useful, and you can also use the zikr in such a way that when you have a therapeutic situation with a person coming up, you do your personal zikr for 15 minutes before the meeting. This will increase your energy and programme you to communicate with the person at a deeper level.

So, I will send you this material three years from now.

Q : Please, not three years; three months.

Q : Three days?

A : One month.

Q : Was that a personal indication or can we all of us use this material?

A : It's for everybody.

Q : Is it possible to get to know the human brain completely?

A : Yes.

Q : But if it's not available in western knowledge, how can we know it? Can we learn it?

A : You can learn it, but I'm not going to teach you. The responsibility is very great, the load is very heavy, and it is very dangerous.

Those who know the functioning of the human brain have a great responsibility, because it is an area of great danger where mistakes are not allowed.

Q : Is it useful or worthwhile to undertake therapy in spite of us not having this knowledge?

A : Yes. You don't have to know everything completely. If you know a little and use this little gently, you can produce useful results.

Look, if you knew the complete functioning of the human brain, it means that you would know the secrets of life and death, and those are secrets that are very heavy to carry.

Do you know why everybody has this mark under the nose? Fariduddin Attar explains it to us, and I am not arguing with Attar. The story is: before a baby is born, he knows all the secrets of life and death, and as soon as he is born an angel places its finger there.

Q : I have two questions. Agha, you have said that no therapy is complete, yet there are some therapies that do mention the word "cure". Nevertheless we do have problems with the persons when they finish them. My question is: when people finish a therapy like this, should we accept the idea of cure or should we insist that the patient go on working with what we have to give him?

A : It depends on the individual patient. If that individual patient is convinced he is cured, you tell him: "You are cured and I don't want to see you again." If however, there is a little doubt, again it depends on your knowledge about the patient, you can suggest that he continue with some directed reading that could be, depending on your decision, from the Tradition. But making that suggestion to the patient is a personal decision of the therapist.

Q : The other question is similar but it concerns people who are already in the Tradition. What does one do with them?

A : The answer is evident. They do the therapy and go on with their studies in the Tradition.

Q : If friends of the Tradition do ask for assistance in receiving another therapy after they have gone through the basic therapy, because they still have emotional conflicts, should the therapist indicate some continuation?

A : He should indicate the continuation of their work in the Tradition because, as a solution, I prefer the Tradition to any therapy. In the Tradition we already have everything. By this I mean that I don't think I would apply therapy to the group. But then, I am old-fashioned.

Q : One question concerning body-oriented therapy. I feel the Tradition does not give much importance to the body. What could you say about body therapy and bio-energetics? I work with these techniques.

A : The reason you don't find many works on body movement in the Tradition is because we are dealing with the generation and accumulation of energy, and since physical body work uses up energy, we tend to lessen the physical work.

Nevertheless there is nothing against the use of physical energy, be it as a treatment, be it in the form of posture or as a discipline of movement or dance.

People say it's possible to calculate the biorhythms of the body. I also think so, but I don't think it's very useful. I don't think it's bad or negative, and I don't think it's totally useless, but I don't think it is as important as some people say it is.

The body controls its own biorhythms. So what should be very carefully taught to the client is to use physical energy in physical situations, and the more valuable energy in deeper activities. Because that deep energy you produce is too valuable to be used in dance, movement or other physical activities.

For example, some of us who are old-fashioned think the zikr should be done silently, because we are so miserable that we need to preserve the least little portion of energy, and we think that in pronouncing the word, we are perhaps using this portion of energy to energize the throat and vocal cords to emit a sound. So why should we not hold that energy in by pronouncing the word inside? I mean, the difference is minimal.

Q : I have a personal question. Concerning the specific locations on the body and chakras, as the yogis say. I would like to ask about the Lataif. It is said they are not physical locations but at the same time, we receive indications about where to concentrate on, using the body. Is this a subtle way of using localized energy? How does it work? I mean, if it isn't a physical location, what is it? And why do we have to concentrate on a physical part of the body?

A : This is because those areas on which we concentrate are areas of energy recollection, and the energy is stored in physical locations, about which we don't talk, for the following reasons:

First, it's not necessary, since that energy is collected in the recollection-center, and it is transmitted to one of the physical centers according to its quality, so that you do not need to know where they are.

Secondly, you don't have to know where they are because you would make a big case of it. Suppose it's the cornea of my left eye, for example, it would then become something important: "Oh, the cornea of my left eye!"; and people would paint it gold or something; perhaps even take it out. So just do it and shut up. Democracy.

Q : For me, the most mysterious things in psychology are the dreams. Can I consider some kinds of dreams as a contact with another dimension?

A : No. From the point of view of the brain, physical sleep is a time in which blocks of cells that were exhausted or damaged are replaced, and of course, this also applies to physical activities which happen psychologically.

Q : You have sometimes said that some kinds of contemporary music can be dangerous. I would like to know what is the danger of such music. How can we distinguish between what is harmful and what is not?

A : Well, the simplest way is to hear it and observe oneself, and if you feel that tension is being created, it is probably dangerous. I'm not talking here about the kind of hits that make you stand up and dance, but only when you observe that there are small signs of tension.

In fact, the system generally identifies with or rejects the tone and the rhythm, and the general reaction is then one of hostility.

For instance, many of you here know that all of those sparkling strobe lights in discos are harmful: they spark according to the rhythm of the brain (68 cycles per second). It is equivalent to drinking a bottle of whisky: after a while, you feel smashed.

It's destructive; people know it and go on doing it. There is no control, no law forbidding it, and I think it's terrible.

Q : Many musicians are trying to create different kinds of music, but in my case, I have observed that I became used to a certain kind of music I listened to in my childhood, and when I listen to a different kind of music for the first time, the first reaction is to be astonished, and only afterwards do I get used to the new music.

I would like to know whether it usually happens or if it could be dangerous to the ear, particularly with the new kind of music after Stravinsky?

A : Yes. This really can be a destructive thing. When people are hit with more and more volume on the inner ear, which is delicate, it becomes dampened when they get older. There is nothing that can be done concerning it, but fortunately, the impact of the sound is monitored and filtered internally, and it's not allowed to arrive at the delicate areas where it could be destructive. So you listen, but do not be afraid of it.

This leads me to another point that I am sure those of you who work in psychology and psychiatry come across. Very frequently, one of the bases of a neurosis is fear.

This fear is something very real for some persons. You can't tell them: "What are you afraid of? There is no reason"; because for them it's something real and concrete.

I have two stories about fear. One of them is an old story by Solomon Schwartz and the other is mine. He said: "Fear knocked at the door. Faith opened it, and didn't find anything."

On one of those sorts of nights, my children Amina and Arif were crying in their bedroom, and I asked them: "What is happening?"

"There is a wolf in the garden," they said, and to them, it was real.

So I told them: "All right, I don't like to have wolves in the garden, that's deplorable. Put on your dressing-gowns and I will take a flashlight and a gun, and we are going to go to the garden together and we will look under each bush and around each tree, and if the wolf is there, I will shoot."

I would say to Arif or Amina: "Is there any place we should look at?"; and they would say: "How about those trees, let's take a look".

We'd look, and there was no wolf. So I said "The wolf is gone"; and the result was twofold: firstly, we looked for the wolf for about ten minutes and, as a result, the children had eight hours of sleep. Secondly, they knew that if the wolf were there, or a bear, or any other horrible thing, Daddy would take care of the situation.

But this kind of fear can become something quite real, and has to be dealt with very carefully and lessened. It needs to be delicately diluted and not just ignored by saying "What do you mean, fear, there is no reason for fear. Let's go into your problems now."

Q : Do you mean we mustn't contradict what the person is saying? That we must not go against what he is saying?

A : This is true, yes. If it exists for them, we have to accept it, in different ways. Such as looking with a flashlight and showing or convincing them that it doesn't exist.

A direct contradiction produces: "This person is not sympathetic; he doesn't understand me; how could he understand my problems if he doesn't understand this? If I'm afraid of crossing the street, I'll take a taxi."

You see, you can find a balance between first approving the person's fixation and then sabotaging it.

There is a very delicate way of doing it, and it is the only way it can be done: by means of observation and judgement of what you are doing, and seeing how it is working. If you are going too fast, slow down.

You see, if you establish a patient's picture, this picture must include the expressions produced by your client. If his pulse is beating normally, then it's all right and you come back to it. If the look is expressing something, or the mouth something else; all of these things are signals that you observe, and according to them, you go on, stop, or return to it later.

Q : Could you say something about essence?

A : Yes, I could talk a lot about essence, but your question is very wide.

Q : Some indications of how we can know when we are working with essence or with personality? I recognize that I have asked a very vague question. Three directions, please.

A : All right, three directions.

To begin with, basically, you are using the essence each time you are using any technique or any context of the Tradition. This is in the first place.

Secondly, you are working with the essence, if, before beginning anything, you invoke what we call a "Nyat" or intention. It means 10 or 15 minutes of zikr. If you concentrate yourself on receiving thehelp

help of the Tradition, then you will be using the essence.

The third and most difficult part is when you are treating someone or doing something and suddenly you have no idea of what to do. And then, without you really knowing it, it comes to you. That is the essence working. That's the third. Then there's the fourth, the fifth and the sixth, but let's wait until next year.

Q : This kind of thing has happened with me, since I have come into the Tradition. Suddenly things come to me, and often I tell things I never realized I knew, and that actually could help people.

A : That's because you read something, because you have gone somewhere, because you bought a tasbee, a rug, or an object of the Tradition, and at the moment you really need it, the energy of this thing comes to you.

Someone might say: "I read something and I don't understand it." That's all right, you don't understand it now, but when you have the necessity of understanding it, you will. It's like an investment.

Q : Agha, could the exercising of Rule number 9 (Ukufi Zamani, the time halt) be a way of getting closer to the essence? Of getting to know it in another way?

A : No, you only feel the presence of the essence and its deeper effect when you receive a feedback from the surface, an echo which says that the essence is working. But it's a very light echo, a very soft one.

The reason for all this is fairly obvious: you use the essence in deep centers of the body by charging and making use of that essence. If you bring that concentration of essence to the surface, to the level of your conscious mind, it will explode in the top of your head.

Q : Does the essence work in an unconscious way?

A : Yes.

Q : During my work, I feel my connection with the Tradition. Sometimes it is very present, but other times it is not present and the work becomes confused. How could I stabilize that connection, neither too much nor too little?

A : Take an interval of five minutes and bring the connection back.

And now, with your permission, I need to see my psychologist.

THT MEETING IN ARCOS DE LA FRONTERA. SPAIN
AUGUST 8, 1986

FORMULATING A GRENADA THERAPY

So far as I can see, I am quite satisfied with the communication and progress being made. I would like to see a little bit more coming out of South America; they have a habit of waiting until they have something really important before they send it out.

The theme of this meeting has been my talking on and on about communication. Communication is absolutely vital, especially in the area of science and therapy. If two or three people are studying along the same lines, they should obviously know about it and cooperate, otherwise it is a treble effort towards a target, rather than three efforts directed within the same thing.

Most of our friends will be aware of the fact that there is a publication coming out of Madrid, and if people don't have enough material to produce a publication by themselves, they could send papers to Madrid for publication. In regard to publication, my advice is to send them papers even if you get no reply, because you finally either encourage them to reply or shame them into replying.

Unfortunately, I don't think I will have the opportunity to go to the Girasol drug addiction therapy centre this time, but I do feel that the treatment and activities in Girasol should be given more and more publicity, and of course, what is being done in Girasol might very well be a model for other countries. I am sure you do this automatically, that is, keep a record of any technique or treatment you use and which is beneficial, in order to be able to exchange information with similar centers in other countries.

This is happening in other countries, of course. Anna recently pointed out to me that a Catholic priest started this sort of refuge for addicts, taking them in from the streets, and for two or three years he went about knocking on doors, begging and trying to raise money to feed and support them. Now he has got some sort of government recognition.

What I am saying, in a way, is not only can one develop what one might call a Girasol treatment, but one can also develop one inexpensive enough to be copied and used in less developed countries which have similar if not worse problems of drug addiction.

If it was possible, one could then define a reasonably inexpensive treatment and offer the presence of somebody to various countries in order to set it up with their resources.

This is not just a humanitarian gesture to the rest of mankind : there is a distinct drug problem in Europe. At the same time as one is trying to do something about the problem in Europe, it would be valuable for other governments, who either ignore or even get revenue from drugs, to treat their own addicts and make a sort of sanitary cordon around Europe.

This may be a Utopian idea, but the severity of the problem will eventually reach such proportions that something drastic will have to be done. When that point is reached, millions and millions of dollars and pounds will have to be spent.

You may say: "Yes we know this, tell us something new." At some time, at some point, the countries most affected must come together and look for some sort of internal solution. If one has a solution or even a possibility to offer them, then one could hopefully get some backing or establish other centres.

Any therapy of the sort practised at Girasol includes all aspects of therapy, from the physical to music, ionization, diet and all these things. But again, it should try to be as compact and concentrated as possible, so that it can become the basis of something that could be set up somewhere else, so that it could then expand without great difficulty or expense.

This idea is something apart from the Granada Therapy, which I hope everybody is working on. Of course, it can also be a part of the Granada Therapy, because the Granada Therapy will or can hopefully be used to handle different situations.

One thing I've been noticing more and more in papers and

magazines is the attention which is being given to questions of diet. You are all familiar with the great fashion for pure food which swept the United States a few years back, in which people ate only brown rice and ground their own flour or grew their own fruit because they were worried about phosphates and other things being used in the soil.

One way and another, manufacturers and farmers were forced to use less chemical fertilizers, although to my mind, they still use too much. But the present debate on diet I have been noticing deals with the question of food additives for preservation, coloring and taste, and as you all know, certain additives can provoke very severe reactions in some people.

Now why do I bring this particular thing up and what can one do? To begin with, if you buy something, it should say by regulation what additives are in it, and quite obviously one would try to not recommend products with certain additives. But it is one thing to avoid additives and another thing to balance the input of additives. This means that you try and avoid the ones which are more harmful, but since one inevitably eats a certain amount of them, the diet should be modified to compensate for or cancel out those noxious additives.

I am not telling you your business because this is a medical question, but one does see certain additives producing certain symptoms which might be identified as the absence of certain vitamins or a bodily malfunction. It is therefore a thing to watch out for without becoming preoccupied with it, and it certainly is important in a situation like Girasol.

I don't really have anything else to say except to encourage you to communicate between yourselves to the maximum possible extent and exchange ideas, however impractical they might seem. An idea which might be impractical here might easily be practical and useful in another place, so keep communication, the production and exchange of ideas to the maximum, and I will be very interested to see what happens.

Q : What do we do with emotions in a therapy situation, both as therapists and also as members of the Tradition in our groups? What about in general conditions amongst friends?

A : These are two separate questions and they have completely different answers.

The way you handle emotions in a therapy situation is different, because it usually involves a person or patient who is ill.

The contact or relationship between a therapist and a person who is ill creates a different emotion, because the intention of the therapist is to use the therapy to cure that person.

Between two people who are normally healthy, the particular energy of curing is not present. The question of what to do about emotions between people in the group under normal circumstances is really too a big question. I would like to keep to the therapeutic aspect.

Emotion between a therapist and a patient has to be watched very carefully. You are all very aware of the dangers of over-identification with the patient. Certainly, you do identify with the patient during the therapy. You make clear and technical use of the maximum amount of conventional therapeutic techniques available to you.

In the Granada Therapy, you also introduce the energy of the Tradition as well as different techniques you may have discovered or heard about from other therapists. You are always in control of the situation: the situation does not control you.

You all know perfectly well, especially when dealing with mentally disturbed people, that if you are tense or nervous or in an emotional state, you can telegraph that to the patient. You must therefore always keep a certain technical detachment: you have to watch yourself as well as the patient.

Nevertheless, you can use a certain amount of calculated emotion. You might say that this is a contradiction in terms; it shouldn't be.

If you find a situation where you feel that there is a possibility of too much emotion, either detach totally or for a period of time. Never forget that patients, especially those with a psychological problem, will try and establish an emotional relationship with the therapist and they will use that emotional connection in order to abuse it.

A patient with psychological problems is usually enormously self-centered, selfish and preoccupied with themselves, and they can very easily become emotional vampires. Not only does that exhaust and knock out the therapist, but the patient will demand and want more and more from them.

So you can feel emotion, but you don't show it. You can control this emotion by keeping a slight distance, because you are aware of how much emotion you are feeling in a situation.

If you get into a situation where there is too much emotion, detach yourself from the patient and ask for help, use a zikr, use a repetition. Come out of it, and then go back.

This a technique which is in the Naqshbandi rules called the "stop" or heart-halt. The "stop" is not a stop to breathing or a stop of thinking. Mind you, some of you stopped thinking years ago, but the question we are considering here is that the stop is to provide an opportunity to re-think and look at the situation very quickly, within seconds or in minutes.

The next question is: how does a therapist protect himself or herself against becoming a trash can for psychic garbage?

There are two simple ways.

Firstly, and this should become a practice every morning when you wake up: remind yourself that you are a person in the Tradition. Repeat to yourself what your intention is and why you are in the Tradition. Secondly, ask for help and energy and it will come, you will get it. There should be no fear of your becoming a trash can of psychic garbage unless you voluntarily take it on yourself and carry it about.

Q: In an interview, you talked about the dangers of bio-energetic gestalt techniques, saying that these methods could create artificial crises. Could you please make this clearer?

A : Any crisis in a patient which is provoked in a therapy situation, whether by chemical, psychological or electrical means, can of course be extremely dangerous. I personally am not in favour of precipitating that sort of psychic crisis.

The reason for this is that it is a question of the judgement of the therapist and such a judgement can be influenced by many factors. It can be based on the amount of time the therapy has taken. It can be based on observation of the patient and on the decision of the therapist.

I am totally against provoking crises of this type because I consider that there are other methods which produce a beneficial result without provoking such a crisis. Don't forget that some shock therapies can be irreversible. All of you have either seen, heard or read about the electro-convulsive incident shock. Any shock is a shock to system as a whole.

It is possible that a particular part of the system at that particular moment may be slightly weak. And while the outward evidence of the shock may be beneficial, there may be a deeper damage.

While dealing with that subject area of shock, I hope to talk a little bit more about this in Mexico in November, because I personally use shock all the time and people usually don't notice. The word or concept of shock is something I can and do use, but there are all the stages before that. Next question.

Q : What cures, what heals?

A : Really, what a question! I mean, a question like that is enormous. Look, I won't make a general statement. What cures, what heals? Ayy! Ouch! Okay, here is forty-five seconds worth:

Illness is not a normal state, but an imbalance somewhere in the system. Not everybody is born with a perfect system, but if they do live in a physically balanced way and they try and live in a psychically balanced way, any weakness that they might have been born with is usually repaired. The work of a therapist is to help the system repair itself and attain that balance.

Positive energy, positive action, positive intention cures and heals. The techniques or the medicines are and should be the instruments of that positivity.

Q : What are the limits of psychotherapy?

A: The patience of the therapist or the life of the patient.

The limits really are not defined because they exist individually, according to each individual.

The limitations a psychotherapist should impose on himself are slightly clearer. If, in relation to a particular patient, a psychotherapist finds himself in a curious area, which one might call being "lost" in the sense of being in a territory where he finds himself maybe feeling a little bit afraid; there is no particular measure for how a therapist feels. It is very much up to the individual therapist in the individual situation. One could say, again, watch yourself, don't go to far, don't push too hard.

Q : What type of energies exist and how can we work with them?

A : Oh, that's a global galactic question.

Q : Some of us have worked with different techniques like laying of the hands, mesmerism, techniques of reincarnation and spiritualistic approaches. Should we continue to work with that?

A : Reincarnation and spiritualistic approaches are not really useful and I would not encourage them to be used. There are more positive and more useful therapies to be used instead of those.

Q : How many different types of energies are there?

A : Well, when I stopped counting, the number I had got to was about one million seven hundred and eighty thousand and a few. That was when I was younger and used to collect things.

Q : How do you use the different energies?

A : If you are in tune and harmonize with the energy of the Tradition, you receive the different energies that you need and you pass them on by contact. If you are in tune with and harmonize with the energy of the Tradition, you will use these energies automatically (which is a word I don't like) or rather, naturally.

Again, what is most important when you are in a therapeutic situation, or even before you go into it, is that you affirm to yourself that you are in contact with the energy of the Tradition.

Q : What is a sane person? How do you define a sane person?

A : Opinions differ as to what a sane person is, and people use different measurements or justifications to point to what is sane and what is not.

Some people use curious methods or terms of reference to determine the degrees of sanity or insanity. Also, some people delude themselves as to the degree of their own sanity or that of other people. For example, I think I am sane but there are other people who don't think I am. But since all Afghans are insane by definition, there is no way of comparison.

Concerning what is healthy or unhealthy, as I said before, it is a question of a balanced state of health: a harmonious existence, harmonizing with the galactic totality.

There are some conventional tests to prove health or lack of health. Some of these measurements are precise and some are more or less arbitrary. One can measure blood pressure, temperature, rate of breathing, i.e., certain average measurements, but these measurements are subject to movement or fluctuation.

DIAGNOSIS

The most important thing in therapy is diagnosis, which is of course also the most difficult thing. If you know that a person is suffering from typhoid fever, anybody can look up a medical book and see what the treatment is, and the most important aspect of diagnosis is, of course, observation

You have blood tests, liver function tests, X-rays and all the technical examinations. Those tests will probably show you if there is a particular disease or condition. If such tests do not indicate something specific, a patient may be taken under observation for a time and talked with to establish whether there is some family or work problem or some other problem.

The period of observation consists of watching what they eat, how they sleep, so that the therapist builds up a picture of the person, and, putting it together with the technical tests, comes up with a diagnosis which shows what the person is probably suffering from, and perhaps what contributory factors from the home, family or work might help or create help.

You can observe different people in different situations. I'm not giving away my secrets when I say that if I look at a person, I look at the eyes, because of course, they say that the eyes are the doorway to the soul.

Maybe I look at their hands, and since I am a man, I probably look at her legs as well. The so-called American term of "body language", if it is observed carefully, can really communicate a lot of information to a therapist.

That is why the "assembly line" technique of dealing with patients doesn't work very well. It's all right if you know that person has come in to have another lot of tablets or medicines, but you need to spend a minimum time, both to talk with somebody and t o get them to talk.

You are looking for signs of tension, and also what type of tension is involved. You need time to look at that person because different people show tension in different ways. You talk with them, encourage them to talk a little and perhaps also you try and get them to laugh. The tone of laughter shows a great deal.

In successive visits, you see by visual scanning whether there is any change. If you have retained a mental picture of that person in your mind from the last time, you bring it out and compare it with the present situation, and you should be able to see any change very quickly.

It should be very swift, very quick, because you really don't have to go through a lengthy technique to do this. You start by looking at the hair, the ears, the eyes, the nose and the mouth and so on, doing a comparison of each piece before it fits, taking a total picture compared with the new picture.

And again, you make the audio comparison, the sound of their voice or the sound of their laughter.

Of course, that doesn't mean to say that you have to make people hysterical every time they come and see you.

THT CONGRESS, SEGOVIA, SPAIN
October 21 to 25, 1985

CONSTRUCTING A UNITED THERAPY

We have a common aim. An aim is essential, because it provides a focus for your research, for your attention and for your activity.

This factor is the theme of the conference: it is also a contributory factor to 85 % of the problems of the world, whether social, physical or economic. As a factor, it is becoming increasingly present in every human activity, to the point, unfortunately, of dominating many aspects of human activity.

It is not hidden, secret or extra-terrestrial; it is a factor which people know about and recognize, and they say that yes, it's unfortunate, but it exists and we have to accept it. My answer to that is that even though it exists, we do not accept it.

If we accept it, we are helping it to develop. Thus, if we accept it and then suffer from it, we are guilty as well. With your various therapeutic techniques, as well as using the tactics and techniques of the Tradition with the energy which can be made available to you, it is up to us to start constructing a single united therapy, now.

THE GRANADA THERAPY

All the various therapies you are representing here today should not be in competition with each other. They should not be contradictory, nor should they be in collision with each other. We must work out a coherent, cohesive therapy so that all aspects of human problems can be handled.

This may sound like a very ambitious idea. It sounds enormous. True, it is ambitious and enormous, but the factor we are setting out to conquer is also enormous. The theme of this congress, and the factor which we aim to conquer is tension, and we will do so.

As I say, we recognize the existence of tension in individuals, groups and society. Everybody is sorry about it, and various people have various ideas and tactics about how to deal with it. Very often their efforts are directed at the symptoms of tension and not at the cause. I say sometimes, not always.

What we must aim to do is to put together all the techniques and see how and on what level they relate to each other, how these relationships can be made stronger, and how this technique can then be used practically in everyday circumstances.

Up to the late Middle Ages and in Europe, until the arrival of the blessed Ferdinand and Isabella, a technique did exist. What we have to do is to take the basis of that therapy which existed before and update it to take into consideration other factors which have developed in our so-called "modern" civilization. This is the point at which techniques of the Tradition come together with contemporary therapies.

I must make this point again, and make it very clearly: there is no competition among us. There should be no contradiction. During these three days here, it is necessary for various therapists to talk with other therapists to see how they can establish this relationship and contact, and not just to demonstrate how clever and how efficient their own therapy is.

Let us take as a baseline that we all accept the validity of different therapies. Let us cooperate to take from our various therapies the direct instruments to build one single therapy. As is convenient and useful, this therapy should have a name. So according to my usual and familiar practice, I have democratically decided what this name is to be.

The name I have chosen is very evocative, not only from a sentimental point of view, but in terms of its positive values. It represents history, the Silsila, stability, unity, effort, and it also represents the Baraka. I suggest that we call this therapy the Granada therapy.

NASRUDIN AND THE PSYCHIATRIST

I'm going to tell a joke about psychiatrists. It appears that one day the great father of all psychotherapy, Nasrudin, was travelling in a neighboring country with his faithful donkey, and he went to the chief psychiatrist in that country and said: "I have a great problem."

So the psychiatrist took out his psychiatric spectacles and said to Nasrudin : "Right, what is the problem"? And Nasrudin said "Occasionally when I'm walking along I have a very strong fundamental pain."

So the psychiatrist said "Aha, yes of course". They talked for a half-hour, and the psychiatrist said: "Your problem is that you hate your mother. Go away and come back tomorrow."

Nasrudin was quite impressed with what the psychiatrist said, and since he was quite a simple fellow, he went to his mother and said: "Mother, I have been told that the problem of my fundamental pain is that I hate you." So his mother took a big stick and beat him up.

Nasrudin then went to his wife, and said: "I went to a psychiatrist and he said my mother is the problem and that's why I'm in pain, and then I went to my mother and explained to her that she was the cause of my fundamental pain because I hated her, and she beat me."

So his wife said: "Sometimes your mother has very good ideas" and beat him.

Nasrudin went back to the psychiatrist the next day and told him the story. And the psychiatrist was very happy and said: "Ah, how very interesting, not only is there the problem of the fundamental pain because you hate your mother, but you also have a persecution complex. Everybody's beating you. Come back tomorrow."

So Nasrudin went to his daughter and said: "You know, I have this very strong fundamental pain when I'm walking with my donkey, and I went to your grandmother and she beat me, I went to your mother and she beat me, and nothing has changed because I sometimes have to stay home because of the pain. Are you going to beat me, along with all the women in my family?"

The daughter thought a moment and said: "No, but I am going to give you some advice. Walk behind your donkey and not in front of it. Because when you are walking along thinking, the donkey is biting your fundamentals."

Now of course that is a highly esoteric and meaningful story. But it does show one factor, which is observation. Had the psychiatrist examined the fundamental aspects he would have found the significant factor.

So, anyway, let us concentrate on exchanging and maintaining such an exchange to work out a credible therapy. We know how tension is created, how it is maintained, we know what is meant by psychosomatic, and yet the majority of tensions in the world today are of human origin, which means that the solutions to the tensions of humanity are in the hands of humanity. If you can add the energy of the Tradition to that, you have an unbeatable formula.

I tell you this and I will guarantee it to you, but it requires a united and concerted effort, with the conviction that it can possibly work.

I can and will generate energy because it is my function to do so. You are also able to generate it as individuals and as groups. Put this energy to work and unite in effort. Don't indulge in competition or in contradiction: if you want to comment or criticize, do it in a constructive way. Criticism can be either constructive or destructive.

United effort has no collision factor. It can be done, but if people's effort is scattered or diffused, it can take longer. The Tradition wants and demands that this be done, because humanity needs this therapy,

Keep your target in mind; keep your intention clear and in front of you: that is what you have to do. Remember, with attention, not tension. You cannot teach unless you learn. If you say "I will teach you to relax" to somebody in a threatening way, it won't kill them but it will take five times as long.

COMPATIBILITY

You have to keep one factor in the forefront of your mind, which is also the theme of this conference, tension. The second thing you've got to keep simultaneously in your mind is: how can my particular therapy relate to another person's therapy?

Quite naturally and efficiently, you spent yesterday getting to know a bit more about techniques other people use, so that you can arrive at a preliminary decision on how an aspect of "my technique", together with the other's, will be compatible with another person's technique. The key word here is compatible. Some techniques can appear to be somewhat hostile to each other, but it is always possible to lower the particular level of a technique to find compatibility. After all, if all therapy is based on the same principle, which is to be beneficial to mankind, at some point or another they will have a common language.

If one or other therapist takes up a too-rigid or individualistic attitude, and considers their own technique as something rigidly formalized, the danger is that one could then formulate a single therapy consisting of individual semi-related parts. What we want is an integrated therapy.

One aims for a context in which all techniques are possible. They are not necessarily all applied simultaneously. For example, if you have a person who is in need of a surgical operation , you can arrange the operating room with certain beneficial colours. There's no conflict between the colour technician and the surgeon. You can have music in the operating theatre: there is no conflict between the surgeon, the colour technician and the musician.

A patient may need osteopathic treatment or massage: if, during the operation, the osteopath or masseur pushes aside the surgeon to massage the patient, this can cause friction between the surgeon and the osteopath, as well as being terminal for the patient.

If there is a function for a masseur or an osteopath for that patient, his function can be performed pre-surgically or post-surgically.

If a patient is in need of psychiatric treatment, this can take place either before the operation to de-tense the patient before the operation takes place, or after the operation to help recover from psychic shock. Once again, if the patient is being prepared psychologically before the operation, the psychiatric therapist is not pushed aside by the surgeon who wants to get hold of the patient.

Each area of therapy, the colour, the music, the surgical, the osteopathic or whatever, has its own type of function. It is not a competition, nor should it be. If a patient undergoes a surgery and is put into a positive environment afterwards for convalescence, this may have a marginally more important role to play. But this is not, or should not be, a source of friction or argument among the team. The priorities for the use of a technique in a sick person depend on the physical and mental state of that person.

Before any operation or treatment takes place there is and there should be a conference of the therapists involved in the overall treatment to decide the treatment priorities. If it is obvious that the person needs immediate surgery, as a result of the usual and correct medical tests, that immediately becomes the priority.

The other therapists then decide what the pre-operative and post-operative techniques should be. Either simultaneous colour, music and massage before the operation, then psychological, herbal, or other therapy to prepare the person physically and psychologically. There is no competition in the sense of "I want to get at that patient first." The well-being of the patient is the most important factor.

It is valuable for various therapists to talk with each other. Let's take the example of a surgeon talking with a colour therapist, music therapist or whatever. The surgeon could describe a classical surgical operation, with the pre-operative, operative, and post-operative phases. He can try and describe what he thinks the psychological or physical problems during those three periods could predictably be.

While he is describing that, it is possible for the therapist to consider at what stage he could possibly assist. Assist, not interfere. If the surgeon is expressing a feeling that the tension in a patient taking place during a particular phase, is, from his point of view, extreme, the therapist could then suggest using his technique to diminish the tension during that period.

The therapist cannot or should not tell the surgeon how to hold his knife or where to cut, but he can and should make suggestions which would help what one can call, in a certain situation, the prime therapist.

Of course, during a pre-operative stage, the prime therapist may be a herbalist, a masseuse, or any one of the therapies used to prepare the patient for the operation, physically and psychologically and also to prepare him or her for the post-operative stage. This technique is what, in the Tradition, we call "investment", in the sense that in the pre-operative stage one is treating certain symptoms which are present, and at the same time one is inserting some energy which will surface usefully either during the operation or in the post-operative stage.

In the surgical operative stage, the prime therapist or technician is the surgeon, with the backup of his surgical and nursing team, plus the energy which has been invested before. In the post-operative phase, the prime technician is the therapist who is principally involved in questions of physical post-operative shock or psychic shock.

Each prime technician is complementary to each other. There is no competition. The surgeon is not waiting there trying to get the patient onto the table. The post-operative therapists are not bashing on the door of the operating theatre to get the fellow into their hands. Otherwise you might have a situation which is called tension.

If the three stages are properly decided and each one is given a minimum time, there can be speed, not hurry or tension. Each stage is locked into the next stage.

In the Tradition, the development of a person is of a similar nature. A person develops to a certain level, and he or she doesn't take some sort of sudden jump into another level.

The levels of contact and development exist. As a person develops, the various levels have a greater contact with each other. There is no abrupt "staging" factor. One thing phases into another and there is a gradual perception of this development.

It is not a situation where somebody wakes up in the morning feeling "enormously developed" in comparison with yesterday. There is nothing against feeling marvellous in the morning; it depends what you ate the night before, when you went to bed, whether you dreamed or not.

It also depends on whether you wake up like somebody climbing through a well of treacle to get to the surface. In the morning, some people come to the surface sort of reluctantly. Some people wake up and are completely functional right away. From my personal point of view I think that people like that are horrible. That is a purely personal psychotic attitude I have: if I don't have adequate tea from the moment I wake up, take to the hills.

Today, each therapist or group of therapists will make a brief presentation of their form of therapy. Then I think it would be better to try and break up the groups of similar therapies and exchange with other types of therapists, comparing compatibility with each other. Listen to and be hospitable in your mind to other people's therapies.

We are among ourselves, and we are friends. We are not in competition with each other. We should not have the attitude of: "Although I am a therapist of such-and-such a type, I will listen to that other fellow."

Be open, and listen to other people's tactics and techniques. There is no question or danger here of compromise. Exchange of ideas, flexibility of attitude and unified intention is important, and we can produce some of it. If we maintain a rigid attitude, our own flexible response is lost.

ABSENCE OF ENERGY

Following your conversations, discourses, and exchange of ideas, information, and techniques, there is one other area that I would like to recommend to our attention. It's a factor which, in a person, may be what is called for the moment the absent factor.

From the point of view of the physical body, for instance with nourishment, we all know what can happen if there is a vital or other factor absent.

All therapists know in physical medicine or in the area of psychological medicine what a present factor is. Let us say that a present factor can be the presence of a micro-virus, an inflammation, or in psychological medicine, a fixation, a predisposition or something else of that nature.

What I'm asking you to consider now in your research is the introduction of a factor into the patient's state which is absent. The reasons for the absence of this factor can be many. I'm not going to talk very much about this factor, I'm just going to mention its importance in the context of the Tradition, and also in the context of physical and psychological balance, and therefore health.

This absent factor or element can conveniently be called energy. Everybody knows roughly what the context of energy is. We classify energy in the Tradition very carefully and distinctly, from the basic simple physical energy in its different forms, to the very pure and essential energy we use in the context of the Tradition.

Many of the Tradition specialists in therapies have held very strongly that the absence of the energy factor causes imbalance to the whole system. Absence creates and invites physical and mental disease, and psychological and psychotic conditions.

It can also be absent, although present, for instance, in an unactivated form. And as far as we are concerned in the Tradition, its complete absence, or presence in an unactivated form, is the same thing; because the action of supplying a particular energy to a person or activating the energy which is unactivated is a similar process.

Okay, so I'm not using another Machiavellian trick to disturb your theories and working-out. I'm merely putting this in as an additional aim, to fill possible gaps which may exist. I'm suggesting to you that if, as a result of your combined studies, there are still two or three questions which are not clearly resolved, think of the possibility of there being an absent factor.

This is not to give you an excuse of stopping short or really pushing your research, it is in fact to remove possible areas of confusion which can be explained by the existence of such absent factors.

So, if you didn't have enough complications in your researches to start with, here is another one. But there's nothing vague to worry about; if you worry about it, you know what it is you're worried about, and so do I.

TENSION IN BABIES

Finally, very shortly, I have just now had the first opportunity of reading a report which I received from a medical team in Mexico. This medical rescue team was a British army unit, trained in rescue and resuscitation work after natural disasters.

The report is quite large and I haven't yet read it all, but one factor was very interesting to me, and I will condense it for you. It's something which is very simple, very striking, and in a way, very astonishing. What I'm talking about is the extraordinary survival of extremely small babies who were buried under the ruins of Mexico City after the great earthquake.

As I say, I haven't read the whole report, but one of the initial conclusions is very interesting. Some people may say that this conclusion is simplistic, but I'll tell you what it is. It is that these babies were very tiny when they were trapped. They were so small that they didn't know that they were trapped; they had no tension factor in the sense that even if they were not happy, they had no conscious knowledge of how many hundreds or thousands of tons of masonry were on top of them.

To an older child or an older person, the psychological impact of being under thousands of tons of rubble can be catastrophic in itself. But these tiny babies had very recently gone through the traumatic experience of being born. In a physical sense, they were also depending on themselves. So it could be said, psychologically and physically, that they reverted a little.

So here's another question: was their survival a question of physical tenacity, or was it just the absence of a tension complex ?

WEAVING

In two years time from now ... don't think of this in terms of now, plus two years' time. Think also of what you are going to be doing in that time. A person making a carpet has a projected idea of what that carpet will finally look like, but during that time, he weaves. So weave.

I don't know about Spanish but in English the word "weave" can be interpreted in two ways. One is to weave like this (gesture of weaving carpet), and the other is to weave like this (staggers). We've had enough of this (staggers) so let us have more of that (weaving gesture).

PROLONGING LIFE

To get down to certain specific questions and answers, one question is: how can one live longer, prolong human life?

You can stop smoking, you can stop drinking, you can give up women. Will this prolong life? It will not make it actually longer, it will just seem that way.

IONIZATION

Regarding the effect, influence and use of ionization. For six months I have been testing different ionizers to see which basic model I can rearrange the circuit on to get the maximum output of ions.

The majority of ionizers manufactured in Europe and in America, measured from the point of view of the efficient output of negative ions, are unbelievably inefficient. Of the ones that I examined, fifty percent produce less ions that you would produce having a shower. The other ones produce a reasonably adequate amount of negative ions, but because of their circuitry and physical construction, the output falls off very abruptly.

Many of the companies making ionizers make them from a theoretical circuit diagram, and when they have made them, most of them have no way of measuring the output. Now this is both incredible and dishonest.

I narrowed my research down to one unit, the circuit of which could be modified so that the ion output could be kept at a specific level. With reasonable weekly cleanings it can be kept reasonably functional. It is small and convenient for travelling. From the point of view of electrical security, for instance, when children touch it, it is completely safe, and if properly placed, it does not blacken the walls.

As produced by the factory, this unit can be counted upon to give out between 900,000 and a million ions per cubic centimeter. With a little modification to the circuitry, I've got it running at about four-and-half to five million, which is a useful saturation level.

As you probably know, there is no such thing as an overdose of or over-exposure to negative ions, so if one is using it, the unit should run twenty-four hours night and day. When it is first started in a room, depending on its construction and the materials, it can take between ten and twenty-one days to clean it and start to impregnate it with negative ions.

This is important, because you have an absorption factor. Materials which hold positive ionizing with a low-power ionizer will absorb the negative continuum. So what you have to do is use the full power of the unit to clean the place out and saturate everything in it. After some days you have a minus situation, at which point you can start to build up the necessary negative ionization.

Negative ion saturation can be and should be used in all situations, especially in therapy situations. Everything from the medically surgical to all areas of psychology and psychotherapy.

The practical physical benefits of heavy negative ionization are very well known, and the clinical tests and reports exist.

An area that interests us very much more is the other, deeper, effects of negative ionization.

Negative ionization produces and maintains an energy situation, acting as a carrier-wave for energy. Just as you have sound waves or light waves, so you have energy waves. Negative ions clean and polish these lines of communication, and constantly check, develop and maintain them.

Furthermore, wherever an efficient ionizer is working, you have a microclimate. This microclimate exists on a gigantic scale in some parts of the world. This is quite palpable in the Alhambra in Granada where the combination of natural materials with plants, flowers and trees complement each other, while using water as a catalyst. As you know, flowing water produces a negative ion area. In microclimates, you have a physical cleaning of the body systems; it's like a sort of psychic vacuum cleaner.

I'm going to suggest that an ionizer be used very specifically in tekkias, and also in areas of therapy: consulting rooms, surgeries, doctor's waiting-rooms etc. Why I mention therapist's waiting-rooms is because you have what is called an anticipation factor in waiting-rooms. "Good or bad, this person is going to help me. Excellent."; or "This person is going to drill my tooth or do something and it's going to be terrible."

The presence of a heavy negative ionization in an anticipation situation means that the effect goes in very deeply, because the person is in what we call a primal situation of anticipation or fear.

So you can have a preparation microclimate before the therapy and during the therapy. A part of your therapy is already taking place in the waiting-room, therefore in the therapy area I would certainly recommend the use of these ionizers.

I would also widely recommend their use in the home as far as is possible. Primarily in the sleeping rooms, nursery, bedroom and, secondly, where food is cooked.

BRINGING PEOPLE TOGETHER

During this congress, I will answer some questions, the answers of which would be of general interest. Additionally, both today and tomorrow, I will suggest to you certain areas of thought and research.

We are building the basis of a coherent therapy, At this time we need to exchange ideas and to compare theories within groups and from person to person, but this is only the beginning.

During this congress you will be speaking to people who live in other parts of the world, and the relationship and contact you have now made should continue and develop by exchange of letters, cassettes, and other things. In another year, I hope we can have another congress.

During that time we will aim to refine our techniques, so that next year people can present an updated, more coherent technique, so that eventually, after the third congress we will have a more precise idea of the Granada therapy.

INTENTION AND ORGANIZATION

I would like to see a continuation of this congress on a smaller scale in each of your areas. So I would suggest that when you go back to your own countries, you form a small therapy study group in each area. This basic therapeutic group will relate and correspond directly with other therapeutic groups. It would also diffuse therapy throughout their local overall groups.

Building a therapy group within a group is basically exactly the same as the organization of a group in the context of the Tradition. It is not a hierarchical situation, but an efficiency situation. As with the therapy gatherings, there is no competition. A person is given the authority to organize and maintain a group. This authority which they are lent is not a debatable authority. It is either accepted or not accepted.

The person in charge of a Tradition group or a therapy group needs backup. This backup can be of a technical nature, which includes the production and sharing of energy, or an ordinary, efficient, what I call nuts-and-bolts backup, that is, assistance in the general sense of the word.

In a chain, the links are working together to hold something. They are not pulling against each other. So when you establish a therapy group, support it and give it energy on every possible level. Action is more important than discussion. Exchange of ideas is perfectly good. A certain amount of critical comment is valuable. We cannot function against tension if tension exists among ourselves.

Briefly, to restate the intention of the congress: it is to develop a therapy, which we will call the Granada therapy. This does not entail abandoning your own technique of therapy, it means adding other therapies to your own therapy which are helpful to it. Using an additional therapy does not diminish the importance of your own therapy.

Surely, if the intention of therapy is to heal, there is no confusion and no contradiction in using a similar intention. If, for example, a person is using colour therapy, there is no problem or confusion if he uses a musical therapy at the same time. It is an additional technique, not a replacement technique.

You have to be open and honest enough to appreciate the validity of certain aspects of other people's techniques.

If a surgeon is performing a surgical operation, there is no problem for him to have a subliminal sound or music. If you use a musical therapy, (reacts to loud background noise) an intrusive sound like that one is obviously not welcomed by the surgeon. He probably tenses up, so it is counter-productive.

I have a small note here regarding trace minerals, which are important in the correct functioning and balancing of the system. They are the usual familiar ones, but the important thing is the chemical form in which they are given, broken down into the form of amino acids so that the human body can assimilate them, which means basically that they are encapsulated by amino acids. As I say, they are the familiar minerals: iron, zinc, iodine, copper, manganese, chromium, selenium and molybdenum.

Incidentally, there's another cutting from a newspaper here, which is a report from Los Angeles. This is a very important area of study because somehow, extraordinarily, somebody has finally decided that state of mind may help cancer patients. They are calling it auto-immunology and other Greek words.

What they are repeating is a factor which has been known in the Tradition for thousands of years: that a balanced physical or mental system has its own latent defense system which can be boosted up as a reaction to the invasion of something detrimental and dangerous to that system.

Everybody says "Yes, we know that already" because of the normal production of antibodies. But this is probably the first time that the concept of cancer has been treated as a very serious and very bad disease, which it is, but treated in a way that it should not have the sort of death syndrome automatically attached to it.

TOWARDS A UNIVERSAL THERAPY

To a small degree, I am satisfied with the progress being made. If I say I am very satisfied, people will relax, so I will say that I think you have established a formula of contact. It is how you use that formula which will make this therapy work.

We can aim for a book or a series of reports. We can also write more and more reports and stack them up, and be satisfied that our work and research has produced this kind of material.

Now, gathering together peoples' papers and publishing them is certainly important, but when you are treating a patient, you don't, I hope, hold out the book and show it to him so that he is cured.

Like all practical and useful things, it is their exercise in the form of action which makes them useful. When a thing like a book or a therapy becomes familiar to you, you use it more easily.

These reports or books belong to all of you. This part may belong to Chico, this part to Pepe, which is fine. They have produced the report, their name is on it and they get the credit for doing it. They have produced reports for your use, but the ultimate and final beneficiary of these reports is your patient.

Never lose sight of the fact that the most important person is still the patient. Certainly, through your function and work, your own fame and authority can become greater, as well as your reputation as a therapist.

As therapists in the Tradition, you must be your own judge of your ability. This means that your judgement must not be based on the number of patients you have but on the number of cures you produce.

Some therapists say: "We have an 80 % success rate". As I have said, another way of looking at this statistic is as a 20 % failure rate. If you keep that 20 % failure rate before you, your aim is to diminish that percentage. By meeting together and exchanging ideas about therapy, you are all working to diminish that rate of failure.

Which single individual among you gets more credit is not important. You know personally and privately how good you are at your therapy, and you should be saying to yourself: "I can be better. I have the energy to help. I am in close relation with the energy. I must receive it and use it." Again, not stacking it up: "Oh, look how much lovely energy I've got."

"A wise man who does not use his knowledge is like a donkey with a load of books." Let us certainly produce these reports regularly; let us go through these reports critically each time and see what unnecessary factors can be taken out.

I'm not saying that we should examine them in a hostile fashion: "I am looking for some rubbish to throw out." You are certainly not, I hope, looking at it and saying : "If this is by Pancho Gonzalez, it must be rubbish"; it possibly is, but try and prove it first.

If somebody says to you: "That paper you gave or that point you made is very interesting. Ahem, there are some points I don't agree with". Now there are two attitudes therapists have to this sort of comment.

One is to say: "You think that some of the things I wrote are not very good. I think you are garbage!"; in other words, the defensive attitude of: "I am going to defend my piece of therapy." There is, understandably, some degree of jealousy and competition.

If somebody who is not a therapist criticizes something in a therapist, the reaction is usually either one of pity: "How stupid!" or else it is: "Of course you don't understand, you are not a therapist."

But when two therapists of different therapies talk together, the first thing to do is establish between themselves that they are talking about cures. When you come here to meet and talk together, forget your identification with your own therapy as much as possible. By this, I am not saying: "Ignore your training", nor am I saying that you should feel so humble that you excuse yourself, saying: "I'm sorry I'm only a psychologist"; but you should not be thinking that the reason you are here is to defend your own therapy.

If your attitude is one of defense, you automatically create a certain amount of negative influence.

If you come here thinking you have to defend your therapy "against all comers", you are of course paranoid. Leave your paranoia outside. All you have to think about when you're in here is that you are among friends.

You share a common aim in your activities. You participate in the baraka and in the energy of the Tradition in order to help people.

Last year I said how necessary it was going to be to create a therapy. Day by day, week by week, we see the necessity growing greater. You have the spread of disease, tension, malnutrition, with all its effects. Social situations can and do produce tension and disease, because an undernourished person is vulnerable physically and psychically.

If they have no hope, people go to extremes. Extremes produce, in fact, more tension because one extreme will automatically oppose the other extreme.

As the problem becomes larger, we have to work hard.

Years ago when aspirin was first invented, it was used very widely for many years because it was a useful drug. When new diseases or physical conditions were identified, that simple aspirin had to be updated, and people looked at the basic chemical formula of the aspirin, salicylic acid, and said: "How can we develop it and change it in order to use it in new or newly-identified conditions?"

The discovery of aspirin was only the first step, because its purification and the further development of its use was and is continual. No therapy should remain static. It does and must develop according to the requirements of the world population.

Such developments have to take convenience into consideration. For instance in my own country of Afghanistan, a very old treatment for children with measles was to take the seeds of a pomegranate, boil them in water, and give that child litre after litre of this juice. Now this therapy worked, it brought about a cure.

If you look at that method, you also have to compare it with the convenience or practical factors. If you are treating a child for measles and you give the mother or father a medical prescription to be taken to the pharmacy which says "250 litres of liquid", this is inconvenient.

Over the years, the constituent element that produces the cure has been identified. So now this decoction of pomegranates exists in the form of little tablets, and of course everybody says: "Yes, yes, we know that."

What I am getting at is that the same thing applies to these reports. We want to boil them down until we have one therapy which can be applied in the beginning within all the therapies you use, and which, eventually, can slowly replace therapies.

We are not going through the reports for the sake of rejecting bits and pieces of them. We are simply trying to take out the valuable parts and protect them, and since it is you who make practical use of those techniques, it is only you who are able to use them selectively and flexibly.

What we want is a flexible therapy which can be used under any circumstances, where distance is no problem, where the amount of money available to or for the patient is no problem, and also where the type of climate they live in or food they eat is not a problem.

This is not a Utopian therapy we are looking for. It has to be an extremely practical therapy without imposing any limitation on ourselves.

Having established the fact that we can put different therapies together, and by using a little politeness and patience, we can see they are not really hostile to each other. Let us take, not the next step, but the step after that.

We can say now that this is the second official therapy congress. But what has been happening between the first and the second? Has that space in time been empty? I don't think so.

I think that during the time between the first congress and

this one, you have had many smaller congresses. Now what makes a congress? Is it a meeting of minds, an exchange of ideas? Is it a combination of your various energies? If those factors have been present by letter, telephone and meeting since the last congress, you have in fact had congresses. If your label for a congress means that there must be more than 25 people otherwise it is not valuable, you are imposing a numerological limit on yourself.

The value of numbers exists in external things. For instance, it is said that a king must travel with 50 people because he has to show that he is a king. If somebody says "That is a king", everybody looks, and if they see 50 people milling around they will say: "Yes, certainly." But if he is alone, they will say: " It's not possible, kings don't go around by themselves." There is a certain exterior value to this judgement. Why not have 50 people travelling around with you? If you are a king, you can probably afford to feed and clothe them and pay for their tickets.

Of course, there is another aspect. If a man is really asking himself the question, he doesn't need 50 people to tell him he is a king. Maybe he looks at his little badge and says: "Yes, that's me" like Nasrudin, who once went before a judge with documents to be certified. The judge said: "You say that you are Nasrudin, can you identify yourself?", so he took out a small mirror, looked at himself, and said: "Yes, this is me."

Of course that is what is called reassurance therapy, which is a new addition to our canon. But I'm sure that even if I hadn't thought of it, one of you would have produced it.

As I say, therapies do not and should not remain static. In every area of research people are doing what is called "pushing forward the frontiers of knowledge." Certainly, one should be satisfied with one's knowledge up to a point, but that satisfaction has to be based on something real and solid. In order to carry out a therapy, you must be fairly sure of what you are doing.

If you constantly have to question yourself: "Is this right? Am I doing it right?"; you'll come across as neurotic, and this neurosis will communicate itself to your patient: "Do you think I'm doing it all right?" Nevertheless, the feeling that you are doing it right should not be an end in itself. At the back of your mind is always the possibility that "I can and want to do better."

It is indeed always possible to do better, which means that you go on further exercising and developing your therapy. You don't say: "Since I'm not 100% sure I'll stay home and go through it over and over again, and I'll only go out and do it when I feel it's 100% sure." You develop it further by doing it and exercising it.

We are trying to develop our therapy by introducing new things or parts of such new things as you go along. When you feel that the situation is right, you don't get up in the morning and say: "Right, I'm going to try this new thing with anybody and everybody that comes along" because it's a recipe for chaos. If your attitude is flexible and you're testing a patient, a moment may arrive when you think "This may be a good moment to try this."

This is not irresponsible experiment. It is a feeling which comes to you based on the rapport you have developed with that individual patient.

Every patient, every person is broadcasting out on different levels. One of your skills has to be to tune in on that patient or person: in other words, you have to pick up the right signals and analyze them. Every good therapist has first to be a good diagnostician.

If somebody comes into your treatment room and they have a thing around their neck which says "I have cholera" and you look and say: "Just a minute" and you look it up and say "Cholera, that's right. Good-bye, next!", this is a reaction, not a diagnosis. When a patient comes to you for consultation, you look at them, talk with them, notice their mannerisms and get a picture which you feed into and compare with your past experience of symptoms of the disease.

You must seek to deepen that technique and make it more profound. You don't reject all the diagnostic tests you have already learned, you are keeping them and adding other ones to those.

If you say: "I am going to form a diagnosis on the basis of a person's profound problems", and that person then comes in to you and you see them sitting there holding their jaw and groaning while you're trying to think out what their profound psychic problem is, you have a problem and he most certainly has a problem. He can easily solve his problem by going to another doctor, or rather to a dentist, but that problem remains with you.

You're looking for and projecting an analysis technique outward on all these levels. And you're picking up all the transmissions that this patient is voluntarily or involuntarily sending out.

Very simply, you tune into a series of different frequencies.

I'm sure you've all had a situation where you've been treating a patient and there is something missing, that you feel, but that you can't really identify. Very often it will be because that person is transmitting something on a level which you are not receiving.

It may be on such a low and basic frequency that you ignore it. Or it might be a frequency higher than you are actually receiving on. If you have a situation like that, there are several possible reactions. One is that you say, either for your own satisfaction or in self-defense: "Oh yes, that is the Mount Fujiyama syndrome", finish. Or else you can make a mental note to check out that particular area the next time you see the person.

Concentrate on that area, try to identify and tune in on what it is that is missing. But if you begin to worry about that missing element or signal, your worry will transmit to your patient.

Perhaps next time you see the patient, you will have a mental picture of the patient and also of that one area you want to concentrate on. You may say: "I will now try and produce or provoke in the patient a stronger signal coming out" so that hopefully he or she becomes able to receive it and identify it. You are flexible, and unless you are completely sure, you don't just decide: "This must be the Fujiyama Syndrome."

Certainly, those of you who deal with people who are psychologically disturbed have to be very careful, because as you well know, they can send out spurious or false signals. You must be careful not to be diverted by a false signal. But if you have identified and decided that this is in fact a false signal, then you ignore it.

You're maintaining the flexibility while not reacting to that person's actions. You are simply identifying and using a technique.

So, let us now try harder with attention, not tension.

In a way, we are in a race against time, but that should not necessarily frighten us. There's no need to think: "The world will come to an end before we can do anything" because there is the possibility of stretching time, although in fact this is not really stretching time, it is simply making better use of it.

When you do this you are using concentration of energy. If you are talking with another therapist engaged in a different type of therapy, start by considering the similarities between your different therapies. Don't start by looking at the differences.

For instance, you can say to somebody: "Let us start on two or three principles about which we can agree." Maybe then you will find one or two on which you disagree, but you leave those two or three aside for the moment, because as you get to know that person better, as you start to exchange and mix your energies, then you can compare notes or justify your theories and feelings more and more openly and clearly.

You do not get into the area of defending your own point of view or your own therapy because you are not together to destroy or criticize each others' therapies. You're not expected immediately to accept 100% of another's notes: "So-and-so is doing more" or "less" and "these notes go into my secret black book."

Should I feel sorry because such-and-such a person is not working efficiently, and then phone them saying: "Look, you're not working correctly"? Or is it not better that they should feel and know this for themselves? i.e. without either guilt, neurosis, "mea culpa" or sitting in a corner and going mad. It means recognizing it and doing something about it.

This responsibility is yours and the therapy is also yours. At each point where you make a further development in this therapy, you connect with another source of energy of the Tradition, which can and does push you one stage further ahead.

Don't forget that you don't just go from congress into sleep, and from a state of sleep into congress. Each congress is a formal and useful external gathering together of friends, but the continuity of effort must be maintained.

It is not for me to chase you up between congresses. If I gave way to my personal inclinations, none of you would ever sleep at night between meetings, but then, that would be a personal indulgence I am not allowed to have, although the temptation is sometimes very great. So when it happens I just beat my wife or kick the dog.

Start on a solid basis. Progressively establish not only a higher and higher but also a deeper and deeper relationship, so that each congress is not like a graph in which each point is one congress and then another, and you then draw a line between the two. It's true that a congress may be a high point with more energy, and maybe it then goes down a little bit afterwards, but this line should be maintained and then go a little bit up to the next congress, then take off from that point and go a little bit further upward.

The energy and concentration you put in is not of a frenetic nature, it's a constant momentum. Carry it through. You must push, all the time.

Experiment with techniques; not recklessly, but when you feel the situation and time is right. If you come to a situation where your official therapy leaves you with a question, call for, connect with, and use the energy of the Tradition in that situation.

Believe and know this energy to be present. Feel it. Don't keep it as some abstract idea. Bring it out and use it. You have no excuse for not doing this. It is only stupidity or laziness which prevents you from doing it. If you hesitate out of some sort of fear: "Do I have the right to use it in this circumstance? Will it be a waste of the energy if I use it?"; there is no basis for this fear or hesitation. You cannot waste it because you don't control it; you never control the amount that comes to you.

The energy of the Tradition exists in all sorts of different forms and qualities. Its quality can be that of sugar, money or psychic energy, but just try to get into the movies by using the energy of the Tradition to buy your ticket: they'll just call the police or the men in white coats.

If you say: "I don't use it, not because I'm afraid, but because I don't know whether I have the right to use this or whether this is the right moment"; in other words: "I can't judge what type of energy or how much." In fact, I judge it and you don't.

It doesn't work in such a way that there is a situation in which you say: "What type of energy? How much? Do I take two cc's and inject it intravenously or subcutaneously or what?"

This is because, if you are solidly in contact with the Tradition, you are automatically in contact with its energy as well. You become the channel between the energy and the person or situation you are involved in. You establish the connection, but the quality and quantity of energy which passes along that connection is my business, not yours.

If the decision as to how much and what type of energy was up to you, then you might be in a situation of fear. You would hesitate and say: "I think we need this much of this quality, and just to make sure we'll add a little more and bang it through quicker"; as when somebody has a headache and they take two aspirins rather than one in order to cure themselves more quickly.

The judgement involved has to be qualitative and not quantitative. Okay, does that mean that I'm sitting here before a sort of control panel with little dials and knobs connected to everybody waiting for one of the dials to go ping? No, such a system would not be efficient enough. The energy is much more subtle and precise, and much more efficient, than this.

It works on the basis of need and the automatic answer to that need: the need involved here being the profound need. That profound need, as well as the recognition by the person that "I am in need" or "this situation is in need" is what pulls the switch, not me.

But once the switch is pulled, you might say: "What is to stop the quantity or the quality of the energy? Maybe I get too much?" This is also not possible because energy has an existence and a quality of judgement of its own. It arrives, it judges and it acts.

You can always ask for 75 million kilowatts of energy, but what kind of requirement and judgement is that desire based on? On the idea that "More is better" and "More powerful is quicker." In fact, the energy is too valuable and too dangerous to be left in the hands of people who make such subjective evaluations.

Every time you do something where you have expressed your intention before doing it, you are attracting the energy of the Tradition. This is not a superstitious thing in the sense of "I'm going to start this now, and I hope it will work".

It is done in order to make the connection and affirm your intention to yourself, in other words to remind yourself of your intention.

And then, you will see that it works.

CONSTRUCTIVE CRITICISM

Once again, do not have a critical attitude towards each other's therapies. The absence of criticism among you does not mean to say that there will be a complete absence of criticism in the congress.

There is hostile criticism and constructive criticism, and I am going to be constructively critical of you, firstly because I know you, secondly because I can be objective, and thirdly because you can do nothing else but listen to me.

One criticism (and they are not in order of importance or priority) is that, in general, you are not narrowing down your areas of therapy quickly enough, and you are still introducing a lot of unnecessary personal factors. Yet if, like the one I have here, you have a therapy which can be expressed on one page, I'm not saying to take it and cut bits and pieces out of it just to make it smaller.

You cut selectively, and only for a useful, not a destructive, purpose. If a gardener wants to cut a rose tree, his intention is to benefit that rose tree. To make it smaller, he cuts selectively, he does what the English call "pruning"; which means he looks at the street or area around it in order to have an idea what shape he wants it to grow in. He looks at the old branches and the new branches, he looks at the balance of the tree. Then he has to make a judgement about which branch is to be cut.

With his experience and knowledge of plants and trees, he knows that there is a correct time during the year to cut, and in what season. He knows that it is sometimes necessary to cut a very young and strong growth in order to encourage it more. By doing that, he is not discouraging a new growth: he is allowing the vital energy of that tree to recycle itself correctly, so that when the season of maximum growth comes, the energy will flow to the right places.

So when you examine your own therapies or techniques, examine them in that way: in order to direct them, strengthen them and focus them. By cutting down the overall area of your therapy you are not limiting its effect, you are rather increasing its potential and deepening its effect.

You might say: "But this sounds contrary to what you've just been saying. You said that we should add other techniques to our own techniques, but now you're telling us to cut them off!"

In fact, there is no contradiction.

Say you have a particular area in one of your therapies or techniques which you are satisfied with; you consider that it works and that it is efficient. If it occupies a given amount of space in your technique, try and concentrate it. You are then not making your therapy as broad, but more concentrated, so that if you take some aspect of another therapy and add it to your own, and that aspect of the therapy has been concentrated, you are not then adding another big chunk of other therapies to your own to get a broader coverage, you are acquiring a altogether stronger, more energetic and concentrated overall technique or therapy.

When I say I intend to be constructively critical I'll explain what I mean by giving you some examples. Somebody said to me yesterday: "I have been treating a patient for fourteen months and I don't really know this person very well."

Well, my reaction to a statement like that is to be critical. Not in the sense of a critical illness but it is indeed a criticism, because it means you have not been functioning correctly. A therapist should most certainly be able to know a patient within that amount of time, otherwise they are not being efficient.

Of course some treatments or therapies take longer than others, depending on the condition of the patient. But since the person who put this question to me had told me more or less what the problem of the patient was, I thought that if this therapist had been functioning correctly, it should have taken a probable maximum of fourteen hours.

One of the main reasons for losing time in a therapy situation, especially in psychological treatment, is that very often people start off the treatment on too sophisticated a level.

In many therapy situations, you go first to the basics as you identify them, and as soon as possible, you establish a relationship with the patient where you can tell him or her about these basics.

Sometimes a therapist may think or feel that going straight to the basics may cause a psychic or social shock to the patient. I'm not saying that the therapist should automatically be rude or brutal, but remember that you are in the business of therapy and not in the business of politeness.

One extreme is rudeness or brutal shock. The other extreme is going round and round the problem very delicately and politely and kindly without ever getting to grips with it. Again, there is a balance between the two, and the place to go is somewhere in between.

At any point, you have the flexibility to use either of these extremes, but since you know that they exist, you don't have to go backwards or forwards and through all of the steps in between.

You're taking them out of the practical aspect under certain circumstances. Any therapy, be it surgical, psychological or whatever, has certain preliminaries, which are dictated by the state or condition of the patient. The necessary examination by the therapist begins with an evaluation of the person's physical, psychic and psychological health, and the establishment of a rapport where it is necessary.

Once those preliminaries have been correctly and precisely done, then go into the therapies.

Another recommendation which is not a criticism but a suggestion or recommendation is that a therapist should broadcast confidence to the patient. You can say: "Yes, I think I can and will help you." A patient will then be quite happy because that's what they want to hear, it's what they are hoping for.

But they only listen to that reassurance for a short time, because they already expect you to say that. They don't expect you to say: "You're finished. I'll try and do my best but there's not much hope."

They know you are going to say that you will help them, so they are thinking about their own problems and listening to the tone of your voice like a sort of background violin playing, and finally after that five or ten minutes they know you are going to say: "Right, come back next Tuesday and we'll continue" or "We'll operate" or whatever.

In a way, they are almost in a trance, they are actually disconnected. They are really just listening to the tone of your voice and also planning what they are going to do after the consultation is finished, like the shopping to be done or the children to see to or something. They are listening with half their mind.

If during that time you start screaming with horror about their condition, they come back to consciousness.

So during the time that you are establishing the initial relationship with them you are doing the usual formal reassuring explanations or making reassuring noises.

Parallel with that you must broadcast and transmit to them that it really can be done. If the transmission of confidence is sent out correctly, they will receive it. As I say, maybe they are in a trance state, but the deep and fundamental protection system is still working. That is why they wake up if the tone of your voice, which was reassuring, becomes a scream.

You can increase that confidence factor by scanning that person on different levels. You're looking at them, noticing the way they talk, their mannerisms and you communicate most strongly with them because they basically want a cure.

You identify the level on which this need and desire exists. You relate directly with that, and you pump the confidence in.

Let me give you an anatomical analogy. If it is necessary for you to give a patient a large injection of 2 or 3 centilitres, you do not, I hope, try and do it through a capillary; you look for a larger vessel which can take a larger needle, so as to absorb a larger quantity more quickly and more efficiently.

You can therefore see the value of putting together the strong need with the strong possibility because you then have a strong type of communication.

Once you have established that you can use this very deep link constantly during the therapy, you can then stimulate and re-energize this need of the person to be cured. You do this deeply, strongly and automatically.

If for reasons of a change in their physical or psychic state, they are perhaps a bit low or depressed, you can certainly say to them: "Look, do you want to get better or not? Take a grip on yourself. Pull yourself together. Make an effort!"

At the same time you are doing that, you are pushing in the same message of "Do it" on that level, but not as a question. During a therapy, everybody wants and needs reassurance at various times.

It is true that they also want you to show them that their condition or situation is important. Not important in the sense of serious and terribly grave, but it is possible to give people a little bit of reassurance, and if you can tell them that their condition is significant, the responsibility shouldn't be too much to bear.

Years and years ago I was on a ship going from one place to another, and somebody came up to me on the boat and said: "Somebody says that you seem to know something about therapy and things like that."

Then he said: "Can I tell you about all these problems I have which need therapy?"

Since I couldn't really escape, I said to him: "All right, tell me."

So he talked, and I went back to thinking about the fish and all the other things down below. And at the end of about half an hour he said to me: "What do you think?"

"I have heard of worse conditions," I answered.

"What do you mean?" he said, "I am the worst possible case!"

A patient or client will always give a greater importance to his own situation or problems than anybody else, because of course, they are very personal to him. He is the one suffering. So you recognize this: you don't help him to increase the importance, but you give him the impression that you understand and appreciate that this is a serious matter.

But again, on a parallel level you try and get them to diminish the danger of their condition or situation.

Everybody knows that there is such a thing as supporting and helping a person with psychic energy. This should be precise and concentrated. General reassurance is good: "We are doing all we can" or "I can help you, this will work" is fine, and people want to hear it, but they also want to feel something.

They want to feel better, either physically or emotionally, or else they want to feel that "something good is happening to me". You are helping them to increase that feeling.

Not only can you help them to feel it, more importantly, you can help them to use it. If there is a situation where a patient may say: "It's funny, I'm feeling something"; depending on the patient, you have to be very careful how you explain that.

You should also watch, observe and then actually see whether they are feeling something and perhaps not telling you. They may be feeling something and be afraid to tell you because they are afraid that it is something negative which is developing in them.

You can say to them, whether they echo it back to you or not: "There is something working in you within yourself. It is not mysterious, magical or supernatural, but totally natural. Maybe you haven't felt it because you haven't tried to develop it before. It is in fact something which your own system is producing in order to establish a harmonic balance. Remember, illness is not a natural state. It means there is a disturbance somewhere."

For various reasons, the system needs help to reestablish its own balance. A system can sometimes reestablish itself without assistance, but if a person or system needs assistance and this is given to them, they must always be told that their own system is also working towards the cure.

So illness is not a natural state, it is a disturbance of a normally balanced system which has had some ups and downs. By reassuring a patient, you are helping them to help themselves.

You're also helping them to help you because you, as a therapist, also need help from them.

Here again, you cannot have any competition between patient and therapist. Putting out a feeling of confidence and expressing it is one thing: dominating and totally directing them is another. "I will cure you if I have to kill you!" With that approach, yes, they might, but this is another problem.

In every situation, in every therapy, maximize the possibilities. This doesn't mean that you overload a patient with every possible therapy technique that exists. Apart from the fact that working this way is too complicated, if you've used every type of therapy on a patient and they then recover and are restored to health, you'll probably say: "Which was the one that worked?" The answer, of course, is usually a combination of different therapies.

As I have said before, therapy is a little bit like cooking. You know more or less what you want to put on the table. You know more or less what raw materials like meat, vegetables, and so on you're putting into the pot.

As it cooks, you add various things in various proportions. If you say: "These are potatoes, they need salt", you don't say to yourself: "This is salt, I'll put in two kilos of salt, and wham."

Salt is salt. You put in a proportion and then you taste it, and then you check and see. And then you think "Maybe it would benefit from a little bit more of this or a little bit more of that" or else maybe a little bit more time.

The result, hopefully, should be something which tastes nice and satisfies the hunger.

TALKING TO PEOPLE ABOUT THE GRANADA THERAPY

This morning I would like to give some words of advice and a few words of warning. The warning is this: we are working to produce a therapy, but we do not have a complete therapy. Therefore while we can use the words Granada Therapy among ourselves as a kind of shorthand and know between ourselves what we are aiming for, we cannot or should not be describing this particular therapy to anybody else.

This is not because it is a terrible secret, but because it is not yet complete. You cannot or should not say to somebody, and most certainly not to a patient: "I am using the Granada Therapy on you."

We are saying to each other that are working on the development of a therapy. Be very careful about this because it is a very specific warning.

The second word of advice is in the same area. As I said at the first meeting, you are not being asked to throw away your particular therapy and the next day start up business as "A Granada Therapist".

The practical reason for this is that if people come into your office and look at your plaque and it says: "Pancho Gonzales, Granada Therapist", they will say "What the hell is that?"

If you're a therapist and you use a therapy whose name is more or less known, that's all right. When we finally start to introduce further techniques of the therapy, you don't use them secretly under the cover of your original therapy, because when the therapy is complete, it can be offered to patients as a complete therapy.

When we have a complete therapy you will be able to say to people: "Yes, I am a Freudian, Jungian, Adlerian therapist, or whatever, and I also practice another therapy." You can then say to them: "In my opinion, this is a very special, particular and useful therapy." If they then say: "Fine, if you're satisfied, I trust you and I would like to do this therapy", then you can try it on them.

They can also say: "Look I'm sorry, but I don't want to be a guinea pig to be tested on. I would like to stick to a conventional therapy you represent." In that case, whatever he or she says, if you feel it valuable, you use the Granada Therapy.

If your intention really is to try and cure, this is not being dishonest, because the name of what you are doing is ultimately almost irrelevant. It has a value for you because of what the context or name of Granada implies, insofar as it signifies that you are operating within the context of the Tradition, but to the patient, this name Granada is not particularly evocative. They'll say that "Granada" is some sort of new Spanish therapy or something. You don't convince them of its value, you simply show them that it works. As I was saying, you have to transmit the confidence you feel in the therapy to them.

If you say to them: "This is a new therapy, let's try it out, it might work or it might not"; you can forget about it. More than half of your function as a therapist is to give confidence to people. To do this you must have confidence in your technique and confidence that you can use the technique, thus helping their inner being to have the confidence to help you in the therapy.

In therapy situations, many of the techniques used will be the same tactics as the basic tactics of the Tradition itself, based on what is not very elegantly called press-button tactics.

If a teacher in the Tradition establishes a relationship with a student, he works on, and also with, this student, because he has to press the right button in the student to activate something. This is a button which activates a circuit that the teacher is working with and on. It reawakens or reactivates a circuit which has possibly not been used for centuries or generations. When that circuit is reawakened, energy can then be fed to that circuit to be used. You then have a situation where the teacher and pupil are working together harmoniously; the point here being that the relationship between a therapist and a patient can be similar.

The human system has the capacity to heal itself. Depending on the situation, it needs more or less help to do so.

A therapist aims to create a situation in which there is exchange and feedback. Part of this is to explain to the patient as much of the therapy as you think he or she can understand, telling them as much as possible how they can help you to help them, and you also have to convince them gradually that they really can help you.

If you have somebody in a state of very deep depression who is saying: "I can't do anything, I'm good for nothing, I've tried but I'm inefficient in everything"; you can say, up to a point: "Why don't you try to help me in a depressing way? If your depression is so intense, why not see whether there is any limit to the depression?"

Now, of course, this is not an invitation for them to go to the extreme of depression and commit suicide.

So if they then say: "Fine", and take a pistol out of their pocket, at that point you say to them "No, not as far as that."

Use a sort of technique where they themselves examine their depression. And then, while you're examining areas of depression, you ask: "Is that state of depression a normal, usual human state?"

What you're doing, in other words, is encouraging them. You're not saying: "Get rid of your depression" or "You don't have a depression"; you're saying: "Examine and see if you've got anything else besides." And then, "Okay, but in addition to that, is there any other area which you have?" or "Examine yourself and see whether you are really totally full of depression"; because after all, the psychological situation of a person is only part of a whole system.

You can say something like: "Okay, you're suffering from deep and total depression. Now, for instance, look at your hands. Are they depressed? How do you judge what is a depressed hand or a not depressed hand?"

Of course that's a bit of an esoteric question, but it does at least deflect the attention away from the depression, and you then start getting a comparison. And you could continue in this direction by saying: "Are your ears depressed?"

You can go through the whole system like that. It is certainly a form of trick, but what you are doing here is diverting the importance of "my psychological depression", and, by not treating it as a distinct thing, you're taking it apart. You're distracting their attention or fixation.

Of course, this technique is and always has been applied in different ways. The person might say: "No, I'm not concerned with my hands or my ears, it's my brain there is something wrong with." So you can then reply: "Right, let us then examine the brain and its function. The brain controls and monitors the physical functions of the body, therefore let us see how much of your brain is truly damaged or inefficient"; because this damage or inefficiency can also be shown by certain physical disabilities. There are certain normal physical examinations like reflexes, temperature or blood circulation.

If your hands are not showing physical signs of degeneration or lack of function, it will be possible to say quite accurately that the part of the brain which looks after the working of the hand is functioning all right. So that is a "plus one" brain function, therefore the brain and the rest of the system is not 100% destroyed.

With the same technique, you can go through a person's ears, nose, feet or any other parts of the physical body, and you can say: "I notice, for instance, that you can flap your ears so that is plus a half." So at the end of this list, we find that we've got at least a plus 8.

Supposing you say to the patient: "Why don't you go away and do your own examination along the same lines. Make your own list of plus or minuses, and bring it back next time I see you."

It is very interesting to see what sort of list they produce, and how much plus or minus they give to the various presence or absence of certain physical functions. "My nose moves in all directions gracefully and wonderfully, that is plus 25"; or else,

"My nose does not move in all directions, which is a minus 25."

Of course, you might say: "But this type of reaction or answer happens to our patients all the time." Nevertheless, in many ways, you are establishing a common ground of discussion or measurement as to their condition.

If you have their list, you don't then say: "Come on, scoring the fact you can't move your nose at minus 25 is ridiculous"; because there you can provoke an aggression and defense situation in the patient. Maybe you can discuss the relative importance of being able to move one's nose gracefully. This is especially useful in producing and maintaining a dialogue with somebody who is closed or who doesn't speak.

There is a technique used in some psychotherapies which is to provoke a reaction, either by harsh criticism or a shock or something like that. This can be used very carefully and very delicately in some situations, but by using this technique, you can also get the reaction I have just described.

It may even be that after several sessions with this person, when you've put the same type of question to them and they haven't replied or you haven't established a dialogue, they might even say to you: "You know, I think you're crazy. What is all this about my nose being depressed?"

What you want is a reaction, but without a shock or any violent move on the part of the therapist. Perhaps you're even getting the person to think: "What the hell is he talking about?" I've seen this sort of thing work even in very extreme cases of what is usually called a vegetable state.

When some very basic emotion in the patient comes to the surface, it can be called a form of astonishment, especially if they have gone through a long period of therapy and are almost self-hypnotized by this therapy. The sessions probably follow the same pattern with maybe the same impacts upon the person. There may be the same or similar questions, and the person is accustomed to the tonality or tone of voice and they are only half or a quarter listening to the questions and the conversation.

If they then hear a question like "How depressed are your

fingernails?"; the reaction is one of astonishment or curiosity, and they may even say: "Of course not!"

As I say, even in the extreme case of a vegetable, you have extracted a reaction. You've pressed a button and something has restarted to function.

This is one aspect of a technique which can be used, but not in isolation and not alone. Don't forget that we have talked, for instance, about the use of sound, colour and ionization. If the patient is experiencing a colour therapy, a background sound therapy and is in a highly ionized situation at the same time, all these things are pushing buttons as well.

If you get a positive and useful reaction with a combination of these therapies, it is important at that point to experiment. If you are simultaneously using three or four of these therapies you should see if there is one of them which has pushed the button harder than the other.

The next time, diminish or increase the level of ionization, colour or sound. Measure the reaction and do the same the next time, but always keep note of which therapies you are using at a particular time, because even if you are using every one in the world, you don't really know which one is working the best. You can start with one, two or three of these basic therapies: diminish one, increase the other, or possibly use another therapy.

Set up a situation or a place like a therapy room where you can control or monitor therapies. This should include the use and positioning of an ionizer, or else the ionizer's position in relation to some colour you may be using. You can bounce ionization from a colour and send it out with the qualities of that colour as well. If you do it in a random way: "Well, I'll put the ionizer there, and I'll paint this wall green and do something else": you become unable to analyze the result because your setup is imprecise.

If you decide to use an ionizer, colour and sound in a situation, arrange them and place them very precisely in the beginning, according to your own theory or feeling as to how they should be arranged. Do it in such a way that, after a consultation with a patient, when measuring the results, you know exactly where that patient was in relation to the various technical tools you are using.

As far as possible, you should try to explain simply to the patient what you are doing: "I'm using the influence of colour, ionization and harmonious sound to help you and me and our relationship."

If you have certain scientific or technical instruments in the room there should not be a situation where the person feels that these are sinister or dangerous or anything like that.

You don't have to explain the theory and practice of every instrument to them, as that can take a long time. They should feel that they are okay, that these things are there to help them, and that it's possible to sort of just accept or ignore them.

It also avoids a situation which I once witnessed with somebody who was using an ionizer. The therapist was sitting at a table with an ionizer on it and the patient sat down. The doctor then said to him: "What seems to be your problem?"

The patient looked around, looked at the ionizer and said: "The problem I have is this"; because it looked like a microphone, and the patient thought the doctor was recording him, which of course produced a confusing situation.

You want to create a situation in which, even if patients are not familiar with all these things, they should at least not appear to him or her to be anything threatening or menacing.

So briefly, use as many techniques at the same time as you can conveniently handle.

Add to them, subtract them, buy or keep a manageable number of them.

Get the patient working with you and convince him that everything you are using and everything around him is working for him and with him.

He is part of the therapy, not just its subject. Press the interior buttons which will help him to function for himself.

FEMININE INTUITION AND THERAPY

It is useful to be able to talk with the women because there are certain aspects of therapy which concern them. In a therapy context, a male therapist naturally brings in a masculine attitude, along with all the masculine attitudes that go together with his masculinity.

And of course some of you are saying: "Of course, he's talking about the chauvinism men automatically have." But women who practice therapy can use one thing which is very particular to them, which is a quality which everybody accepts that women have called feminine intuition.

If this intuition is used and focused in a correct way, it can become a precise instrument and not just a vague quality.

Now, women will usually identify or come to the point of a problem more directly and quickly than the average man.

If they use this faculty in a therapy situation with decision, they can start a therapy much more quickly; but it must be used with precision.

If a woman looks at a situation and this situation is a problem situation, if she can then establish a state of reasonable tranquility and calm when looking at such a situation, she can get a very close idea of what the central cause or problem happens to be.

But right here you have the beginning of their problem: perhaps because of a certain conditioning or other feminine attitude, they don't hold onto that perception.

Because women are sometimes naturally more delicate than men, they may identify a problem or a situation and then try to do something about it in a very delicate, nice and feminine way.

If the situation is not a serious and deep one, the light touch or delicate hand will probably solve it. But if the problem is more difficult, more objectionable or nastier, they may just delicately cover it over. Naturally, this is a compliment to women. Unfortunately, it can also be a failure or weakness in a situation of therapy.

I'm not saying that women should ignore their femininity and try to react to a situation like a man. They would be uncomfortable in trying that, and because of this, it wouldn't work.

How then do you use this feminine intuition? How can you use and be in touch with it? How can you be feminine and not feminist, because I've been asked by your husbands, sons and boyfriends to tell you: "Don't be feminists."

Femininity is a delicate and real quality, and not just an abstract quality. So how do you develop it so that you can use it?

Most women are either trained or else unconsciously learned from their mothers how to use their femininity. If it is to become an efficient quality, it is not only a surface delicacy, it is a quality which is capable of development. And if it is correctly developed, this feminine intuition is stronger and more flexible than male intuition.

And believe me, men, there is such a thing as male intuition. But since it is not masculine to say: "I have male intuition", it gets called superior intellect or superior intelligence.

Now why? Why is feminine intuition stronger and capable of more development than its masculine equivalent?

It has to do with the physical composition of a woman. Basically and physically, the female body and entity is stronger than the male.

Again, we are not measuring this in terms of muscularity or size of bones. We're talking about things like stamina, because yes, stamina is an energy which is capable of being used over long periods rather than over sudden periods. One of the most obvious reasons why a woman must have this extra stamina is because women usually have to go through the process of giving birth to children and raising them. This shows their long-term strength, stamina and capacity. When a woman becomes pregnant, or if she has a condition of particularly feminine illness, her whole system mobilizes to support or control that situation. When the requirement or situation of urgency does not exist, then that extra faculty and extra energy can be used and directed in a positive way.

It is really not possible to measure feminine intuition, in the sense that "She has 10 degrees worth , she has 5 degrees and that one has 20 degrees." Feminine intuition can only be measured by that intuition itself, in other words by that feeling.

In western society, if you talk about feeling something you can't measure, it is usually connected with emotion, hysteria or something like that. So it's the old problem; you can't weigh it, you can't measure it, you don't know what colour it is, "therefore it doesn't exist." -- "You say you've got feminine intuition? Show me, do something."

A man went to Nasrudin one day and said to him: "Nasrudin they say that you are a wise, capable, and knowledgeable man. I'm very busy and I've a lot of things to do and you're always talking about the existence and power of God. Look here, I don't have much time, so show me God."

Nasrudin took off his shoe, hit the man on the head and went on talking with his friends.

The man went howling to the judge and complained: "I asked Nasrudin a perfectly normal question and he hit me on the head!"

The judge called Nasrudin to him and he said: "Nasrudin, this is not correct. The man asked you a perfectly normal question and you inflict pain on him."

So Nasrudin said to the judge: "If he will show me the pain, I will show him God!"

If a person says something like: "Should we as women, or should a woman always be guided by intuition in all situations?"

The answer in lots of cases is no, because then you've got a lack of correct balance. Intuition is one factor we use among others. You should try to know yourselves, so that you can identify exactly when your intuition is to be used and differentiate it from the times when your own experience or even your own conditioning needs to be used.

If you can try and find out in what way your intuition communicates itself to you, you can identify it when it starts to speak. It doesn't speak all the time and it doesn't communicate in every circumstance.

If you observe yourself in certain circumstances, your intuition shows itself in certain ways and you can feel it acting. If you can develop this in a situation when it doesn't seem to be talking to you, you can look for it or look for how you think it may communicate, and you can then either see if it is doing something or else encourage it to do something, all the while reminding oneself that it has its own being, and that there are a number of situations where it is not talking to you because it does not have to. This is because in those situations, you can use conditioning, training, intelligence or whatever other ability you have.

It's value is that it supports or opposes an opinion which you have.

That is to say, you look at a person or situation, you examine it quite carefully from your experience, training, background and other things and perhaps at that point your intuition will then say: "Yeah!"

Or else again, your intuition may not say anything at all, and then you go ahead with whatever you have decided, according to the situation.

Sometimes, though, you have not been able to make a total decision about this situation. You're not sure. There may be an element of confusion, so you look around for an intuition and you get your intuition to establish a balance about what you felt. If you're familiar with, and have enough confidence in your own intuition, it will help you to make the proper positive decision.

Sometimes you will say, in a situation or something: "This is okay, that looks all right, but there's something that is still not quite right." Before you then say: "This is my intuition and it probably says 'no' with a red light against that situation, see if you already have an internal red light against that situation.

In other words, before you do it, you have to look at yourself and ask: "Is there another factor influencing me, which I think is my objection? Is there a physical factor, an emotional factor? Is some other factor present? So then you examine the situation again.

If there isn't any physical or other reason leading you astray, then listen to your intuition. Don't be controlled by your intuition, and don't try to control your intuition.

If you become familiar with it, if you are familiar with the circumstances when it is there to guide, advise or push you, then intuition becomes a perfectly normal and usual way of handling situations: "I examine the situation from the professional, social, political and intuitive point of view."

If you like, when you examine a situation all these factors have a proportional vote. If it is a technical situation, your technical experience has a greater percentage of influence. The same applies to social, educational and other situations. You give your intuition a correct portion out of that overall total.

There are no rules as to how much weight that intuition has. The importance or proportion of the vote you give has to be based on your own experience with your intuition.

If you find that in certain circumstances your intuition can be a little bit emotional, then you can delicately diminish the influence of that particular intuition in that situation.

So take advantage of this very fundamental and useful power you have.

And finally, I've been asked by your husbands and boyfriends to ask you to be very patient, kind and understanding towards them.

THT CONGRESS SERRA NEGRA, BRAZIL
March 31 to April 8, 1990

LISTENING AND TALKING TO BODY AND BEING

In these few days, I would like to try and do quite a lot of intensive work. When I say intensive, I do not mean with tension, anxiety or some sort of great hurry or urgency.

We have already had several therapy meetings, and we should now be devoting ourselves to producing something more concentrated, useful and less diffused. If we are to encourage our therapists to use particular aspects of the Granada Therapy, they must know what they are doing. At this stage, we may not be able to give them the whole thing, or even 60% of it, but we should at least give people a basis on which to build, in order to allow them to use the tactics, techniques and energy of the Tradition through their own therapy disciplines.

Beyond a certain point, research and discussion must be put into action.

Of course there are always areas one can call "pure research" in which a person accomplishes a research project and amasses information, but the function of that pure research is to provide information for people to use in practical areas, i.e., in our case, for us to be able to use this Granada Therapy in a knowing way, meaning that people know that they are using it, and when they have used it, they know what they have done.

Otherwise, during the course of a therapy or activity, they may use various elements from the Tradition and not know which was the one that really succeeded.

For instance, depending on the physical and psychological health of that patient, a person may decide: "I will treat this patient with a particular intention and particular attitude" and during or after the treatment, he or she should be able to monitor what was done by asking themselves "Did the particular aspect I used work? Did it advance the cure?" Otherwise, if several different aspects or techniques are used simultaneously, you get an area of confusion. We are therefore talking about specifics, and our terms must be precise.

One of the main factors I think this congress should concern itself with is listening to the body and conversing with the being.

As such, the human body is not silent. All of us know that there are certain physical signals which can always be monitored. You have the pulse rate, body temperature, the rate of breathing and all the other standard measurements that can always be applied. In this way, the body is communicating with you. The subject of this congress therefore applies between all of you as therapists and your patients, and also between you and yourself.

A therapist examining a patient will note all the normal signals: pulse, temperature, etc. There are other tests like sound, X-ray, putting cameras down the throat and all sorts of other ways of testing as well.

All of these tests are in fact communications between doctor and patient, and they can also take place between a person and their own being. After all, by means of nerve impulses, every part of the human body is signaling all the time. Certain sets of nerves signal a pain: that signal is picked up, the source of the pain is identified and then we will look for the reasons for that pain and so forth. It means that a communication of signal is taking place.

Depending on the physical state, you have an almost perfect communication system built into the human frame. When I say this, I am not saying that you should ignore sophisticated diagnosis techniques like X-ray, ultrasonics or whatever; I am simply saying that one should develop or enhance this natural communication system.

The physical system or body is very much interested in the health of its own physical system, and the being which exists within that physical body is just as interested in the health of that body as the body itself.

So when I say "listen to the body", I mean that one begins by using the conventional tests, but one then enhances the method of testing by enhancing the method of feeling. Encourage the system; encourage the body to transmit. At the same time, you have to persuade and convince the being that, in fact, you are listening. And not only that you are listening, but that you are encouraging further and deeper communication.

If one increases this communication within oneself, many of the confusions that people complain about can be identified.

On a very deep level, the being is a very private entity. Certainly, there are techniques which have been developed in the realms of psychology and psychiatry to allow certain closed areas to be perhaps opened up. But sometimes the being will defend its privacy so strongly that a therapy will sometimes have a reverse effect. That is why you have to convince the being that "Yes, I can listen, and I do want to help". You use this method of communication with the being of a patient, when being is communicating to being.

How do you convince your own or somebody else's being that it is safe to confide that secret to you? If the essential being of a person enters into a deep communication with another essential being, that becomes an area of total security. Both essential beings have the same scale of values. They are talking, if you like, in a profoundly different common level of language.

In the area of therapy, this type of communication has the deepest value, because it saves time, effort and energy.

Another value to this is that in a being-to-being communication, a form of energy can be exchanged. This energy is of a nature which can adjust and change the being either of the transmitter or the recipient.

Everybody here has had the experience where, after two or five minutes of speaking with somebody, one says to oneself: "Here is a person who can help me" or "This person gives me comfort" or "Here is a person whom I can trust".

This very often happens by a form of thought contact. I am not talking about telepathy here, it's something much more profound, much stronger and more valuable. It can happen accidentally, for instance when two people are studying something together or having a conversation, and suddenly a harmony is established.

This is what can be called involuntary harmony, but it does happen. So how can one produce it or provoke it?

In the case of a therapist and patient, it can happen by creating circumstances which can attract this sort of accidental contact: ambiance, colour, all the factors we have been talking about before when discussing therapeutic contexts.

For instance, your own attitude and intention as a therapist can help towards this: "I want to help this person, I believe I can, I know I can, I know it is possible".

This intention you are saying to yourself is something you feed into yourself before the therapy. During the period of contact and therapy, you also have this turning over in your mind.

You have to believe in yourself and I hope I don't have to tell you not to approach a patient with your hands outstretched to strangle him while saying "I'm going to cure you", because he might get the wrong signal.

When patients are in a situation where they are in need of therapy, they are in a psychological or physical state of imbalance. Very often, since they are in a rather defensive state, they can pick up any agitation or tension from you. As a professional, you are obviously using tactics and knowledge and what is called "bedside manner" with the patient. At the same time, on a deeper level, you are not pushing, you are just transmitting. This is exactly similar to an exercise or zikr you might do in the Tradition.

To do a zikr or an exercise, perhaps you wear a robe, sit in a particular position, take the tasbee and repeat a word or phrase. This is your intention, it creates and influences the ambience and it attracts energy. During that process, on deeper and deeper levels, you are receiving, producing and working with the energy that is there. You are talking to your essential being and you are showing to your essential being: "I am sitting here wearing this, I have a tasbee in my hand, I am taking this position and I'm doing something for myself." So you have the physical being and the essential being working together harmoniously.

If a person is in need of medical treatment or therapy, they know it. The cause of a physical or mental state may be well-concealed, even from oneself, but deep down, the essential being knows exactly where the imbalance and problem is, because the essential being monitors and receive every fraction of sophisticated signal from every nerve in the body.

If just one gland is not functioning, if there is a drop or an increase in the corpuscle count, the person's being records that factor in a millisecond. Equally, if you are doing an exercise or producing, receiving or processing energy, your being knows to a fraction of a degree how much.

Establishing, maintaining and developing contact with the essential being is a constant activity. You have to convince and persuade your essential being, or that of somebody else, that you are the warden of this conversation. You may say "This is ridiculous, because the physical human body contains the essential being and the essential being should know that the body is the warden of this contact or confidence." But don't forget that the essential being is also witness to the abuses, stupidities and other things performed by the physical being and the so-called intelligence.

Furthermore, the essential being has to be sure that any signal that it sends out will be properly understood and hopefully acted upon.

"What signal should I send?" "About what?" "How regularly?" "Does this so-called brain want to know that two corpuscles have just died in my left leg and that three corpuscles are not doing very well in my right arm?"

"How many signals?" "How often?"

Well, the answer to this is quite simple because you don't have an "all or nothing" communication, but a communication based on necessity, urgency or need to know.

The essential being does not take over the lower functions which the human frame can usually perform on its own. What it does is use them in a different way. For instance, if persons with normal and reasonable hearing hear some music, the tone is pleasant and that creates a certain calm and harmony within them. As you know, we use music very widely in the Tradition because, as we say, we know there are ears within ears.

What we would ask the communication with the essential being to do is to inform us when or how or how better to do something. Or how to feel or analyse conventional feelings in a different way.

Very many of these tactics or things I am talking about are already well known in therapy, so "what else is new"?

What is new is that you are focusing more precisely with the energy of the Tradition on what you are doing. And when you're doing it, you don't just say "Well, I'm in the Tradition, so I'll do it and get back-up."

What you say is: "I know it works, it will work and I will make it work."

Also when listening, you yourself are more refined in your listening. The listening itself is more refined, (not more selective, because you could be ignoring things): it's both more subtle and more precise.

What I would very much like to do in these next few days is to consider this particular point of listening and talking, and I would like for you to think and discuss with each other about how you can apply this in your own discipline or therapy.

This may appear difficult to some people in relation to themselves, because they may say "I'm not quite sure I know my own essential being." This is a very familiar point which has been put to me many times, and the answer is that you have to know and believe it is there and get to know it adequately.

Discovering the totality of one's essential being is a life's work and more.

Progressively, as one tries, one discovers more about one's being. So you don't wait until you arrive at a point where you can say: "Right, I'm satisfied that I know my essential being completely." Get to know it better so that you can speak to it better. Convince and persuade your essential being that you are its warden, and that it should share its secrets with you.

And if it does confide its secrets to you, what are you then going to do with those secrets?

It is up to you to persuade your being that you'll use those secrets usefully, that you will go about using such secrets without boasting or telling everybody about them. You'll keep them secret because they are personal to you. Certainly, there may be some of them that you might wish to confide to somebody you trust. There may be surprising or even unpleasant discoveries to be made about your essential being. You may discover, for instance, that you're an idiot and that, of course, is a secret which you would normally prefer to keep to yourself.

Those of you here who have read and remembered the Naqshbandi Rules will find that this area is covered in those rules as well. In a therapy situation, you are taking this a step further. While "travelling within yourself" and getting to know yourself and your own being, you are also harmonizing and making contact with a patient's being.

We are talking here about two active factors, listening and talking. Both listening and talking can be excuses for time-wasting, or they can be usefully employed. We are in the Tradition to act in an active and not in a passive way. There are no excuses for laziness or inactivity when one identifies an area which needs work.

In the next few days I suggest you examine ways, circumstances and techniques in which you can enhance this listening and talking capacity with people who will basically be your patients.

OBSERVING THE BODY AND BEING

Yesterday I talked about communication in terms of listening and talking. I would like to add another factor to that, which is observation.

It is quite obvious that any therapist, before and during a treatment, must carefully use their powers of observation for the purpose of diagnosis and to observe how the treatment is progressing.

To that, I would like you to add an additional area of

observation, which is observation from the point of view of other disciplines of therapy than your own.

You might say "This is a little bit difficult because if I am a general practitioner or psychiatrist, how can I look at a patient through the eyes of a surgeon, a dietician or from the point of view of somebody in another discipline?"

"Are you asking us to learn all the other disciplines, and apply them all in addition to our own at the same time?"

The answer to this is of course no, because it would be both time-consuming and confusing. What I am suggesting you do is that you tap into and establish a connection with the reservoir of knowledge of all the other therapists here.

Certainly, we have reports, papers and archives which are available to be circulated and read. But, there is another reservoir, another source of this knowledge and experience. Since the year 1982, when we started the Granada Therapy, I created a special reservoir of energy to be used by therapists in the Tradition. In order that you can make a contact with and benefit from this therapy reservoir, you must know and believe and feel that it exists. "What do I switch on, what is the phone number, is there a fax line?" No.

In a given state or therapy situation, once you have repeated your intention to yourself, you focus and put yourself in contact with that reservoir. This is not magic, nor does it mean that you have an entire picture, i.e. an immediate neurological and anatomical knowledge of every therapist here or who ever was. All you need to know and all you need to get from that contact is how the knowledge held in that reservoir applies to that particular circumstance or patient, at that time.

How your access to that knowledge and how the energy coming from that reservoir operates is in form of slight indications; not categorical in the sense of "You are now to do that!", but a feeling or indication that this technique or that aspect should be followed.

When you start the activity, you repeat your intention and then commence the actual activity; you do not wait for some sudden illumination to come from somewhere. As you commence your therapeutic activity, be it in conventional or holistic medicine, you are doing your activity as well as you can, and, having made the contact, you should feel that the energy is coming to you. You don't wait to get the feeling; sometimes the feeling is more obvious, sometimes less, but you go on doing the activity.

You may commence an activity and then by knowledge, experience or intuition, introduce another factor or a variation of that technique. Don't forget that you must always be watching, monitoring and checking yourself as well as the relationship between yourself and the patient.

The amount of contact or energy you receive varies from situation to situation. The quality and type of energy you receive varies according to the time, the situation and the patient. After all, in every area of a patient to therapist relationship, in every situation of this type, the factors will have changed slightly; the time is different, today is different from yesterday, the patient has changed slightly and so have you.

This means that there will be always slight variations in the type of energy or activity. The type and amount of energy is self-monitoring in exactly the same way as the Tradition's energy is available to you if you do a zikr or exercise; it works according to how well you can use it.

The factor of observation is important because you are observing the situation, the patient, and yourself in as many ways as possible. It is important to observe yourself in the sense of "How well am I doing?": not in a self-critical or defensive way, but in a confident way, in order to remind and repeat to yourself: "The energy is there, it can be used and I can use it". You are transmitting that feeling of confidence to the patient in conventional ways and also communicating from your being to their being.

I must say this to avoid any kind of misunderstanding: when you are in contact with this reservoir of energy you do not "become somebody else", you do not get halfway through the situation and ask yourself "Who am I now?". So avoid this kind of question, otherwise you'll find yourself writing your name on the back of your hand to remember who you are.

But joking apart, you do not become a sort of a marionette or instrument. You are yourself, but functioning a little bit better.

This reservoir of energy has been produced, and part of your function is to add techniques, aspects and details to this reservoir. You do this through your own therapy meetings, and also as individuals, by repeating your basic intention to yourself and adding to it the intention that you want this experience, tactic or technique to be added to the reservoir of therapeutic knowledge.

The energy which exists in this reservoir is of two different types. One type is what we call colourless, i.e., without colour or type, which means that it can be used for any type of therapy.

The other type of energy is coloured, which means that it is mixed and specific. In your own particular areas of therapy, its function is to encourage you to try, to encourage you by gently indicating to you that it is present.

Without being too dramatic, what does the existence of this reservoir mean? It means that any individual therapist is representing all the therapies of the Tradition, in other words, the ones you already know and the ones you don't know. In that situation, the whole energy is being channeled through you at that time.

It is not dramatic in the sense that there might be some sort of "certain cure" or "instantaneous" effect, but it does mean that in a therapy situation, you have hundreds or thousands of options of activity. Nevertheless, this should not cause you confusion or cause you to move significantly away from what you really know best. If you are a surgeon and you have to operate on an appendix, it would not be efficient to try and use an osteopathic technique for this job.

There is a difference between being open and having access to all of these techniques, and being confused because there are too many techniques. This is why it is absolutely necessary to have as much exchange between yourselves on therapeutic techniques as possible. It is not only useful, it is absolutely necessary, for instance, for a surgeon to consider what could be done in pre-surgery, pre-operative or post-operative situations.

As therapists, you also have another function which slightly widens your professional function. As people in the Tradition, your contact with the Tradition influences your family and the society in which you live, so that your social impact and responsibility is also important. You must be in a position to answer any possible question which patients or other people may put to you.

I say this because the majority of people who are in need of some sort of therapy or another have a heightened degree of perception. This perception is actually based on self-preservation, and they are very quick to identify a positive quality in the therapist.

They may conceivably say: "Your conversation, tactics or techniques are a little bit different from others I have experienced", because their perception is very keen at that moment. They can be both encouraged and given strength, or they can be deeply frightened, depending on your answer. So if somebody puts a question to you, you can explain yourself to them, according to your knowledge of them, and in a way which will encourage them without giving them any sort of fear or anxiety. You can make the answer very simple, for instance by saying to them: "Perhaps my technique or attitude is different because I want to cure you." Of course, they might very well reply "What do you mean, everybody and his brother says that, no therapist says 'I want to kill you' or something like that."

So part of your skill is to believe it yourselves, and say it in such ways and at such levels that patients also believe it. If you are confident in your own mind, not over-confident, but confident enough to feel that you can advance this person's well-being, you can and must broadcast this fact on all possible levels. You do not say to them: "I am going to do this that and the other thing, and in any case, the post-mortem will prove me right." There are truths you say and there are truths you don't say.

The factor of constantly monitoring your own feelings and performance is important, because this factor is also transmitting a positive energy. It has to be a confident monitoring, and not of a hostile and critical nature. It cannot be a doubtful examination in the sense of "Is this right? Shall I do this or that?", because the critical or the doubtful transmits equally negative impulses.

The relationship and contact you build up with the patient should be based on certain positive basic factors. And, throughout the therapy, it should be modified according to the state of the person.

This modification of the tactics you might be using can be dependent on signals which you are receiving.

There is a little bit of a difficult area here, because you do not necessarily have to, and sometimes you should not, explain to the patient that you have access to a particular energy, because it might frighten them away or create confusion. Nevertheless, you should get a message over to them that they are coming into contact with something new and beneficial.

A conventional and useful way to do this is not to say to them that "Your state of health, your condition is such that it will benefit from my using certain aspects of the Granada Therapy, which is not a new, zippy, Californian cure-all therapy", because everybody says that sort of thing and everybody hears that. So maybe you say: "This therapy is a result of considerable study and discussion, and it is a very pure, direct, and specific therapy."

In fact, the way you explain it depends on the person you are explaining to. Some people will say: "No thank you, I am not going to be a guinea pig. Go try it on somebody else".

So it depends how you present it. You have to convince them that you are interested in them as a human being as well as interested in curing them. They are listening, their being is listening. You have to talk, and your being has to talk to them.

At every moment, at every stage in a therapeutic situation, the word you should keep in mind is "alert"; you have to be alert to what people are saying and to what their being is saying, alert to how much and what form of energy you are receiving back from them, alert to your own observation.

All these areas of alertness should come together in an inverse pyramid formation and turn into an activity, an action. It is up to you to put the Granada Therapy into function because it is not an abstract therapy and it does not function in a vacuum.

COPYING UPWARDS

As I have already said, I both recommend observation and use observation myself, and I also tend to back up the different levels of observation I make with visual observation.

Over the period of a congress like this I can modify, hopefully upwards, any technique or use of energy according to how you assimilate it. I can do this in several different ways: the two most obvious ways are to do it and tell you I've done it, or again, to let you have a little glimpse, a little glance of how I am doing it.

Of course, if I give you a little bit of an idea of how I am doing things, this is not necessarily how I am really doing things.

When I say this, it's not really a trick: what we are dealing with here is that people, like monkeys, copy.

Even if people are right to try and copy what I do, it involves a complicated equation which I ask you to try and understand. If they imitate what I'm doing, and even assuming they are right in the way they copy it, if they do copy exactly what I have done and reproduce it exactly in the way they do it, it will still be wrong. Even though they had a good intention in copying it and a good intention in doing it, it is still wrong.

Part of the reason is because I am doing it and you can't do what I do; but the major factor which has changed is the time. By the time you have understood what is going on and copied it, we are already 5 or 10 milliseconds later and the time has already changed.

If I suggest, recommend and teach you to do something, I have to allow for your doing it at a future time, when you have learned how to do it. So I am thinking ahead on your behalf.

VISUALIZING A THERAPY WITH PRECISION

As part of a therapy situation with access to the reservoir of therapeutic energy represented by the Tradition, in your mind you should think of or visualize a triangle or an equation. The equation is made up of the therapist, plus the patient, plus the technique, plus the energy either equalling or hopefully resulting in benefit.

In the triangle situation, you have the therapist and the patient, and at the apex, you have the energy of the Tradition.

By any definition an equation is neat and tidy and it also takes a fixed and rigid form. You have to think more and more in definite and precise terms in order to benefit completely from this extra available energy, because it is a precise energy and it can only be used in a precise formulation.

Certainly in an equation, the therapist plus the patient plus the energy and techniques of the Tradition equals, hopefully, recovery or benefit. Obviously the resulting factor of $A + B + C = X$ depends on how usefully you function and how beneficially the patient reacts to your own functioning.

If you are working on the basis of an approximate sort of A, plus a precise B, plus a C based on hearsay, it won't work, because your result will be a "more or less" one, and it is not a result worth trying for. I know that this thought-process sounds manifestly silly, nevertheless this is the way people do think.

If you're going to be expected to use energy of a very refined quality, you must obviously make your attention and technique either of the same precision, or it must at least come close to the same precision.

I have said before that the most important factor in a therapy situation is not the therapist nor the technique, it is the patient.

Of course, the therapist and the technique are also certainly important. By using valuable and useful techniques, the therapist benefits himself or herself, because the very use of positive energy and intention spills out into other situations close to that therapy situation.

Everywhere a function and activity of the Tradition is used, the influence remains and is felt. This is another factor which one can introduce into the relationship between oneself as a therapist and the patient.

I have already suggested how one could explain or introduce a patient to a therapy of the Tradition if there was a question. You don't have to explain the whole thing, because then you get into an overlong explanation, but depending on the patient, you could use certain aspects to explain certain fundamental ideas, like that it is not just the person as a patient that is being dealt with, but you and the patient together with a whole activity.

I am not saying that you have to feel guilty, defensive or hide the contact you have with the Tradition from patients. But people who are ill or who need a therapy are usually in a nervous or possibly unbalanced condition, and if you are trying to conceal a Tradition technique you are using because you don't think it necessary to talk about it to them, they may consider that you are trying to hide something from them which is fundamentally important.

At that point they might consider that you have a doubt or that you don't know what you are doing, or again, that you don't want to tell them how seriously ill they are. So as I say, if you have a reasonable explanation which you can give them in simple terms, this will probably go a long way to overcome the normal and basic primitive fear they might have.

ENGAGING THE PATIENT'S ACTIVE COLLABORATION

You can use another gambit or trick, as it's been described; and I'm sure this is familiar to most therapists. When a patient has an idea, or has heard of some treatment or something, and they want either to have it used on them or else to use it on themselves: "I have heard that there is a tonic made out of boiled boots which is good for hacking cough" or something like that.

The wise therapist will always have an unmarked bottle under his desk so that he can then say: "Yes I have it". (Agha picks up a bottle from under the table and puts it heavily on the table).

Of course, that doesn't mean to say that you agree to and accept every suggestion put to you, however outrageous or stupid it may be. What you are doing is simply demonstrating or proving to them that you are on their side, that you are with them and do identify with them.

Of course every therapist knows that if you can get the patient identifying with and enthusiastic about the treatment, this is a very valuable relationship to have with that patient. What you want is a situation in which not only is the patient enthusiastic and identified with the treatment, but where you are also giving them a contact with positive energy for them to use as well.

A therapist can and should provoke or produce as many circumstances as possible where they can use tactics or techniques from the Tradition, but of course only in relation to the situation.

We have touched upon the use of colour and one can add other useful tactics or elements of the Tradition to that. But from that point on, one is also adding the other factor which is very much "person to person" and being to being, with the addition of the energy reservoir.

THERAPISTS WORKING TOGETHER

I would like to make a small variation of the programme: we will have the usual discussion this morning, but before you break for lunch I would like you to make a certain arrangement among yourselves. This is not really a change, it is what I would call a technical adjustment or fine tuning.

When you finish this morning's session, select twenty-four people from among your number. The selection can be just a representative one, it does not have to be based on any particular criteria. Then subdivide those twenty-four people into four groups, and those four groups will meet separately in four convenient and private places in the hotel, i.e., not in the public rooms or the bars.

From four o'clock this afternoon until five o'clock they will do the Ya Shifa exercise with the intention of helping to reinforce the connection between all of you here and the therapy energy I have arranged.

They will do this exercise between four and five, and then they will come down and join you in the congress discussion as usual. How you select these people and on what basis you select them I don't know, I'm not suggesting anything, I leave it entirely up to you. There should just be a representative number of twenty-four people.

Now as you know well, I don't often explain things, I just tell you and if you understand, fine, if you don't understand, you eventually will. But one of the functions of this small group meeting this afternoon is for me afterwards to be able to check that the energy is flowing correctly.

AWAKENING THE ESSENTIAL BEING

For this morning, let me continue a little on the topic of listening and speaking to the essential being, both your own and that of a patient.

You all know, especially those who are involved in psychological or psychiatric counselling, that a patient can very frequently show a different or even several different personalities. Equally it is possible that a person, especially somebody who is psychologically disturbed, can show such a very strong deep personality that a person might think that it is their actual being.

So fine, we have put forward the idea of establishing a relationship with the person's essential being. But how do we know that this is the correct one, the real essential being?

This judgment or identification by you is simple because, fortunately, this choice or decision of yours does not in fact consciously exist. It does not exist on the conscious level because you are not trying to communicate with it in a conventional way.

Being speaks or communicates to being in a completely different or unknown language. There can therefore be no element of conscious misunderstanding or trickery, because it is on a different wavelength and not in the form of a spoken or conventionally heard language. It is in fact a wavelength; it is a communication of a human nature in the form of a commonly shared wavelength.

When I say common I mean there is no variation between the wavelengths of Brazilians, Argentines, Germans, French and so forth, otherwise you would have a conventional confusion.

To be more correct or more specific, one calls it a harmonic and not a wave. Because if it were as inefficient as a wave it could be interrupted, but if it is a note or harmonic, it is something absolutely fixed with no degree of error. Conventionally speaking, anywhere you go in the world among musicians, if you say that a note is a high C, everybody understands that what is meant is that note, and nothing above or below.

So the communication harmonic of the essential being transmits and receives in a very precise frequency and recognizes its counterpart. This communication and reception apparatus or harmonic is a very fundamental and functional part of the essential being. It is something, which, if it has not been used properly and correctly, can remain in a dormant state for generations and even centuries. It isn't lost, it doesn't become destroyed or injured, it just remains there.

But even if it remains dormant, it is at the same time alert and receptive to a signal on the right harmonic.

This is one of the reasons that we use the phrase that people in the Tradition become "awakened". People do become awakened this way, and the more this function is exercised, the more familiar it becomes, the more usefully it can be used.

It cannot be overused, burned out or abused, because it has a protection in the form of a series of filters which prevent any negative or abusive material coming in.

Information and energy can be fed to this essential being in certain specific ways. You feed or nourish it by offering it information or energy which it recognizes as being useful. Which means, of course, that you must put yourself in contact with sources of energy and useful information.

And then, in it's own way, the essential being, having identified the fact that you are awakening, will also point you in the direction of this information or energy.

There are also other ways in which a teacher can, to use a conventional phrase, force-feed or intravenously feed this being. One of the reasons why a teacher might do such a thing is to increase the capacity of a person.

Now just in case anybody is thinking about it, the application lists for this technique are already full. In this context, some people have mentioned reading about a method in the Tradition called the Shattari method, which is also called "the rapidness".

Such a method does exist but, again, before people start putting their names down for it there is a story about it.

There was a well known Shattari Sheikh who was visited by a student who said "Will you accept me as a pupil to follow the Shattari Method?"

So the Sheikh said: "Well, yes, but you should have time to think. Go and sit in that room there and I will call you."

The man went and sat in the room and he was there for two or three days, after which the servant came and said: "The Sheikh will see you in his formal reception room."

The man was very happy because he thought this would be a marvellous experience, especially since it would take place in the formal salon of the Sheikh. So he dressed himself in his best robes and went in. He entered this enormous reception room and the Sheikh was sitting on a pile of carpets and all around the room there were ashes and burning coals, things like that.

The student said to the servant: "But how can the Sheik be comfortable in this room full of ashes and half burning coals?"

"No, no" replied the servant, those aren't ashes. Those are the remains of students who didn't qualify."

So we are not told whether the student continued with his application or not.

Apropos of nothing at all, last time I was in the States I saw some of my cousins and their small children. And one of my cousins had one or two video tapes of me talking at one of the meetings, I don't know where. They showed this film and afterwards one of the small girls of about four said to me: "Agha, you change very much when you're out of your country".

And I said: "Well, maybe yes, because I'm getting a little older and I'm losing my hair, and so forth."

"No, no, it's not that" She continued, "Every time we see you on that video you have a very, very long nose."

So, I promised her that the next time I would have one of those clip-on microphones.

So you see, all observation is relative.

Observation is relative because the diagnosis and analysis of a patient's condition may obviously be influenced by one's own therapy discipline. As I have already said, this is perfectly valuable. I'm not saying "ignore the training of your own discipline". All I am saying is "add to, increase the levels, and increase the different points of view of your observation".

Communication and contact with the essential being of a patient, if it is well established, is really the key to treatment. While this is true in the case of a patient, this is also true of the essential being of every person, therapist or not. If a person is physically ill, mentally disturbed, depressed; whatever their condition, the essential being of that person knows exactly what is wrong.

Of course, knowing what is wrong and being able to do something about it requires first communication and then action. If I am sitting here with a headache and there is a box of aspirin, I have to do something in order to put that box together with me in order to resolve the situation. I have to initiate a movement and take an action. This means I have to make a decision; a circuit must work.

This is what the essential being is trying to tell you. It is trying to push you into action, but your conscious being must be able to receive those signals and identify them correctly.

You may receive the signal consciously and then perhaps analyse it or interpret it incorrectly. Again, the harmonic of communication between your essential being and your conscious physical being must be not only correctly established, but used regularly in order to keep the line what we call "clean". This is part of what is called knowing oneself. This communication applies within oneself, within the therapist and also between therapist and patient.

Imagine a situation, context or ambiance where the essential being of the therapist can be in contact with the essential being of the patient, and that essential being of the patient is communicating exactly what is wrong. I ask you to imagine this, because this is in the realm, not exactly of fantasy, but perhaps it is not solid enough from a Western point of view. So let me change one word: instead of saying imagine, let's say focus your thinking towards the situation.

Techniques exist, the discipline exists, the energy exists. In this formulation the therapist is a catalyst.

In every useful activity in the Tradition you must set yourself certain goals or aims to be achieved. The goals and aims you set yourself should be realistic, and they should be objectives which are of a common human benefit. There may be some people in conventional medicine, psychology, psychiatry or holistic medicine who wish to psychoanalyse a stone or to analyse the relative muscularity of a tree; because this is the West, they can be assured of a place in history and big volumes in all the reference libraries: but what has been their contribution to the galactic human condition?

Always keep certain achievable aims in front of you, always stretch yourself a little more. Your function is to advance yourselves in the Tradition and to further yourself in the therapy of the Tradition.

DEALING WITH NEGATIVE FEEDBACK

All of you in the Tradition engaged in a therapeutic activity should take note of the Naqshbandi rules. Of course, everybody in the Tradition should already know, study and be conscious of the rules, but more particularly, people who are engaged in any therapy will find that there are certain rules which they can apply more closely to their own activity.

For instance, a rule which is of considerable value is Safar Dar Watan or "travelling in the homeland" i.e., travelling within oneself.

This rule is especially useful for people involved in psychiatric or psychological therapy, because they come into contact with a factor I have spoken about before but which I'll repeat again. They can come into contact with people who have a considerable negative potential or negative charge, and if they themselves have a slight worry or fear, it is quite understandable that perhaps some of this negativity may transmit to them as therapists.

This fear or preoccupation may become stronger if the therapist is thinking: "If I am putting my essential being into contact with this person's essential being, is this negativity dangerous to my own essential being?"

We will deal with the two beings, the essential being and the conscious physical being in two parts. Regarding the essential being, there is absolutely and categorically no circumstance under which a negativity can transfer from person to person on the level of the essential being. I repeat categorically that there is not one single circumstance where such a communication could take place on a negative basis.

Secondly, as far the conscious or physical being of the therapist is concerned, there is the possibility of receiving a certain degree of negativity, but fortunately, such a negative charge, if it has been transmitted, is small and insignificant, and such a transfer can only take place if there has been over-identification with the patient.

Nevertheless, if that transmission does take place, its effect is limited to being a surface effect, in which this transmission's negative charge or capacity is like a form of static electricity on the person. In fact, it is a very low and insignificant charge.

If it does exist or if a person is concerned or worried that it might exist as a result of a therapy session, this is what they should do. They can do exactly the same as any person in the Tradition does who encounters some negative energy and wishes to get rid of it.

The best and most positive way is to hold the tasbee, and the tasbee will absorb the negativity and discharge it to the ground. The tasbee does not hold the negative or become negative. In the absence of a tasbee or if one does not have immediate access to one, there is another simple equivalent which is to pass the hands over the arms as if you are wiping perspiration and touch something of natural origin: wood, stone, a natural material. This will remove and ground any negative charge.

This is a technical activity, not superstition, and you can see the memory of this in the West when people touch wood for good luck. Somehow they know that they must get rid of this charge, and the most natural material which is everywhere to touch is wood.

There is a third alternative, perhaps in the absence of a tasbee or a natural material to touch, because you have your own inbuilt way of discharging negativity. You use your contact with the Tradition by repeating your zikr to yourself, because your zikr or Sirr is another connection, another bridge between you, myself, and the Tradition.

Communication with a patient or the connection a therapist has to a patient should be carefully established and monitored.

You all know this. You have been taught about the dangers of over-identification and other hazards. But to be more sure and more confident that this relationship will not develop in any negative way, you add another tactic. This tactic or technique does not replace the one you have learned in your own discipline. It simply consists of starting every therapy session by repeating your intention to yourself, and occasionally to call this intention up again in your mind during the period of therapy.

Each time you do this you are establishing a filter between yourself, the patient and the situation. This filter is not an obstacle to communication. It is there to allow useful feedback from the patient while preventing and stopping any negative or confusing impulses coming through.

Certainly, when dealing with a patient one can experience various personal feelings: impatience, frustration, anger, sorrow, any number of human emotions. And the filters I talk about do not prevent these emotions from coming up from you or from the situation itself, because they do not prevent them from arising.

If negative or confusing impulses do appear, you have to handle them yourself. But if you are quite sure and not worried about the possibility of negative contamination coming to you, the very small amount of energy you might use to worry about this possibility can now be focused on any of your own personal feelings or reactions.

YA SHIFA AS A CONNECTION TO THE SOURCE

In an analogy I have used before, I have talked about the initial amount of energy you use to start a wheel moving. In a therapy situation the same form of activity exists, on the basis of contact between one essential being to another.

Once the initial and right type of impact is properly established, the communication will continue automatically on its own impetus. Now I don't like the word "automatically" because it suggests something mechanical, but in any case, the communication continues with less of the original effort, and at the same time, the degree of communication is being constantly monitored. It can therefore be increased or decreased according to the need of that particular situation.

You are all familiar with the phrase or zikr "ya shifa" we use in the Tradition. The word "shifa", like all the other attributes of God we use in the Tradition, represents not just a word, but an overall concept. By repeating this phrase or formula, you are affirming that a source of health and healing does exist. By affirming this, you place yourself in a specific relationship with that source.

Once you have made this affirmation in the context of your therapeutic activity, you are then acting as a reflector between that source and the patient. This energy, which you are both receiving and reflecting, is an energy like a fuel, and like any fuel, it has to be fed into a mechanism, just as glucose is fed into the body to be burned.

You therefore use this affirmation as a way of increasing your capacity and potential to heal. You become part of the healing function.

You don't use this affirmation in isolation, it becomes part of your therapy discipline. You don't call in the patient in and go and stand over him or her and say: "Ya shifa, next!" This might be an interesting mass-production technique but it would also be self-deluding. Nevertheless, it is an extremely powerful base on which you can stand and build.

Once you accept it as the basis, it does not remain only in this basic state; it percolates and travels its way through the whole of your therapy activity. If you read, study, and think about what is represented by the whole concept of "shifa", you will consciously and unconsciously find a situation in which you can use these aspects. You will find situations in which an option seems to be offered to you, and people will say it happened "by coincidence."

You do not have graphic dreams or visions, and even if you did, you would certainly not tell your patient that you were treating them as a result of a vision or dream that you once had. Otherwise, the resulting reputation you would develop might not always be the best.

VISIONARY EXPERIENCES

Let me comment very quickly on what one might call visions or visionary experiences. If a person experiences a particularly vivid visual or dream experience, assuming there is as much recall as that, it means that it is something that should be examined in very considerable detail.

Certainly, there are volumes and volumes that have been written about how to interpret dreams, from Freud, Jung and all the others on, all of whom go into every possible way you can look at them. But the first examination of a visual or dream experience should be not exactly hostile, but done with a critical and doubting attitude.

If the dream can then be ignored or dismissed, on that

basis of that examination, so be it. "It was the cheese I had for supper" or "Maybe it was the funeral I attended" or something else. If it passes the initial doubting phase of: "Was it something I ate? Yes.", then it can be examined in another way.

Did it contain any positive and recognizable elements from the Tradition? If it does contain one or more of these elements, how does that element relate to one of the 99 names? Was it a suggestion, an indication, an order? Does it relate in a positive way to my therapy discipline or to my own life?

While on the subject there is, as usual, a Nasrudin story about dreams.

It appears that he was travelling through the Gobi desert with a companion, and it was very hot and they were running very short of water, until a time came when they had just one bottle of water left. They were both terribly thirsty, their mouths were dry and they were semi-hallucinating. So they decided to sleep early one night and get up very early in the morning and share the last bottle of water the next day before trying to get to the next oasis.

They both woke up early the next morning, and Nasrudin's companion discovered that the bottle was empty.

He croaked to Nasrudin, because his throat was so dry: "Why did you finish the water? How could you do such a thing?"

Nasrudin said: "You know that we are both dervishes and that we are sworn to follow the orders of our masters, of our teachers. Last night I had this dream. In this vision, Maulana Rumi said to me: "Nasrudin, drink your water; drink your share, now."

So the other dervish said to him: "Yes, but he said to drink your share of the water. Why did you finish the whole bottle?"

"Well, it was obvious", said Nasrudin, "my share was the lower half of the bottle."

So you see, dreams can also be relative.

THERAPY AND TRADITION TACTICS

In your therapy situations, you are supposed to be exercising certain techniques from the Tradition. And of course, by practicing these techniques in therapy situations with patients, you are also using them on yourself. In such situations, you are making an opportunity where you can use as many techniques as possible.

There are obviously some situations where you can use more of these techniques and other situations where your choice is more limited. Before the commencement of a therapy activity, you can decide what you are going to try and use. Then, during the therapy situation you then see whether you can add other techniques to the one you began with.

You use these skills or techniques in a perfectly normal and flexible fashion, because quite obviously, if you decide "I'm going to use this and that" before a therapy situation begins and the opportunity does not develop, if you are not careful, there may be a temptation to try and force more and more techniques into a situation.

Alternatively, perhaps you may have decided in advance what technique you were going to use, and then during the therapeutic situation you find you are using something else or one or two other techniques. This should not cause shock or confusion: "I had intended to do that, now I find myself doing this, I have to stop and start all over", because if you have started by going into the situation with the correct intention (at least to a certain degree), you and the situation itself will attract the right activity.

That doesn't mean to say you have lost control of the situation. It means that something within you or something in the situation has provoked a particular tactic.

I repeat this point: you do not and have not lost control of the situation because, of course, you must not.

COMMUNICATING FUNDAMENTAL POSITIVES

Let me recommend an aspect of a technique to you. It is not new; you all know about it and use it. It is an aspect which you use normally and I'm going to suggest a way in which you can use it in a more specific and focused manner. It's a very simple thing called the tone of voice.

Everybody uses it; it is not limited to therapists and all of you know the necessity of establishing a rapport and influencing a situation by the choice of words or tone of voice you use. Now I'm not going to teach you voice projection or tonality, because even with my skills, with some of you that would be impossible.

The question here is not so much of changing the tone of voice or producing a harmonious reassuring tone, it is what you choose to say in what tone of voice.

You all know that in therapy you choose words like healing, curing, getting better and you say these words in a reassuring tone and manner.

Certainly, continue to use these phrases because they are also expected of you, and the patient wants this reassurance. If you are talking to a patient and reassuring him or her with these phrases, even though they expect them, they are not really listening to them. They are simply the normal preliminaries or opening people expect and which are understood and appreciated by their conscious being and mentality.

We have been talking about the dual contact. In the course of a conversation, or any comments which you might make, introduce certain, what I might call "trigger" words.

These trigger words are a very positive and strong aspects of the whole idea of health and cure. In a conversation you might say to somebody: "you are looking better today", but better is not good, better is not right, correct and balanced.

What you want to introduce into the conversation, to be picked up by the person's essential being, are the fundamentals: good, right, improved. Note how my voice becomes beautiful immediately. You are feeding, giving and providing constant positive to the essential being, which deals with and uses extremes of positive. It does not want relative or comparative words.

This may be very basic, but after all, a great part of the essential being is fundamental, basic and simple. If you are using fundamental positives, in other words phrases such as these, the essential being understands that you are speaking to that being in an adult way. You are respecting its degree of understanding.

The difference between speaking to or encouraging a child and teaching or disciplining an adult is, if you say to a normal adult: "Come on, finish up your vegetables, you will grow up to be big and strong", the person will say: "This man is a lunatic" or "He's selling vegetables". But if you say to a reasonable person: "You know, for reasons of health, a reasonably balanced diet is required and vegetables contain this that and the other thing" the person appreciates it because you are considering that they are intelligent enough to understand.

You are thus adding another technique to establish and deepen the relationship between your essential being and that of the other person. This is necessary, because the reverse situation, the reverse signals from that essential being back to you will also be on that positive fundamental basis.

The essential being of a person knows intimately what the minute by minute and second by second state of the body and mind is signalling to you, and it sends signals to your conscious being in a very simple and also very sophisticated way.

This is logical, and it is possibly even one of the few logical things in human beings, because the essential being of the person is interested in the quality and good state of the body. It knows those signals, what type of signals they are, and in what way it can communicate and be understood.

It may choose how to signal to you, either by some physical change or physical manifestation, or else it can signal to you with a series of strong ideas coming back over and over again into the mind.

Thus we return again to one of the Naqshbandi rules: "Knowing Yourself". Knowing yourself also means knowing the signals.

Certain signals are, if you like, physical signals which people already know about themselves and which are obvious to them. For instance, some people say: "If I eat eggs I go blue in the face". This of course is a fairly unsophisticated sign of low tolerance to eggs, and, for the purpose of diagnosis all you really need here is a mirror.

But signals of a less obvious nature are coming back to one all the time. They can come quickly and pass, perhaps because of a lack of alertness by the person.

After all, don't forget alertness does not mean that you spend 24 hours in front of a mirror to see if your face has gone blue. Alertness is a state of scanning which is constant in you and it should be encouraged, because if the essential being wishes to send a significant signal, this signal will be repeated over and over again.

APPLYING TRADITION TACTICS

Applying the Naqshbandi Rules to oneself encourages you to become conscious of this constant monitoring of yourself. A very familiar technique of enhancing or increasing this monitoring is the zikr, and this technique can be expanded to include a patient.

As you should all know by now, there is an optimum physical position for doing the zikr that we call "joined together", in the sense that in the classic position, the hands are placed on the knees, either in a sitting position or in a cross-legged position on the floor. This way there are no "loose ends" and the energy is circulating within the person and not flowing out. If a person is sitting in a position of doing the zikr, the energy is flowing and mixing within the person.

Involving a patient in your zikr can be done simply in a sitting, standing, or any position, with the right hand on your left shoulder and the left hand touching the patient. Obviously this can be a quite normal thing to do, supposing a therapist or a doctor is taking the patient's pulse. In that situation the patient is involved in a circuit of the energy of your zikr.

They don't know this and they don't have to know it. To help the energy flow more efficiently, you repeat the intention, which is something you normally do before doing the zikr, and you add the fact that you want to include the patient in the flow of energy.

You are using the word "flow", not the word "give", "take" or "exchange". The operative word is flow.

Consider this, and make a place or a note in your research for the idea of using the tone of voice and the choice of affirmative, positive words.

People may think that they have all gone deaf, but one can carry on in a certain way, which is a little bit of a trick. Nevertheless it is sometimes useful, because in my case at least you can very easily get a sort of hypnotic attention from people, so it's also a way of testing whether their attention is really there, or whether they are just looking at you.

Again, you can check out the same phenomenon by a variation in tone. If they are nodding in rhythm to your words, it is usually indicated that you should change the tone or rhythm. If they are still nodding after you have stopped talking and left the room, you either have a full hypnotic situation or a very solid member of your fan club.

So examine other aspects of any technique you use, whether it's using music, tone of voice or colour, by asking "What is the basic quality of this technique?" And then if a particular use of colour or music has not produced the optimum result you were hoping for, see how you can go back to its basic component or element, and see if there is another aspect which you can use. Don't forget that in these cases, as from now, you are connecting with or tapping into a new and special type of energy.

RE-INVENTING MEMORY

In many areas of almost every activity one does things like classifying, sorting and arranging.

Doing this is of course necessary: one has a filing system, one imposes a categorization under different headings, but there is a point beyond which this categorization or filing away becomes a sort of end in itself, at which point, instead of helping, it becomes an obstacle in the sense that you produce a filing system: A to B, B to C, C to D and so forth which is perfectly useful and logical;

if you are looking for something on an alphabetical basis, you know the initial letter and can find it. This is an obvious fact.

But this is not useful beyond a certain point, because you begin to get subdivisions of the subdivisions and then section 2A of the second subdivision and so forth, and there comes a point where it is miraculous if you can find anything at all. So you introduce something called cross-referencing, and when that becomes too complicated, people put everything into a computer. All you have to do then is go to the computer, type in the subjects you want, and the information appears on the screen or starts getting printed out.

So there. Western civilization and philosophy has re-invented the human memory.

Now certainly, in some areas, from the point of view of a certain kind of efficiency, computer records and memory banks are perfectly useful. But the danger here is not that, as people were saying in science fiction, computers will "take over" the world, it is that people either become or don't become; they start ignoring certain things which come from within.

If you go to the biggest computer bank in the world and type in "Essential Being", out comes something that says "Wrong Entry". Therefore, while technical advances in the area of computers are an asset, they should not be allowed to replace certain deep human faculties.

POOLING RESEARCH

Different people, and also peoples, have different areas which are more developed within themselves, and it has nothing to do with race, sex or geographical location. This means that in the context of the Tradition, you recognize and use these different qualities in different people.

It is certainly possible that some of these capacities which are not so developed can be developed further in order to be brought up to an equivalent level. In the Tradition, this is what we aim to do where there is a significant absence of certain qualities. Then, if you take a group of people from any geographical location, you can harmonise them together and they profit from each other's qualities. And of course the difference here between the human being and the computer is that the people who have a certain different advancement can help the others to advance in that area as well. The equation will then be complete, because the people or persons who have this low degree of quality are not kept in that position, they are helped to push it up.

This is why one tries as much as possible to involve people with these different qualities in a similar activity.

When I first started proposing that you develop a therapy, I suggested that you should compare your different disciplines and see how you could learn from each other and perhaps incorporate parts of your own discipline in other people's activities.

In the same way, putting together people like yourselves with different degrees of capacity produces a current and a movement inside the overall group. To improve the circulation of this current, you do need more connection, correspondence and interchange of ideas. You need to think of each other and also for each other, but not in the sense that you are doing somebody else's thinking for them.

If any of you therapists read an article or come into contact with a situation you think could be interesting for somebody else, you are thinking about them. When thinking about them, make a copy and send it, with or without any comment, note, or thought you might have about the subject.

We must cover a wider and deeper area of therapy research. Very often you hear or read in magazines or professional periodicals about an area of research being done in a particular subject, and sometimes the conclusions to this research, if there are any at all, may be either unclear or disastrous. I have read many scientific, medical and other research articles where they say: "We did this, that and the other thing. It took us so many years and the results were inconclusive". And sometimes, when I have read the terms of reference they used, it is obvious that the research had to end with an inconclusive result.

In a majority of cases the reason has been that they have not allowed for certain aspects of the being of the person. Of course in Western research, there are certain factors of the being which they cannot measure and test, so that for them these factors do not exist.

I am therefore suggesting to you another area of thought: read as much as possible, look at it and see whether you can add something. Whether the result has been conclusive or inconclusive, try and see if there is a factor which you either might introduce or that somebody else, say a therapist of another discipline, could possibly introduce.

The division or arrangement of different people in different groups has many functions, but there is an additional function I would like to explain.

Sometimes it is such a simple thing that people ignore it or don't notice it. If you have people of different disciplines in a group, there may be situations where you are explaining a very small point of your own discipline to a person who is not of that same discipline. In doing this, you very often find that you are also clarifying that point for yourself.

On the conscious level the clarification factor is operating, while on the deeper level of being to being, the harmony is increasing, because, again, you are dealing with exchange on the level of very fundamental and basic realities.

This is not really the occasion to deal with questions like: "What is reality?" As far as your understanding of reality is concerned, you can take as a basic factor that the important aspect of reality, as far as the therapist is concerned, is the focusing of harmonious energy. The therapist actually functions as an instrument and equally as a condensing lens to focus on a point.

Your developing skill is and has to be on what you focus. If there is an illness, do you focus on a theoretical, practical or obvious source of the illness? Do you focus on the patient generally?

You can do both of these things and add one more. Let us say that hopefully and necessarily the energy that you are focusing is of a positive and healing quality. And if the receiving element in the patient is the person's essential being, it will attract and even manifest itself to the energy as the point of reception. This is because this receptor will or at least should identify the energy as curative and positive. It will then do everything it can to attract and assimilate this energy.

DESIGNATING SITUATIONS

A subject I would like to talk about tomorrow morning and introduce as a subject for discussion among yourselves is a question which touches upon children, and on the young generally. It would be useful to talk about various possible, necessary or useful therapeutic aspects concerning children.

I use the word aspects or situations and not problems, because we should try to be fairly precise in designating situations. All problems are situations but not all situations or aspects are problems.

So again, regarding classifications, don't automatically classify something as a problem in the sense of "I have a problem" because that is already taking it into a slightly negative classification.

"I am in a situation, there is a situation, such and such a person has a situation" is a better way of looking at it.

It's the reasonable examination of that situation which decides whether there really is a problem or not.

So, secret number seven hundred and eighty-six. Classify positively where possible.

PRIDE AND HUMILITY

There is one factor I would like to talk about before we commence the main discussion. In Tradition activities we place a lot of importance on the aspect of humility. This is not necessarily limited to the suppression of pride or arrogance, because a large part of humility is the feeling of gratitude, in the fact that a person, whether they function as a therapist or in any beneficial area, should be grateful for the gift or ability they have.

Certainly they can very well have a pride and confidence in a personal ability they built up, but with this feeling there should be a feeling of gratitude for the simple fact that the possibility or ability has been given to them. Along with this feeling of gratitude there should automatically come the feeling of humility, because however accomplished they are, however intelligent and clever, by comparison to the source of their knowledge and ability, they are nothing.

Certainly in any profession, whether in a therapeutic area or as an engineer, architect or any disciplined professional, a true professional builds up and gives off a public face for show. This is necessary because in a competitive world a professional must most certainly show that he has confidence in his own abilities. But the outward show or image-building done by a professional should not confuse or impress the person himself.

It shouldn't impress a person, but certainly one is allowed to encourage oneself. One examines himself, one feels confident in what one is doing and within oneself one says: "I'm able, I'm capable."

One should therefore do this because it is necessary. At the same time, within himself or herself, a person should guard this valuable, important and very delicate thing called humility.

HELPING THE YOUNG

For this morning, let us start looking at certain aspects of therapy which concern young children and adolescents. You have heard me say many times that in the Tradition we are very much preparing a way for the young.

Certainly and fortunately, everyone in the Tradition can pass on a strong and real contact to children. Whether their own or other's, all children also come into contact with a therapeutic context.

Let us divide this contact into two approximate areas. Let's say that one is the external, surface or physical area, and the other one is the deeper area of contact involving the use and transmission of energy from the Tradition.

Questions like diet, pollution and exercise have become more and more a matter of public concern. Some of this preoccupation or interest has been used commercially to sell doubtful or weird diets: slimy diets, putting on weight diets, getting taller diets, getting smaller diets and all permutations thereof. So the interest is there, especially in young people, because young people by definition follow fashion: fashion in dressing, culture and also fashions in health consciousness.

So let us try and consider in which way an aspect of the Granada Therapy can take advantage of this awakened interest by young people. Apart from the area of encouraging a correct and balanced diet, another unfortunately significant phenomenon is in what I would call the abuse area: drugs and alcohol being the two main areas of abuse.

All of you involved in therapy or just in social activities have evidence that these two problems are going to predictably increase and not go away. And of course, because there is so much money involved, certain areas of drugs are going to become more and more sophisticated and cheaper and cheaper. So the problem basically falls into three categories: prevention by education, treatment of the addict patient and post-recovery.

We have two or three centers working on the treatment of alcoholism, drug abuse and the recovery process and I hope there will soon be some useful reports that I will circulate. For the moment I'll leave aside the area of actual treatment and not comment on that aspect in detail for the moment.

What I would like you to think about and work on is a way of presenting information, a form of psychological presentation of prevention.

I know that this has already been done. There is publicity of the "Using drugs is not smart" type, or "Smoking is bad for you" and so forth, which is in progress. But what I would like you to think about is a similar type of presentation with the addition and taking advantage of the extra energy available from the Tradition.

You see, such energy as can be made available for this type of project is communicated through therapists to the young. It can be transmitted through parents who are in the Tradition to their own children, to their brothers' or sisters' children, and to other children in their families, but it is very difficult and very inefficient, at least for the moment, to try and transmit such energy through publicity, posters or television advertising.

Certain images, symbols and combinations of colours can be used to divert or deflect the attention of the young who are going towards drugs and alcohol. But if you expose such symbols or colours in newspaper advertising or on television, they wouldn't function correctly, because these colours or symbols need what we call a "trigger" for them to function on the person.

So in a place where one might be receiving and treating young people who have such problems, if those colours and symbols are already there, the trigger can take effect, because the ambiance and situation is of a therapeutic or curative nature, but if the symbol or colour is just seen in the abstract, it doesn't create the relationship.

Through some friends of ours, I tried to get a pop star in a television program to wear a T-Shirt with a particular symbol on it about a year ago. It wasn't a symbol any of you would recognize, it was a sort of pop/psychedelic symbol. It was part of an overall pattern, because I was thinking: "Everybody copies what this person wears and thinks (although if the truth be told, he doesn't think anything) but young people do imitate what he wears or what he does.

Now where was the trigger here? Where is the connection? The connection was in fact that he was a former heavy user of drugs who had publicly stopped. Unfortunately his agent, who was approached by friends to ask whether he would wear this for a thirty minute intercontinental programme, said he would be very happy to do so and that the price would be 6 million dollars.

Since under normal circumstances this could be considered to be an obstacle, I reverted to a less sophisticated form of gambit which did do the job, because as the pop star was being escorted to the rostrum through the screaming and dancing fans, a very enthusiastic lady fan tore off his shirt and handed him another one, which was a saving of six million dollars.

All right, it's true that one can't really build a whole drug programme around that particular type of gambit.

What you want to try and do is to take advantage of these empathies or awarenesses among young people, lecturing at them, talking to them at their level, monitoring them and obviously correcting them. This is always being done, and has been done in the past. Again, take advantage of the additional energy factor which can be available.

In many quite public and obvious areas of increasing political freedom, things like the green lobby, the anti-additive food consciousness, can be brought together into a formal programme. There is a momentum building up in the world. In every case, if you trace it back you will find that the source of that movement is the realization that there is something which boils down to an individual and collective being.

Understandably, young people want to be modern and "with it". So we have to give them something which is with it and modern.

Okay, if you like, here we are getting into the area of selling a product or marketing. But what will sustain our product is the energy. We want to try and aim at a product, if you like, which is constructed and which is also timeless.

If it is a product which is fixed in time in the sense that they can say: "That was last year's diet" or "last year's hair-do" and "we want a new one", then we get into the situation where we can say "All right", which means that we sit down and update the product.

This is possible, of course, but there is also another way: if you have a good product, you don't necessarily have to change the colour, shape and form every year. You can show different aspects of the same product. And since each aspect is just another aspect of the reality, there aren't any stronger or weaker aspects involved.

Additionally, if it is constructed carefully enough, the young people who accept it will hold onto it because it remains modern. Basically, such a programme or product would be permutations on a theme.

So this is the subject I would like to suggest to you today.

EARTHLY EFFECTS

For people who know what they are doing and what they are using, it is possible in many therapy contexts to make use of some factors which, according to conventional understanding, are mysterious and inexact. Therefore if a therapist is taking advantage of these factors, it is usually better not to confide in the patient, especially as some of the factors you might use have a bad reputation for reasons of having been previously abused.

Of course the planet Earth is part of the galaxy; it is part of the cosmic system, and the beings that exist on this planet are subject to certain influences. Such influences may be of a cyclic nature or they may be localized at certain points.

You can thus see why I mention the possibility of problems or doubts regarding what I have just said, because it might be considered that I am talking about what in the West is called astrology, and you can appreciate a patient's concern or worry about such a thing. Quite understandably, they don't want their appendix removed astrologically.

NASRUDIN'S COSMIC PHARMACY

Nasrudin was out of a job so he asked some of his friends what sort of profession he should take up.

They said: "Well Nasrudin, you are very capable, and you know a lot about the medicinal properties of herbs. You could open a pharmacy".

He went home and thought about it, and said to himself: "Yes, I think it is a good idea, I think I'm capable of doing that".

Of course, being Nasrudin, at that particular time he was going through one of his moments of wanting to be prominent and important, so he thought: "I won't just open a herb shop or a pharmacy dealing with herbs, I'll open something enormous and make a significant impact".

He bought a shop, installed the shelves and cabinets, and when it came to painting the outside he put up a scaffolding and covered it with sheets and worked away behind it. He didn't let anybody see what name he was giving to the pharmacy or how he was painting the outside.

Then, after several days, he distributed leaflets saying: "The grand opening is tomorrow at 9 o'clock".

Everybody from his own and all the surrounding villages came, and they all stood and waited in front of the new shop. At 9 o'clock Nasrudin came out, removed the sheet from in front, and there was an enormous poster saying "Nasrudin's Cosmic and Galactic Pharmacy" and underneath was written: "Influenced by and harmonised with planetary influences".

A lot of people were very impressed, and he did very good business that day. In the evening a local schoolteacher came up to him and said: "Frankly Nasrudin, these claims you are making are a little doubtful."

"No, no," replied Nasrudin, "Every claim that I make about planetary influence is absolutely correct. When the sun rises, I open the pharmacy and when the sun sets, I close it."

So there can be different interpretations about how much planetary influence effects one, or how much of these influences one receives or uses.

GALACTIC EFFECTS

Of course I am not particularly concerned here with trying to explain this sort of influence upon individuals, but there are certain combinations of planetary aspects which can produce influences upon areas or upon communities. These influences can be conveniently divided into two distinct areas: the positive and stimulating type of influence, and the other influences which are not of a negative character but which can constitute an interference factor.

You can see this on a daily basis at a simple and obvious level. In the morning, when the sun is at a certain inclination, there is a certain tranquility or calmness, and a certain type of light. During the day, when the sun is more intense and higher, a tension factor can sometimes come in. As the sun declines, just before it sets, there is a period of calm with a particular sort of light. This is a very simple and obvious observation which is physically and very basically felt, on the surface.

In the galactic and planetary system, you have something quite necessary, which is a very distinct discipline of movement and orbiting of the planets. This is called something that some of you may remember my mentioning, which is the galactic order. The movements and orbits of planets are to a very great extent predictable, therefore if such movements and orbits are predictable and if they do have an influence, if one knew what these influences were, it would be possible to predict certain influences in certain areas.

Of course the ancient Chinese and ancient Egyptians made many studies of the planetary system, but the only people who codified possible predictable influences were the Arabs, because they developed certain instruments which could measure certain planetary movements and conjunctions to a very precise degree. In order to confirm these observations, they set up observatories in various parts of the world and the information was fed back from them and compared.

Now we are all very familiar with the page in the newspaper or magazine where "Aunt Carmen tells you your stars for tomorrow and the next day". You have the prediction that Jupiter is in Sagittarius and Mercury is in the kitchen or something, and it will be a source of great satisfaction and importance for me to think that my every move is being personally monitored by Jupiter, Sagittarius or whatever.

This is a fairly innocent pastime, and you all know it. It makes the bridge between finishing your breakfast and going out to lunch or supper or work or whatever you do.

But if there is a planet in a cosmic order, and the plant, animal life, rivers and other factors obey this order, so that it is not unusual to ask: "How are human beings influenced?" And if, as far as we are concerned, they are influenced in a significant way, how can one understand how this influence works?

Finally, how, in the area of therapy, can one benefit from such influence, either by associating with this factor or using this awareness to understand the health problems of a patient?

There are certain books of knowledge on this subject. Some of them have been translated and are available. Parts of some of them have been translated, and some of you may be familiar with the Medieval medicinal herb books which say things like: such-and-such a plant or herb should be gathered or cut when the moon is in Sagittarius or some combination like that.

Now of course, you can read a basic and deeper meaning or direction into that phrase if you have the benefit, as I have, of owning the original book on which that one is based. You will then find that the reason for that action is that this particular plant benefits from a certain planetary situation and absorbs a certain energy which can be ingested by the person.

Or to put it in a more complicated way, if that plant grows in a certain place and the person who goes to gather it receives that energy, he doesn't actually have to eat the plant at all.

The reason this was put in such a way is because most people are human, and human beings have a very human greed factor, and if it is written down that at a certain place there will be a certain type of energy available at this or that time, they will go there armed with buckets, trucks and boxes in order to stash it away.

It is therefore what is called protecting people from themselves.

As far as areas being influenced by planetary circumstances are concerned, it usually depends on certain geophysical, geological and geodetic circumstances. You can have a situation where those factors all apply, and a river running through that area can either be the necessary catalyst for the situation, or else it can gather and carry the energy from that area elsewhere.

Now how can somebody involved in therapy use or benefit from this knowledge? You do not have to buy a large and powerful telescope. Like receiving any form of energy or impulsion, the person puts themselves into a receiving state, into a state of alertness, by strongly accepting the fact that these influences do exist. Again, like so many energies, the affirmation of its existence helps it to work for you.

Such an affirmation is therefore another tactic or technique which you can use in therapy. It is another instrument or tool which backs up your own discipline. It does not influence you in the sense that you make your therapy decisions based on planetary conjunctions.

You simply recognize that the function exists, and with your being you ask it and encourage it to communicate. You do not take it to the extremes of hearing planetary voices. Unless it is very urgent, you do not operate by moonlight. It is one of the many instruments you put together to make a mechanism.

SHARING EXPERIENCE

Every activity, especially activities of a therapeutic nature, must have a certain format, certain requirements, and certain instruments.

When we are dealing with therapy situations and the human being, especially with people who are physically or mentally disturbed, it is absolutely essential that the situation, ambiance and instruments all be present. This holds true for any surgical, medical or psychological situation, and it is even more important to have all these elements being used correctly together with the energy.

I have detected certain factors I would like to mention this morning. In certain therapy groups here there is occasionally a lack of precision in timing. Sometimes the meeting starts earlier or later, some people arrive early or late or even during the meeting. In the Tradition, precision of timing is very important and there is no reason why people should not time themselves correctly.

Starting an activity at a precise time helps me to help the activity of that group at that time. I can and do monitor the time at which a particular meeting is supposed to take place. There may be a small margin of error before the commencement of the activity, but I will not constantly recheck for people who are late for whatever reason. If the majority of people arrive and start reasonably on time, anybody arriving late will disturb the situation which has been established. We are dealing with precise activities: let us increase our precision.

Also, in certain Hakim meetings I have identified some lack of harmony and a certain degree of interior aggression. A meeting of a therapy group is supposed to be an exchange of ideas for people to make suggestions as to how their particular therapy could assist other people's therapies. The element of authority or competition disturbs the flow of this contact.

In a way, it is perfectly possible for one individual in a group to dominate a discussion, and that such a domination may exist because their experience in therapy is greater than that of some of the others; but the participation of a person should be measured in terms of the degree of harmonic they can bring into the group.

I do appreciate, of course, that some of you may be following somewhat weird and wonderful disciplines of therapy. Some people may be working or developing their own competence in one of these slightly different therapies, and if their experience in the field of therapy is less great, they may feel shy or reluctant about advancing any of their own ideas or theories. Nevertheless, their participation in a meeting is already a function, and such a person or persons should be given the opportunity not only of listening to other people, but also of expressing or explaining some aspects of their own therapy. Seniority of experience and seniority in terms of degrees and diplomas certainly is a measure, but such experience should produce a considerable degree of open-mindedness.

Some people are involved in therapies which are not yet fully developed, and in studying, using and developing this therapy, they need experience. This means they do and will make mistakes and waste time. One of the functions of having a group of therapists sitting together is to try and help each other to avoid making errors and losing time. This means that the experience and time a therapist has spent in a discipline should be made available to others who are just beginning to develop a theory, in the sense of communicating and sharing an energy of understanding.

When sharing an energy of understanding, different individuals learn or understand things at a different speed. There are some people who will read a book and have some form of total recall of the book. There are other people for whom reading, learning and remembering is a real torture. Yet others learn better by doing and watching.

Sharing an understanding of how to learn is sharing a teaching and helping each other. If somebody has the ability to read a book once and remember every detail, it is no good for them to share that experience with somebody who can learn only by doing and watching. When asked, it is no good saying to that person: "Read that book and you will learn."

So part of the skill is understanding how the other person understands. If somebody says: "How do I learn to do this?", you don't just say to them: "Here is the book, read up about it and learn." You try and explain to them how they put themselves in relation to that knowledge which they are searching for.

The real question here is: how do they produce a state or situation within themselves to attract the knowledge?

If, in a therapy meeting, the ambiance and atmosphere is right, the circuit of connection will be right and the flow of knowledge and energy does and should sometimes influence the topic under discussion, or the way in which the discussion or meeting should take place, i.e., "Should it be a debate about a particular therapy? Should it be a series of short presentations by different people or should there be a period of silence to start with to see what subject comes to the surface?"

When I talk about therapy energy being available it is something already there which is waiting to be used. It is waiting to influence a situation in which you can use this energy in a more familiar way, so that you learn to feel the degree of its presence.

By definition, a person involved in a therapy activity should maintain an attitude of humility and gratitude: gratitude to the source of all healing, and humility in order to avoid any degree of something which is difficult to express; let's call it a height or depth difference between the therapist and the patient. Calling this "height" and "depth" is not really a precise explanation, because it implies some sort of physical difference. It is probably more correctly expressed by saying that the usual equilibrium of the therapist is hopefully slightly better than that of the patient.

Furthermore, maintaining a feeling of humility prevents even the slightest degree of a feeling of superiority or arrogance in the therapist. It can be a natural feeling and it can be present to a very small degree: "This person needs treatment, I can treat them, I am a therapist. At the moment in terms of some sort of conventional measure, I'm better off than they are." This thought does occur or pass through the mind, and quite rightly. It is perfectly legitimate to say to oneself: "I'm feeling better than they are at the moment, thank God."

In every therapy situation, there has to be a very great degree of human and humane feeling, backed up by a very strong and precise energy. Both of these qualities have to be present to compliment and energise each other.

By maintaining certain parts of your own inner being, if you have tried to establish a good contact with the patient's inner being, the contact between the two inner beings will vary in the same way that, when speaking to, touching or treating that person, your exterior manner varies according to their condition. Sometimes you speak to them softly and encourage them to do something; sometimes you are firmer in your instructions. What you do is vary your attitude while monitoring all the time.

Equally, if you are harmonizing with the inner being of a person, a similar pattern of activity is taking place, but with a very significant and valuable difference. Once you have established a reasonable, professional and surface relationship with the patient, you are trying to establish this being to being contact at the same time. To do this, you can use an object, a text, a colour from the Tradition, by its physical presence in your hand or in the room. In a way, that object or colour or book will send out a current through your inner being, which will communicate, in turn, to the essential being of the patient.

This connection is established and continues during the course of the therapy session. When the therapist has established a contact between the colour, the object, himself/herself and patient, there is no need to be continually checking it out or keeping it moving. The patient does not need to be consciously aware of the object, instrument or colour. It is enough for you to be conscious of it; you know it is functioning and you pass it on.

I would recommend to you to be very careful about two factors I mentioned in the beginning: the timing or competitive factors. Any tactic, technique or instrument put into movement, momentum or action by you loses its rhythm or efficiency if it is disturbed by the two factors I've mentioned. Use the energy available to you more precisely by watching the timing and your own state, because this therapy energy is not mine to just waste or throw away. I've worked towards producing situations in which this energy can be provided, and I don't wish to see circumstances where I'm forced to withdraw it.

POOLING KNOWLEDGE AND TECHNIQUES

Concerning the development of the Granada Therapy, I am now reasonably satisfied that most people working at it have a clear idea of what we are trying to do. But I find that there is not enough communication between the different therapy groups in different countries. For example, I receive information from a group or from people about something that they are studying, and this is exactly duplicated by another group. For some reason, there is no contact between these two groups, whether because of communication difficulties or distance, or whether it is that one group wants to do some work or research and be the first to produce an effect and take the credit for being the first.

If the second attitude of being first to develop an aspect of the therapy is held, it would not in any case be true to say that anyone has made this discovery or development on their own. They have done it with a considerable amount of help from energy which is available both from the Tradition and from therapy groups throughout the world. Therefore if there is any credit for development or discovery, it belongs to all the therapists and not just one selected group.

Another criticism I have is that individual people are still promoting their own particular discipline of therapy and giving it too great a priority.

I have explained from the very beginning that no trained therapist, in whatever field, is expected to ignore or abandon what they have learned or been trained to do. In their thinking and activities they will certainly give their own training considerable priority, because it is the area of therapy they know best and in which they operate best. But they should not be so committed to that therapy as to ignore or be even hostile to other therapies. Once again, your function and most important aim is to produce a cure situation on behalf of a patient or patients.

In order to enhance and improve your function as therapists, you must somehow be able to measure what impact would be useful for a patient at a particular time.

This is an obvious factor which is normally used in conventional medicine. A doctor may decide that a particular illness requires a certain amount of antibiotics at certain specific periods. He uses his experience in diagnosis, and he varies the medicine he is using according to the intensity of the condition, the state of health, weight, or other conditions of the patient.

This process is obvious and normally used all the time. But as I've said before, I'm trying to encourage you to look at a patient with different eyes. This doesn't mean there is to be an enormous hesitation factor in any diagnosis or treatment, in the sense of "What would this or that therapist have done?" while the patient is dying or suffering as you go through the alternatives.

We come back to the initial basis: you are observing,

recording, talking to and examining the patient in a conventional way, and you're making a contact from essential being to essential being because you are encouraging that essential being to signal or indicate something back to you.

In the area of increasing communication and cooperation, what I would recommend is not only, as I said before, to look through journals or publications and take out articles which might be of interest, but also to circulate simple therapy experiences to other therapists about those experiences where you feel that you used, and the patient benefited from, some additional factors.

In many disciplines of therapy there are publications in which therapists write articles and make presentations about a discovery or breakthrough in their discipline. I would generally encourage such publication, with the proviso that, in what I might call a conventional paper or presentation of a treatment, very specific measurements, terms of reference, laboratory analysis and back-up always be part of the report.

A therapist in the Tradition might write a short report about a therapy session with a patient, adding that "at a certain point of the treatment, under certain circumstances, I invoked a certain energy, or used a certain visualization or zikr", without being able to specify exactly what that sort of energy felt like or what that visualization or zikr was.

One could perhaps then invite comments from people under similar situations, so that one can identify these unclear factors, and possibly then be able to recreate a circumstance or a situation. One would then, in effect, be inviting other therapists to fill in certain gaps in your therapy.

One would obviously try and be as precise as possible and not have any of these gaps, and one would not expect people to be able to fill in gaps which are too large. Of course, nobody will welcome a letter from another therapist saying: "I had such and such a session with a patient, I don't know what happened, does anybody have any idea?" because you will get many suggestions including "Go see a therapist yourself".

Some of these situations and circumstances leave what is

called a trace feeling. Explaining a circumstance like that may allow 2 or 3 people, each having a trace, to put all those traces together and produce a palpable factor. Quite obviously and necessarily, if one does write such a letter or report, every possible factor which applies in the situation should be noted, so that anybody receiving that letter or report can visualize and recreate that circumstance in their being.

So please really take these two factors I have mentioned this morning into consideration very deeply and strongly. The exchange of tactics, the exchange of techniques must harmonise. There are techniques which compliment each other.

There are some techniques which, when applied with another technique, dilute the effect. Sometimes this dilution factor can be felt, and is objectively perceptible. It may become perceptible by a hesitation in the person, a hesitation in the therapist, or it may come back as a hostile signal from the essential being of the patient.

In the beginning of this congress I said we were talking about "speaking to" and "listening to", which, in a word, is communication. Improve your communication with each other and exercise the communication between yourselves and the therapy energy of the Tradition.

There is still a significant and considerable amount of work to be done, so take the fullest possible advantage of the therapeutic energy of the Tradition in everything you do.

TIMING AND OPTIMIZATION

I would like you to be very careful about your timing and attendance. Being on time is not only a politeness, it allows me to maintain a momentum without interruption once I have started an activity.

For those of you who remember that I said that we wanted to maximize: now we are going to go a little further forward from maximizing to a state called optimizing. Maximizing means using as much real and necessary effort as possible; in other words using the time, the information and energy to the maximum possible extent, and without hurry or tension.

As I have recommended, it is possible to be attentive without being tense. When you have managed to maximize your activities, in other words when you have been able to maximize on the basis of the available information and experience, you then optimize, which in this case, means making the best use of. In maximizing you are using a quantity of energy, experience, information: in optimizing you focus all that information and experience, for instance on a patient, a situation, a person or a place, or on the activity you are involved in at that time.

You are fully focused on that activity. In focusing, in optimizing, you add other factors which either already exist in a situation or else which you can add or bring into the situation.

You might say "This is already covered by maximizing". The difference is that in maximization, you are using a cruder form of energy. Optimization involves a more delicate and more refined type of energy. In a given situation, you are using all your faculties and carefully examining how you can enhance or add to these faculties.

Doing this does not mean you are adding just in order to add. If you like, you are adding refinements, like adding salt and pepper to your basic meal.

Let us take the example of a surgeon in an operating theatre. He must have an almost detached attitude in order to do his work properly. He has the surgical instruments and the assistance of people in the operating theatre, but he then adds to that. He involves his own being in that situation by adding another dimension to it. His involvement or the involvement of any therapist or technician is and must be slightly detached. So you can and normally do have an involvement in the form of a feeling towards the patient, but not an over-identification with the patient as a person. You open other lines of communication with the patient.

As I have said before, you establish a being-to-being relationship with the other person. Then, when the situation is set, that is the point at which you start to optimize in a very precise way. You don't just let your imagination run wild. You survey or look at the situation in a relaxed and detached way, the basic question being calm, not tense or worried, which is: "What else can be added to benefit this situation? What can I reasonably add to benefit this situation, either to improve my own performance within it, or to support, help and benefit the other person?"

There may be answers to this question; for instance, there may be small things to be done like adding sound, music, ionization, or other things you judge to be useful in that situation. It may be something physical you can add, or it may be something in a thought or feeling form which you can send out.

Of course, this all depends on the situation and circumstance. You don't ask yourself "What more can I add?" over and over again. No, you spend a reasonable time at it and get a certain feedback, but this process shouldn't last long. There can be little things which are perhaps technically insignificant: it may be something which is half done by you and half by the patient.

A very careful line should be drawn between adding another element and tacking on extra things without end, because if you don't stop somewhere, you can have a situation that just goes on and on endlessly. You most certainly have to choose what has to be added, because it has to be based on your judgement and decision about what is needed.

But if you are correctly related to the therapeutic situation, you should be able to feel instinctively what can usefully be added to a situation.

FORMAL AND INFORMAL INTERACTION

When I was going back to my apartment last night, I was reminded of the story of Nasrudin when he attended a therapy congress.

It appears that he was invited to this therapy congress in a city very far from his own. He was nervous about the trip and all the strange people and places where he would be. So he went around and asked his friends how he should behave to protect himself from strangers, saying "I have been told that I will be staying in a place where there will be many other people and many beds and I'm afraid that in this strange place with these strange people I might get lost."

Somebody said: "No problem; there is a simple solution. Before you go to sleep, you tie a balloon to your toe. When you wake up in the morning you will look down, see the balloon and recognise that it is you."

He found himself in this large room with many beds and lots of people sleeping, so before he went to sleep he tied a balloon to his toe.

During the night when he was asleep, somebody got up, took the balloon off his toe and tied it to somebody else's toe. So in the morning Nasrudin woke up and looked around. He saw a figure in a bed with the balloon attached to his toe, and he said: "There it is, already. The congress hasn't started yet and I have a problem: if that is me, who am I?"

I was reminded of that when I saw everybody walking around the hotel last night looking where to find their rooms.

You will remember that I have previously talked about the factor of co-action. Co-action can represent an activity of a group within the Tradition, and it can also represent a situation between a therapist and a patient.

For the sake of clarity we have some symbols which we use

to represent these various factors. The first is represented by a circle with two points added to it, which represent the function. It shows that the function is a dual function, that two factors are taking place. You have two points you can call arrows, which show the flow of activity or motion. In case you might think that a circle by definition is limited to just going round and round, this circle represents a situation. Different situations associated with this situation have their own co-action circle associated with it. So what is going on in this situation is the intensification of activity. It is defined as a circle, because it establishes certain precise limits.

If you say: "Well, that's the situation", this is sort of vague, and since it could go in any direction, there is no real point of focus because the point of focus is the entire situation, not just one central point.

In a co-action situation you have another diagram of a similar nature, represented by a circle. This is what is called the interaction, or two-way exchange of energy, the interchange of intention: again with a limit placed upon it so that you do not have the energy or the action just going off and decaying or getting lost.

Both the co-action and the interaction function at the same time. So having established a situation or context of co-action, and having defined the terms of reference you will use in that situation, you then go more into the situation and produce the interaction.

The interaction between the two individuals of therapist and patient has to be established in a gradual way. In any form of therapy, you all know that this gradual interaction is not only established to identify the problem, but to evaluate what feedback you are getting from the individual patient.

In the Granada Therapy we are establishing a different sort of interaction. This can happen because although a therapist certainly goes through all the normal examinations, checks and study of the other person to assimilate the patient's profile, once it has been established, having got the profile, one then introduces the deeper senses, deeper feelings in relation to that patient.

To put it simply: what is their being saying or transmitting?

You all know, especially with mentally confused patients, that they can be transmitting a lot of false signals, sometimes deliberately, sometimes because of their state of mind.

Your particular skill is to identify the following: what are the real signals of the being, and what are the false signals that result from confusion or imbalance?

This is why I have mentioned that the main topic of this congress is the focus and function of the whole being.

One of the functions of activities and exercises in the Tradition is to get to know one's own being more and more. So when I talk about "whole being function" or "whole being focus", the therapist or individual must judge how much of their own being they involve in a given situation.

A doctor has a whole range of medicines which he can prescribe, but he doesn't prescribe all of them at the same time. Equally, a therapist should feel a situation, and then decide: what degree or quantity of their being do they involve in this context? There is a certain objective evaluation or judgement that has to be made.

The temptation can be to involve or engage the whole being as one knows it, but as you know, people who are mentally disturbed will try to involve you more and more, which means that this involvement must be proportionate. The signal coming back from the person is evaluated by the therapist, and the function the therapist then performs is based on how or to what degree one should involve oneself.

Also, to what degree can the therapist encourage the patient to involve himself or herself in the treatment situation? You will certainly try to give advice and suggest to a patient what they should do or what they should take: that is what is called the formal treatment. In the Granada Therapy, we also go through the formal process, because it is what a patient expects, but nevertheless one basically aims at establishing a deeper and more sophisticated communication with that patient, and having established these subtle links, the therapist is dictating the situation in the sense that he or she has control over the amount of deep involvement.

In that way the therapist is protected in the formal situation: a patient can ask for more medicine, more time, and more attention; but on the deeper level of relationship the therapist must be able to control the degree of "deeper level" communication, because as you all know, some patients will absorb as much of your attention, time and medicine as they can get.

So, what is going out from the therapist on a more profound level must be subject to control; otherwise you can get a complete draining of the person's energy.

Here is a question: on a formal level of treatment, to what degree and in what way do you tell or explain to a patient that this is a slightly different therapy? This is a delicate point which came up at the Segovia Congress. If you say to them: "I will treat you according to the Granada Therapy", at the very least you will be involved in long explanations, because they will say: "What's that? Does it work? Do you know that it works? Can you assure me it will?"

If you say to them : "I think it works and it depends a lot on you", the answer could be: "Well, I am the patient. You are supposed to be treating me."

So the simple answer is that you introduce aspects of the Granada Therapy as and when you judge it useful. This judgement of its usefullness obviously means knowing what the patient's reaction could be.

If you tell them that it involves forms of breathing or relaxation, put yourself in their place. What do they imagine breathing or relaxation to be? They may have an exaggerated idea of it or they may think it unimportant. It may not sound to them to be as significant and important as they think they are, because quite naturally, a patient feels that he or she is the most important person in the world. If you just say: "What you need to do is learn to breathe or relax", they will say: "I am ill. I do relax, I sleep at night, sometimes I breathe. Come on, tell me something more important."

There is a very well-known phrase in the Tradition: speak to people according to the measure of their understanding. It is no good saying: "This or that person is adult and has attended

University, they should understand." They want to be treated as somebody special and they have good reason to want this.

It is correct and normal for the therapist to transmit: "I, the therapist, am interested in your health and well-being" to them. This transmission or feeling comes from your being to their being. On the surface it creates confidence in the therapist. On the more profound level it produces different lines of communication, which hopefully are not subject to their conditioned intellect.

You are then conventionally and formally talking with them, discussing their problem, treating them by various conventional means, but at a deeper level you are not just comforting them, you are sending out positive energy and good thoughts. You are sending them encouragement: "You can do it, it can be done" and also sending out the message that the co-action between "you and me" can produce a degree of positive. The person starts off by feeling this positive just in the form of fragments, but the fragments themselves are communicating a message of encouragement to the person's essential being, thus gradually giving them the feeling that working together with a therapist is not only producing something in itself, but that something else can also be produced on their own within themselves.

When one is dealing with people who have mental or psychological problems, you all know that one thing they lose first, or which is at first weak in them, is their confidence in themselves: confidence in their work, in their body, in their system, in their thoughts.

Unfortunately, what they do is actually look for proof of this weakness: "I can't hold onto a job. I can't keep a train of thought. I can't do this or that." If this basic confidence in themselves is diminished, a therapist can use conventional means to try and persuade or encourage them. But again, on a deeper level, you should be sending a message or an energy, not just of encouragement, but actually a series of questions to encourage them to start thinking inside themselves: "Am I really so inefficient? Have I really made an effort to do this? Am I totally lost, confused or destroyed?"

If you ask them those questions formally or openly, they will say yes or no and quote examples to you of how they failed to do this or could not do that, but within themselves, they do know the answers, and they may have to go on asking the questions to themselves until they start getting real answers back.

It's an old familiar thing: you can stand in front of a mirror in the morning and look at your image in the mirror and say: "Is that person really trying? Does that person really want to be well?" The internal being is similar: it is looking at and examining itself.

I have been using the word optimizing, which is a technique we use in Tradition activities. It is also an activity which can be valuably used in therapy situations. As I said, a form in which it can be used is to add details.

With a patient, with a person who is ill or who is in an unbalanced physical or mental situation, you can encourage them to add positive or useful things.

Again, depending on the person, you can say to them: "We are now going to optimize" and depending on their conditioning and background, they will either take to the hills, or else they don't know anything about anything and say "Yes, all right", or what is even worse, they will say: "Aha, would you please explain the concept of optimization to me?" At that point it's no good saying: "Agha didn't tell us everything about it, but I'll tell you what I know" because they'll go away and say: "He is trying something out and making a guinea pig out of me, forget it."

You know that you are trying to optimize and you also know you are trying to encourage them to optimize, but you do not necessarily have to tell them this. One aspect of optimization is in the adding of details. As I say, you are not just adding for the sake of "I think we'll have a little bit of this and a little bit of that."If you are conscious of and in contact with the situation and its context, you add fragments which improve or elevate the situation.

I am probably going to get into trouble from the ladies for what I am saying next, so I have to choose my words very carefully. Ladies know instinctively about optimizing. Using the analogy of the mirror in the bathroom, they look in the mirror and they put a little bit of stuff here, twist something a little bit there and then put a little more stuff down here and they spend a few minutes on that. Then they check the left profile and the right profile and then think a little bit and check out the hair at the back.

It may appear to people like husbands that they are spending hours doing this, especially if you are trying to get in there for a bodily function or a shave, at which point it will take even longer. Of course, the result is marvellous. And just to make sure that it's marvellous, on the back of the front door they have another mirror to check themselves over before they go out.

This is clearly a very natural form of instinctive optimization; it is adding details: a touch here, a touch there, a small amount of perfume as well. They have an idea, or they saw in a magazine what they will look like today. This means that their target, their focus, is specific.

Equally, in any situation between two people or in a therapy situation: a therapist reacts, but in a useful and positive way. One does not react automatically in the way that the patient wants one to react. One reacts according to what one feels would enhance and improve the situation.

It may be adding a flower, adding a colour or adding music. As you all know, it can be a tone of voice, an attitude, or what one wears. You are aiming to produce an effect in a situation within a context. Also, very obviously, there are limits to what details you can include. You optimize a situation for your benefit and on behalf of the other person.

This means you are looking at a situation both from your own point of view, that is from the point of view of what you want to achieve, and also through their eyes. If your contact with a patient is fairly long-term, say days, weeks or months, you naturally take note of some of the normal likes or dislikes they show. For instance, they like a cup of coffee or tea or mineral water; they like you to smoke or don't like you to smoke. These are all things you note automatically, and you create a therapy ambiance which they will enjoy, in which they will feel at home, and which will show them consciously and visibly that you have given formal and normal consideration to their comfort and welfare.

Not only are you increasing their conscious comfort and receptivity, you are also reducing any area of tension which might exist inside them. You are thus using several forms of observation: you normally watch and observe to see if they are comfortable or if they are showing signs of nervousness, rigidity, and so forth. These are all automatic observations you make. Equally, the deep message or messages they are sending out should be observed and replied to when possible. You are inviting them to co-act with you both by words and by action.

We have another graphic diagram we use in the Tradition which can be kept in mind in therapy situations. It is a typical formulation in the sense that in the world you would normally say that one plus one usually equals two, but not in the Tradition. When you see an equation in any text or formula that I write which relates to the Tradition, if it has this symbol on it, it means that it is a significant equation from the Tradition. For those of you who are interested, it is a kind of shorthand for the word Adad, which means item or formulation. These descriptions or diagrams are graphic because they show an action taking place. They are not to be seen as a sort of magical symbol.

So let's say that we have two individuals. Hopefully, what we are counting on is the positive potential in each individual.

This symbol is what we call the symbol for fusion, which means the coming together. It's not an abstract context or idea. Fusion is a coming together on more and more and more levels. And it is possible to go on with this ad infinitum.

One is not just adding more and more on for the purpose of collecting. One makes a contact and then adds to it. You check the contact and then you use it. It is fusion in action, and not in the abstract.

Fusion can also be explained in another way. Those of you who remember your early studies in chemistry and physics will remember a chemical and physical experiment in which you use an anode and a cathode. As you will recall, an anode and a cathode do not usefully function in an abstract sense; they exist in a solution to enable a transmission to take place between the two. We sometimes use the analogy that one and another individual, comprising the anode and the cathode, use the Tradition as the liquid in which they operate.

In a therapeutic situation the therapist is motivated to help, improve and benefit the patient. Both the patient's motivation and therapist's own motivation is hopefully known. The therapist has to chose an ambiance in which that knowledge or feeling can be usefully transmitted.

I would like to expand upon these aspects which you should all learn about and become familiar with, and go through them in detailed and specific contexts in order to see, discuss and exchange ideas and suggestions on how the maximization you have already done can become an optimization, to enable you to work further in these ways.

The energy available from the Tradition can only usefully function if it is directed in a knowing way. Knowing means the feeling which comes from within. In this context and in this circumstance these details which can be quite minor, can be introduced and their feedback or effect analysed.

In case people think that I am introducing more and more factors and details in order to clutter things up, this is not the case. I am concerned about the correct use of detail. Any detail I explain or encourage people to take notice of, is being mentioned because they are necessary details, that, when used correctly, enhance situations. They are details, instructions or points which have been developed in the Tradition.

Remember, I normally don't insist on such matters, I suggest them. If I suggest you follow up certain details, there are very good reasons for my suggesting them to you.

DEEP INVOLVEMENT AND DEFENSE MECHANISMS

There are certain problems about following the therapy in a general situation, because you may be working with people who, although they are not necessarily hostile, do not understand some of the methods or tactics you could be using. They can therefore be critical of some attitudes you are taking or things you are doing.

This should not in fact be any problem, because you are not obviously showing that you are using any of what they might consider unorthodox techniques. You are functioning within yourself and you are following conventional and accepted tactics. It is only within yourself that you are transmitting the energy of the Tradition.

If you are conscious of this fact, you will transmit it. In a clinical or hospital situation, the question has been asked: "How can we be conscious of this when we have so many patients to see? Is it possible?" or "How can we transmit such a thing to that great a number of patients?"

The analogy we use for this is simple: if you have a lamp and people pass under it, whether it's for ten seconds, one minute or five minutes, they will still be getting an impulse or light from that lamp.

Your personal impulse might tell you that you would like to take more time with that person, and because of the number of people you see, it may not be possible to do so. If you are seeing a large number of people, this feeling may build up. You should not allow this to happen because it could provoke a feeling of frustration in you, leading you to think: "I can't reach enough people with enough intensity."

What you must realize is that every person you see will receive a certain impact. You may see them subsequently and often after that as well, but you will already have impacted upon them and it is for them to continue and use the contact, or else not to have recognised the contact and leave it aside.

You are there to offer the contact. Again, it is a two-way exchange. Because of a need, a person will pick up the contact and follow it, or else they will not identify it and just allow it to diminish. If they correctly identify the contact, i.e. what you are emitting to them, they will certainly follow it up, because as we say, heart speaks to heart.

Perhaps they will evaluate the contact conventionally or rationalize it: "It was nice. He or she was concerned and interested", and they can maintain what people call a medical/ social contact.

Or else they can identify what we call a real and profound contact: "He or she was concerned and nice, and there was something else besides". They will sometimes put this kind of thing into words by saying: "I think there is something else." Or for whatever reason, they will disguise or camouflage this by using another justification.

This is where your deep action, your deep involvement comes into being. With your knowledge of the person, you have to respond.

Now this may be a real feeling or it may be a fantasy. As you all know, you obviously do not feed a fantasy, because the moment you become involved in their fantasy, then, as one says, you're dancing to their tune.

If you identify clearly enough that there is an area of communication with that person, don't just say "Yes indeed" and go away. Use that as a basis to check their reaction; use the feedback. If you feel deeply that the feedback is positive, then you can react in a positive way.

How you react is both a secret and a trick. It's a secret because you neither need nor want to tell them the whole tactic. It's a trick because you want them to think that they thought of it.

As a trick, it's a laudable trick, particularly when dealing with people who have some psychological or mental disturbance. When they come to you they have very often been through a lot of different therapies, and they have been given Freudian, Jungian, Schopenhaurean routines, you name it. They have therefore developed what we call a shell defense.

It may be difficult, and in some cases very difficult to overcome this, but the trick or skill is to present yourselves not as "therapists", but as human beings. I am not saying for a moment that there is a difference between therapists and human beings, although I suppose one might fruitfully debate the matter. But the most severe cases one has, particularly when dealing with psychological disturbance, are with people who have developed a resistance to therapy.

Your skill and ability is to identify such people by their

reaction; and to present a therapy to them which does not appear to be a therapy. You are in fact asking them to help you look at their problem. What you are inviting them to do is to involve themselves in a process of co-action.

All right, they come and are open. You are the therapist, so they don't want to do anything. They want you to tell them what to do, so they say: "If I could help myself I would have already done so. You help me, it up to you to make the effort", or again, they might say "You want us to split the effort between us? Right, I'll pay you 50 % of your normal fee." In that case, of course, you double the fee so that nobody knows the difference, but still.

In fact, you are not using their energy, you are inviting them to put it together with your energy to make one single energy.

You should be able to say to them clearly right from the beginning: "You have come to me for help. I think I can help you, but I need to put your energy together with mine to achieve this, so that you can eventually go off and detach yourself from me and be whole, real, healthy and equilibrated without reference to me all the time." You are helping them to create a being which is not dependent upon you.

All right, they can and should and may have a continued rapport with you. You can be and you are available to them, and you are there as a point of stability they can refer to at any time.

Regarding the ability to walk alone: the idea of being able to walk alone can be terrifying to many people, and especially to those who have psychological or other problems. So, according to how you know them, you define what you mean by being alone. Alone can mean lonely, but alone can also mean standing on your own feet. In an extreme case, alone can mean abandoned. So, depending on the person and their state of mind, you have to define to them what "alone" means. If you say to them "You are going to be alone with yourself", they might say: "I don't want to be alone with myself." So here you have the factor of reassurance, but not dependance.

You have to try and transmit a feeling of security to them. On the conscious level, you can explain to them, affirm and talk to them about the need of security and the fact that security exists. Depending again on the state of mind, that reassurance can remain for minutes, hours or days.

But a time will certainly come when they will feel alone. At that time, if they feel this cold loneliness, they will almost certainly panic. How do you get through to your patient to overcome this panic, how do you get this factor through to other people? You have to send out a message and that message has to project security: "I am interested in your health and well-being." You can say that to them a hundred times, write it down and sign it and they still won't believe it. They are afraid for their health, their sanity, their stability and they need to be told something very fundamental and basic: "It's going to be all right" and that has to be a positive signal.

It has to be a positive which you feel, and which you yourself are sure about. You are not persuading them or encouraging them, you are telling them. The feeling of certitude, of being sure, which you yourselves may have, has to be transmitted to another person in perhaps a matter of seconds.

There is a very simple way of transmitting this wave of positive energy: if you feel it, you transmit it. This feeling does not depend on their ability or intelligence or state of being. It is transmitting on such a fundamental wave that no matter what a person's mental or physical confusion may be, this person will receive a sensation of calm, warmth and friendship. Since these sensations are of a very fundamental, basic and important quality, they cannot be artificial. They either exist or don't exist.

A question: if one is dealing with a large number of people, is there any danger or problem here because of the large number? No, because persons who are secure in themselves and harmonizing with their own being will constantly send out a positive signal. It is no strain on their being to constantly emit a positive signal. This question has already been asked, and I'll answer it again: if one is in contact with a lot of people who have a large negative accumulation, is it possible for a therapist to be influenced in a negative way?

The answer is no, because when one establishes a degree of

positive certitude, the negative in another person cannot influence the therapist or the person in a negative way. True, a patient who is very negative can take a longer time to establish a rapport, but the so-called negative danger to the first person or therapist doesn't exist, because in the Tradition one is defended to a certain degree against the negative.

Also, your identification with the patient has a certain distance, and any negative coming from the patient involves what is called a negative projection, which means that it decays quickly.

Furthermore, in a context or situation of considerable negativity, we have certain kinds of support, for instance certain phrases or words can be used. Clearly, your function as therapists is to identify and then make a decision based on feedback from the patient: for instance, in which area can one use the positive more usefully?

You can use what is called a broad-spectrum approach; in other words the initial analysis. You then focus down on what might be called the root problem. Here it is true to say that you are required to make judgements or decisions.

In certain situations or circumstances a person can be reluctant to make decisions or judgements: "Do I have the right, the capacity or the ability? Is this the right time? What terms of reference do I use? What feelings should I employ?"

At some point, one has to make a decision. You cannot defer judgements forever. A great amount of your skill and ability is to be able to make decisions.

Having made a decision and having identified the course of a problem, then you focus on the problem. When you focus on this problem with the certitude you are asking and looking for, then you get the back-up.

The process is therefore focusing towards, looking for and identifying, and then going forth and working for solutions: this applies not only to the patient but also to the therapist. You cannot be comfortable using an instrument unless you have confidence in it. The more familiar you are with this instrument the more positively and usefully you can employ it. You not only use it with enthusiasm but with certainty.

The other part of the therapeutic equation comes from the other person. You are providing them with a technique, you are explaining it to them and encouraging them to use it, and you are supporting them all the time you are doing that. But unless you yourself are sure, unless you are certain of what you are using, you don't use it.

So you have to involve them in it not just by telling them what to do, but by helping them to do it and also optimizing both your performance and theirs, adding any factor which will enhance and improve the situation.

You do not offer them instant solutions. You offer them a way out of problems.

As I say, this is dependant on the other person with whom you are dealing. If it is a co-action, the amount of energy and intensity they put in depends on their physical or psychological state. You may have to put in more than they have to, maybe more than just half. But to encourage them is to increase their participation.

As I said before, this can be a delicate area because they will say: "I have come to be healed or cured, I don't want to do anything, you do it for me".

This of course is where the diplomacy or trickery aspect comes in, or call it what you will. As long as you always maintain in your own mind the end-result of what you are aiming for, there is always a certain degree of maneuver one way or the other, but this end-result is in fact constantly trying to push them, encourage them and sustain your own energy in that particular direction.

You can use verbal communication or diagrams, but you should also try and use a wide variety of tactics.

You should try and establish tactics which you yourself have tried and proved and found valuable.

There are people who can be called verbal people, that is people who have to be talked to all the time, and people who are called graphic people, who react to diagrams.

NASRUDIN AND THE VINES

As always, there is a Nasrudin story which demonstrates this. It appears that Nasrudin was very good at growing and tending to grape-vines, and he had a number of very old and high-yielding vines.

He had a neighbor who had some grape-vines next door and the neighbor used to come out and cut the vines at any old time, and chop them up when he felt like it, and he made a total mess of his vineyard.

Nasrudin thought: "Oh dear, this is awful. I wish he'd cut them at the right time and at the right angle; they'd be much better". So he thought "I'll advise him and give him some help."

So he went and leant on the garden-wall and looked over to his neighbor and said : "Hello", but the neighbor didn't take any notice at all.

He stood there on the wall for a few days and when the man came out to cut he said: "Arrrrghhh!" And the man cut it in any case.

So he thought: "He goes to the tea-house every afternoon for a talk; I'll go and sit there and introduce the subject of grape-vines and give him some ideas."

So for a few days he went and sat in the tea-house, and the neighbor came and looked at him and Nasrudin said: "Hello!", but the man didn't take any notice of him. He thought: "Well, I won't give up."

So Nasrudin thought : "There must be some experts on this phenomena. I will go to the local town." So he went to the local town and there was a whole street full of therapists with their boards: aroma therapists, bone therapists, tooth therapists, ear therapists, all the therapists you can imagine.

Right at the end of a big new board he saw a therapist who was a neuro-linguistic therapist. "Ah, that's a new one, very modern. I will go and consult him." So, he went and explained the situation to the neuro-linguistic therapist, who listened very carefully to the words he had used and to the way he had used them, and he said : "Your neighbor is a graphic man. That will be 5 dirhams."

So he gave the man 5 dirhams and went home. Then he got a big piece of paper about three meters long and wrote on it in big letters: "There is a man not a hundred miles from here who does not know how to cut his grape-vines." And he put it on two poles in his garden facing his neighbor.

After two or three days his neighbor came and knocked on the door, and said: "Nasrudin, I think you are trying to tell me something."

So I just offer this as a suggestion for the moment.

REDUCING FEAR

I would like to talk about something which most people feel in one way or another and which all therapists regularly encounter: the very common and familiar factor called fear.

The majority of people seeking the services of a therapist have this factor of fear present in them to one degree or another. The fear may be a result of the fact that they are physically or mentally unbalanced and allowing their imagination to take over. They fear that they may be more seriously ill than they actually are.

All this is obvious, you all know how patients show their fear. And a therapist will obviously try and comfort and reassure a person: one tries to calm their fears in a normal, understandable and reasonable way.

What I would like to talk about is this: how does a therapist use a focus? How does a therapist make use of the whole being and optimize on it?

Again, having established a rapport with the patient or other person, you start by transmitting what I might call good waves or positive feelings to them on a deeper level. In the beginning, these feelings or this energy you send towards them is a sort of general type of positive; but then slowly, over the course of time, you focus on any specific fear they might have.

Those of you who are involved in therapies which concern people who are mentally disturbed will find that when you try to analyse or specify a particular primal fear, you will find a lot of static interference, because the fear they are showing is mixed up with another or several other neuroses they may have. This particular neurosis does not necessarily produce an identifiable fear signal, so your skill is to sort out the signals you are receiving.

Sorting out, going through and identifying such signals can be time-consuming. Sometimes there is enough time to do this, sometimes there is not. If there is, you can do a parallel operation: you can use your techniques to identify, explain and help them through their neurosis while at the same time transmitting impulses and energies of a positive nature to them.

If you don't have enough time or if the person is in a state of very considerable fear, you make use of the whole being function on that person without necessarily waiting to identify the root or the basic fear.

In order to focus the whole being, you have to know what you are focusing on. Here again we get into the question of detail. Firstly, if you are sure of and basically content with your own professional ability, you then look at yourself on a human level and, without being too ambitious, you link the positive you know you have towards the other person.

This is not a sort of quickie method; it is a method which can be dictated by certain circumstances. Within yourself, within your own being you have hopefully developed certain areas of certainty. These areas of certainty may be feelings of comfort, happiness, love or warmth. You bring together and focus all these aspects which are of a positive nature.

In conventional medicine a doctor/therapist will go through certain tests and explain various aspects of the treatment to the patient. This is necessary and polite, and it also has the effect of calming a certain degree of the patient's anxiety or fear. But you all know that at a certain point after that, you are reacting or acting towards the patient in what is called, if you like, an instinctive way.

By observation or by touch you identify certain things which are happening or which already exist in the patient. Once you have recognised that, you do not have to go back to your textbooks and look up to see what this particular thing signifies physically: you act or react in a way which is instinctive.

What I would recommend to you is that you add another level to this instinct. After all, if you accept and recognise that there are different levels of consciousness, you also have to recognise that the other person also has those levels. The person may perhaps be thinking or existing on just one or two very simple and basic levels, and you might think: "It's difficult for me to communicate with them on other levels because they don't appear to be receptive", but it should not prevent you from trying to establish rapport on those different levels during the course of a therapy or treatment.

You don't act and then wait for some feedback, because if you are functioning towards the person on various levels, any feedback or response will be taken in and any further rapport or signal will continue to be exchanged on those levels.

It is obvious to you all that fear is a very powerful emotion, and unfortunately, fear feeds fear. Fear is not fed by choice. Fear is fed, for instance, by imagination.

A person might have a fear which they roughly identify or approximately define. And then, because you can also have negative optimization, they can then optimize on that fear: "I'm afraid of this. I'm afraid of a particular situation." Then the imagination comes in and adds to it, saying: "Because in this circumstance or in this situation it is possible that this, this and this could happen." This can go on to an infinite degree.

If somebody has an irrational fear, it is, by definition, very difficult to sit down with this person and explain that there is no basis for it.

So if you identify that there is a baseless or imaginative or irrational fear, focus yourself, focus your effort onto that area. Irrational fear such as "fear of the unknown" can be answered by or even cancelled out by a therapist acting in such a way that the being of that person starts to look at and hopefully distance themselves from that fear.

When you have established a rapport with somebody who has a fear, whether irrational or otherwise, the first thing to do is to transmit by speech, by touch or behaviour the fact that you understand that there is a degree of fear.

Because, strangely enough, and I'm sure all therapists will have encountered this: fear defends itself because it has established a form of control over a person, and like anything that has established some authority, it doesn't want to give it up. If, by your speech and action, you seem to be obviously attacking that fear, the fear itself will put up defenses and will manifest itself in the form of even more fear: "It's all very well for this person to tell me I shouldn't be afraid, but there are so many things to be afraid of, such as this, that, and the other thing." While you are sitting there reassuring the person and talking to them in a calm voice, they are making a list of all the fears in the world.

So the trick or technique is that you predict or expect a degree of fear. And you start on the assumption that they are in a situation of worry or anxiety and, hopefully you don't start out by saying to them: "You are afraid, aren't you?" Because it may be that they are, or else they are not, and then they think : "Maybe I should be anxious. Ah yes, so I am!"

As I say, you start with the assumption that there is nervousness, anxiety and fear, and you transmit a confidence wave to the person. What you can be doing on several levels is getting the fear to reveal itself. If it is revealing itself on different levels, and if you are building up communication with the person on those different levels, you can and should establish a profile of their fear. You are getting an impulse back from them and while you are going through the normal, formal treatment or activity, within yourself, you are deeply sending back certain waves or impulses.

Some of them are of a very simple and very basic nature. When you get an impulse back from a person of a fear of a certain type, a certain nature or quality, you can send back a very simple and basic question: "What are you? What is your function in that person? By what authority do you influence that person?"

There is an old saying which I'm sure you have heard before: "Fear knocked on the door, faith answered, and there was nothing there."

Certainly, you can say that to a person and encourage them, as I say, formally and outwardly, but you also have to take into consideration the interior turbulence of that person, which is created and sustained by fear and the negative.

As I have said before, if you put the positive together with the negative, it cancels it out. But it's up to you to be positive: you must be sending out the positive. If you are not quite sure, if you are not quite confident, you might get into a situation which is ridiculous.

But it does happen. Supposing you are sending out questions such as: "Who are you? What are you doing with this person?", you may end up involving yourself with and having a dialogue with that fear.

It's ridiculous, but unfortunately, human beings are ridiculous: "I asked a question. I got an answer which seemed all right. I made a counter-reply and then another answer came back" and the next thing you know is that you are going to a therapist yourself.

When I say that you ask a question or send out confidence, you are affirming. You are not asking this fear "Who are you? I want to know your name". In fact, you don't want an answer. It is a rhetorical question, and by the same token, it has overtones of criticism and contempt, since it implies "What are you? Justify yourself if you can"; and not "Please tell me who you are if you don't mind."

By gradually establishing contact on different levels with another person, you get into the area of co-action. It means you are encouraging them and signalling to them that "Together we can do something", the basic aim being that the person will then, in a phrase we use which is open to different interpretations: be able to "walk alone" in the sense that they do not develop a dependence factor on you.

You should therefore try and co-act with them in different circumstances, all the time watching and measuring to see how you can very gradually reduce the support factor while not obviously removing it, but allowing them to feel that they are doing it themselves.

USING ONE'S TALENT TO CONSTRUCT SITUATIONS

I said this morning that this afternoon we would try and go through some examples of how to employ some of the techniques I have been explaining, but I find that in talking I did not stress or sufficiently bring out one other aspect.

You see, just as I check on all of you I do check on myself as well. As a matter of fact, I am less charitable towards myself than I am towards you, although you might not believe it. When you are employing the "whole being focus" you are obviously including your own training, your own experience and feelings about the patient or the situation within that process.

You can usefully add another factor to those aspects of your own training and experience, which should include a particular sense factor of your own, which some people recognise in themselves, take advantage of, and develop. Sometimes they don't recognise it or else they ignore it, and that is very simply some sort of talent.

In this case, talent does not necessarily imply an ability you have learned. One can feel something and say: "Such and such a person has a certain talent in this direction." People can be musically talented or have a physical talent for movement or dancing. There are many and various types of talents.

The type and degree of talent is very often different in every person. If this talent is recognised early enough, they can obviously be attracted to using that talent as a musician or as a dancer or also be attracted towards something which directs them towards that area. If it is strong enough and identified early enough, the person might perhaps follow that area of activity as a career. If they do follow it consistently, one might classify that as a major talent.

Sometimes the activity or profession they follow doesn't go along with this predominant talent, which means that they don't have the opportunity of using, developing or exercising this particular talent in their work or profession.

But if there is a talent which the person feels or recognises in themselves; a real and natural talent has a way of always coming to the surface and reminding the person about itself, but gently, not in an aggressive way: "What about me? What about this aspect of me you have forgotten about or are ignoring?"

Then you have what I call secondary talents. Somebody says: "I have a feeling for such-and-such a thing" or "I have a touch in such-and-such an area". If their particular profession or job does not allow them to use this major or secondary talent, they can still follow it by doing it as a hobby. If it is followed as a part-time study or hobby, this is obviously more advantageous than trying to suppress it, disregard it or push it into the background.

The question is: "How can I use this talent I follow in my professional activity or as a hobby? Since it is very much part of me, how can I naturally put it together with my professional work? How can I add it to a therapy in such a way that it is not something alien being inserted?

It has to be incorporated if you feel it, if you can do it and if you can use it, in other words, in a homogeneous way. For instance, you can't say "I am Brazilian and like beating drums, therefore I will take my drums to a therapy session and play them". This would be intrusive. Mind you, if your patients are Brazilian, they will probably also have a drum with them, but again, this can get oneself involved in a certain augmentation of the unnecessary.

What you say to yourself is "I am Brazilian and my preoccupation is drums. I have a certain inherent rhythm and a certain natural ability in that area." The central factor here is the rhythmic factor. A person might say, for instance: "I have a certain natural body rhythm, how can I add that to a therapy situation? Is it possible to do so? Does it improve the situation itself or is it that I feel more personally comfortable in a rhythmic situation?"

You see, assuming these talents exist, I am suggesting that you look at them both in a positive way and in a negative way. Positive in the sense that "I have this talent. I would like to interact with and make use of this talent, but is the affinity I want to practice a purely personal one?" If this is the case, it means that although you may enjoy it, it is unproductive in a therapy situation, insofar as it is only making part of you happier and more content.

However, if you think you have a talent or capacity which can be either rhythmic, a touch for something or else a feeling or a communication that can be made use of, at that point the question has to be "How and when?" Another important question is: "To what degree; to what depth?"

I am talking about the prime or major talent and also a secondary talent. A person can possibly have two or three different talents, and if they can construct the right kind of situation, they can introduce two or three of these talents to complement each other. You are not going through them all saying: "I have this and that talent, which do I use?" or "How much of it?" and so forth, because this just becomes another source of confusion. If you are feeling a situation, the answer should come from it; the answer should already be there.

For instance, you hear people say "He or she is a good communicator" about somebody. If, in answer to that, one says: "Yes, I think I can communicate with people", what else can you communicate to a person apart from your particular professional activity?

The word I am using here is the word "construct" in the sense of constructing a situation. In a relationship with another person you should try to optimize, which again means to add to the situation.

It is almost like setting up a kind of theatre set, because if you have people's conscious and unconscious attention on different levels, you are broadcasting towards this person. On different conscious or unconscious levels, people do take note of details. Once they have satisfied themselves that the situation and ambience is positive, comfortable and secure, they will notice and listen. They will use their normal faculties to absorb what is being said or what is being done in a situation.

Now, are they completely concentrating on what you are doing or saying? Not entirely, because a certain amount of their being is occupied by fear, anxiety or other factors. If you like, that part or aspect of their being is involved in a negative situation or a series of negative situations.

What you want to do is to try and bring out that tension in order to focus on what is really happening. You can use a series of simple actions or tricks, if you like, to do this. After all, that part of their being and conscious or unconscious mind is in fact involved in trivialities, but they are not trivial to the person.

If you say to them: "Don't have these stupid little worries, concentrate on me", they will concentrate on you and on what you are saying; and they will honestly and sincerely try to do this, but there is a part of the primitive being which is still preoccupied.

So if you are functioning with your whole being towards them, how do you encourage them to involve or commit their whole being towards you?

I am sorry to disappoint you: I don't know of any instant way of doing it. What really applies here is the time factor.

What they have done is encompass or surround these primitive complexes, and it is the tension factor which keeps them together. This is not a physical tension factor, it is not intellectual or even in a mental area, it is a tension which is at a very much more primitive level. And with primitive things one has not exactly to use primitive methods, but speak to or communicate with them in a very basic way.

This attempt by you runs simultaneously with the actual therapy or activity you are performing with that person. You are feeding it through your deep essential being and out towards them.

Some of you may say: "Look, I am not that primitive. I don't know how to communicate on a primitive level." Well, you are not expected to growl at them like a dog or even think that way. You are merely feeling towards them in a human and natural fashion. How they pick it up and how they analyse it is part of their problem, but it has to be done in a very simple, natural and human way, otherwise that primitive quality or primitive being can say: "This is too complicated for me. I don't understand those big long words."

If this primitive aspect feels a warm and natural wave coming from the person, it will use its own natural and primitive ways of feeling, testing and measuring this wave. Firstly and basically: "Is it hostile or aggressive?" If, by these primitive measurements, this primitive part then feels a relationship with the signals which are successively going out over a period of time and the relative importance to the person of these hang-ups, fixations or problems will diminish.

This is a gradual and gentle process. It does take time but it is a necessary activity, a necessary parallel operation, because however educated and sophisticated that person may be, there are some occasions when they will revert and check back to the primitive: "How do I feel?" No matter how much they may persuade themselves that they are educated, intellectual and everything else, they will always check back to a more primitive level from time to time: "Do I feel safe? Do I feel threatened? Is this all right?" They may check back for a fraction of a second, and if the signal comes back that there is "nothing really dangerous or really hostile here" then it is all right. If the signal comes back that there is somehow some danger, you will get a defense mechanism operating.

It is true that we are talking here about minimal signals or traces, which are very small and light. But don't forget: if we are optimizing, we are aiming both to get more and more situations within ourselves and to provoke more and more situations with other people in which there are less and less obstacles and barriers and more and more points of agreement and meeting. In that way, you have your maximizing, because you are optimizing on various functions simultaneously.

This, in turn, creates and maintains the harmony within yourself or towards the situation.

So recognising, developing and using a talent is a useful

additional instrument, but again, it should be complementary, it shouldn't be only a change of thought, in the sense of: "I'm doing this, but now I am going to use my x or y talent". It should flow together with your intention and impulse, along with your training and technique.

MAKING USE OF THE ESSENTIAL BEING

Those of you who were at earlier congresses will remember that I introduced the subject of the essential being after a certain time. I did not introduce that subject early on in the congresses, but quite deliberately after a certain situation had been established among ourselves. The reason for this was not in order to say to you that you would "all have an essential being as from now" because the essential being has been involved right from the beginning of the therapy congresses, and in fact from the beginning of your contact with the Tradition.

I am re-introducing this subject of contact with the essential being for the simple reason that the essential being is slow to react and slow to trust. The strongest basic motivation of the essential being is of the nature of defense. It is, by definition, deep within the person and therefore it protects itself by hiding. So if you begin by saying: "We are going to involve and understand the essential being," it is as if the essential being is being put out into the open on the table without its natural defense.

It is not that the essential being is reluctant to be recognised or even to be used. It is only reluctant in the sense that it wishes to protect itself and also the person. It therefore has to be encouraged and persuaded, and it also has to feel right.

When the essential being is allowed to function more and more efficiently it produces what we call a dynamic. Here again, one has a slight problem of language, because if you use the word dynamic, it depends on what that idea or word produces in people's minds. Dynamic can imply a constant and even frenetic action, but in our own terminology it means something which is both producing and reacting, in other words something which needs situations and circumstances to react, which both wants to relate and wants to react.

As I said before, it recognises what it can use. The co-active pattern implies an activity and it implies movement. You can have a form of movement which obeys the law of gravity, say when something is held up and then allowed to fall: it then obeys the law of gravity and drops. What this represents is movement as a result of a momentum which has been started off and which continues.

The co-action with the being can be represented by a sort of diagram: we can see it as a hollow circle or vacant space, which, for the sake of argument, we can call a circumstance or a situation.

In fact, this circle is not entirely empty. It contains the activity, energy and stimulation which causes it to move. It can then be taken as just a particular circumstance or situation which we will consider in isolation as if it were an individual, but it is also a graphic illustration of many similar situations which take the form of a chain, because they are all associated with each other.

Each situation and context of this nature requires the use of energy or a tactic, and the way it moves, the momentum it establishes, connects and influences an adjoining situation or context.

There are certain contexts and situations which will obviously require more intention and commitment of the being to make them work. So the degree of intention and energy you use on different situations will obviously vary.

I am not suggesting for a moment that there are variations in the degree of intelligence among you, but I am sure that some of you will have noticed that many of the things I mention in the context of therapy apply to you as individuals as well as therapists. This is useful, because if you can use such things upon yourself, it means you can practice them, let them become familiar to you, and then use them in turn on other people. You then get a feedback in the context of their terms of reference in a more and more precise way.

This means that they may be reacting to a particular situation.

But if you know what your reaction might have been in a similar situation, you add or subtract their surface reaction and you get a clearer idea of what their real feeling is.

Another diagram represents the indication and implication of movements and action, but why is it shown with a circle around it? Surely, if there is energy, movement and development, could this not be infinite movement? Why is there a limitation on it? One shows it this way because the circle represents the time-frame of the activity, which may be just a second or millisecond long. It's a convenient graphic way of putting down a function.

For an action to take place in a context or a situation, certain functions have to be fulfilled within that instance. If those functions are fulfilled, the product of that situation or function transmits and relates to other situations around it.

Most of you are familiar with the analogy we use of the oil-spot technique: if you have a piece of cloth or paper and you put drops of oil in different parts of it, they eventually coalesce over a period of time and come together. They could be considered initially as individual entities which are separated or isolated from each other: but in joining together, each spot or circumstance brings with it the experience of how it travelled, of how or why it came together.

Is there a motivation for its coming together? Whether and how they come together depends to a very great extent on the texture of the material on which you drop the oil. If you drop the oil on a metallic surface it is very likely that the spots will eventually come together in an almost accidental way.

The analogy of the material or cloth we use is that we say that this material is the Tradition. And the Tradition is working through people, since the function of the Tradition is to work with and for people. If one is using, distributing or making energy available, it must be distributed in such a way that it can be used, and the different qualities and aspects can then come together and complement each other.

The human understanding and the human ability to take up and use energy is, in fact, limitless: any limitation is imposed only by circumstance. Taking advantage of and using and benefiting from disciplines in the Tradition means not only accepting those disciplines, but making the effort to make oneself make the effort.

You might say that this seems unnecessarily complex because if one's being recognises that something is useful, there should be no effort in trying to do it or use it. But the factor which is absent is: "In what way?" Literally: "How?"

The concept of the existence of an energy can be encouraging or even frightening: it can cause all sorts of different reactions in people, so that if you explain to them that the energy can be and is used through the human dynamic, does that solve the problem? And do they go out and do it? The answer is no, possibly because the word "dynamic" causes excitement, fear, hate, dread or any other emotion. So there is no point in suddenly saying to a person: "We will now use a dynamic." Some people will dive under the table, others will jump out of the window and you have a whole possible area of reaction.

So, realizing the fact that one is dealing with people who have different degrees and different depths of conditioning, you use (or rather I use) all sorts of tricks. I always update my tricks, so you'll never see it coming. I might say: "Don't worry about the dynamic; I'll do the dynamic, you listen." It sounds like a perfect combination, but it is in fact a two-way street, it's a balance.

You're not preoccupied with "The Dynamic" as a "high-flying concept" because Agha is taking care of it in those terms, but you are involved in the dynamic nonetheless. By being involved, which people are, in one co-action or another, they will feel the existence of an energy and dynamic so long as a function is being performed. Since the need to use this dynamic is deep and natural, they are involved in something, in a situation, in an activity, and they find some extra quality or some extra talent.

They have developed a certain momentum within themselves or within the situation, and as they, the situation or the context improves, they are content, they feel well, they feel comfortable. They don't need to stop and say: "Was it the dynamic?", because by their movement and activity they are drawing out as much of the dynamic as they can use.

Like attracts like. I am not so stupid as to ask anybody a question like: "Did you use the dynamic yesterday?", because you can provoke a whole gamut of unnecessary reactions. People will then go through every minute of the day saying to themselves: "What did I feel or didn't I?" or "Should I have?" I therefore don't ask those sorts of question because I don't want people to ask themselves that sort of question. Before they go to sleep at night they're lying awake saying: "Did I use the dynamic? Was it the right dynamic I used?", and they swallow their Valium and still can't get to sleep. It's unproductive.

There is a phrase we use called "quiet satisfaction", which is an individual feeling. Why, for instance, call it quiet satisfaction? Why not just quiet, meaning calm and tranquil, or why not just satisfaction meaning satisfied and content? Why the two together?

This is because the word satisfaction can also be evocative. If you say: "I am satisfied. I think I am satisfied. Am I satisfied? Do you think so? What is satisfied? I will phone somebody and ask them what it means", and you then start the whole useless questioning process over again.

Or else, satisfaction can be a feeling of: "I am satisfied" which is understood by some people to mean self-satisfied, therefore "I will stop here; I have arrived."

Quiet satisfaction means that you are quiet within yourself and that you do not feel the need to tell everyone about it, to broadcast it or to examine it obsessively and analyse it. The word quiet implies that one is quiet within oneself and not disturbed.

Try and keep these various ideas and symbolic representations in your mind. You should not only use them as objects in isolation, but also as patterns of being, thought and behaviour. They are components, they do fit together and they do function harmoniously over time. They may be on paper in word and graphic form, but they are not just ink on paper, they do exist in a wider sense and they should be functioning within you.

They are not independent or individual concepts in the sense that you take them and carry them around saying "Where is that thing functioning in me and should it be and when?" It does and will function, but you have to allow it and invite it to do so.

After all, I am only functioning here because you invite me and want me to do so.

UNITY, SELF-SATISFACTION AND MOOD

I am always very insistent about the unity factor. I don't have to repeat the value of united effort, united thought and united use of energy. By working together, by co-acting, you learn, experience, and exercise this, so being part of and employing unity is one context.

If you are say, "given" unity of purpose and a direction in which to act, it is very useful and positive and can be very clear, but that is only half of the aspect of unity. If the principle of unity is a fundamental aspect of the Tradition (which it is) and if the importance of using unity is explained by me over and over again (which it is), the other side of the equation comes from you: how do you achieve unity of purpose, unity of of feeling and unity of attention?

You do not achieve it by diversifying your activities, and certainly not in any way which creates a friction. Frictions are caused by rivalry, jealousy, and lack of attention to detail. Lack of union is caused by the wrong attitude.

There is an attitude among different groups which I find is an obstacle to a united activity: an attitude people take upon themselves, not in my presence, but nevertheless I have heard it said: "I am in the Hakim Group." As far as I am concerned, this means nothing. It could be a group of poets, musicians, or dancers. It has happened that because we have a large number of people in various groups who are therapists, I have produced and directed energy in the direction of therapy.

The Tradition contains techniques, energies and applications of therapy, but the Tradition itself is not a therapy. If anybody thinks or says "I am a member of the Hakim Group" using the term with pride or superiority, well, I do not ever want to hear that. In the Tradition, allow me to judge who is less or more inferior or superior. Whether you are a practising therapist, musician or poet, if you are doing it well, I will back you all the way.

Certainly, the function of a therapist touches directly on the lives of people in an important area. In medicine they deal in areas of life and death. But when they are in the Tradition their attitude should be one of united action and united feeling.

I certainly would not deny that a person who has studied and is qualified for a position has deservedly earned a certain consideration or position, but let us leave aside any claim to superiority or inferiority. One can legitimately say: "I am fortunate enough to be in the Tradition and I happen to be in the Hakim group."

I do not just say this because of any personal like or dislike of mine, it is to stop certain attitudes developing, since some attitudes can provoke counter-attitudes, at which point, even if we say we are "in the world and not of it", we get into the same old pattern of claim and counter-claim, superiority, inferiority, jealousy, challenge, etc. Suffice it to say: "I am a doctor, nurse, therapist, teacher. I am happy with it and am trying to develop it. I do not shout it to the whole world. I have an inner satisfaction which I am developing".

Another obstacle to unity, correct harmony and communication can be called "secrets" in the sense of: "I know something you don't know." This is a familiar and juvenile children's game. There are secrets, and I can and do tell people things of a secret or confidential nature. I can and do give people personal activities and things to do which apply to them only.

We should not fall into the trap of rivalry or competition. We have eighty or ninety therapists present here. Supposing a group is established which has eighty or ninety poets or musicians? Are they going to function harmoniously or are they going to count their own importance by weight of volumes published? We are getting into rivalry situations here, and this is for children.

These may be points which people recognise, and although they may then ignore or deny their existence, they do manifest themselves in certain contexts and they are disruptive.

If one wants to make any sort of judgement or evaluation of

another person in the Tradition, let it be based on certain things which can be seen: they attend exercises regularly, they are punctual as well as various other points which can be noted.

"Such-and-such a discipline or punctuality is subject to a certain amount of flexibility. Such-and-such a detail depends on how I feel or how I interpret it": this is untrue. Details are details, functions are functions. If a person is habitually late for an exercise or activity, they should leave home earlier. There is absolutely no point in me sitting here talking about details when people ignore them or take them as being unimportant.

If the intention and impulse is there, people can achieve the most amazing things. If you are a smoker, have no money and the nearest tobacco shop is ten miles away, I guarantee that you will go to the end of the world to find the money and get to that tobacconist before it closes.

People are motivated and focus their intention because of an understanding they have: if their own intention and motivation is not clear enough, it would be contrary to the discipline of the Tradition to impose force upon them. They are and should be their own force or own impulse: "I want to be there at a particular time, I understand the reason and I focus on that particular achievement with the whole of my being".

I can write letters, threaten people and do all sorts of things, and I might get a result insofar as people would say: "If I don't do that, something awful will happen." In fact, it would be ridiculous to do this because the person would rightly say: "I have freely entered into this activity and now I am being threatened."

So the impulse must come from within the person themselves. You don't sit by your telephone waiting and saying to yourself: "It's time for me to leave for the exercise, but I'm waiting for Agha to call me and tell me to go."

I'll help you on the way, I'll suggest what you could do, I'll make energies and other things to do available to you. The agreement we have is that I will provide it, but you have to use it. If you do not use what is available to you well and usefully and take maximum advantage of what is on offer, the only punishment is what you are imposing on yourselves.

This being said, in case anybody missed it the first time around, I repeat that I do not promise heaven and I do not threaten hell.

That was the bad news. Depending of course on how you take it, the good news is that we are focusing more and more on certain activities.

THE MOOD FOCUS

In the optimizing phase, I do take into consideration a factor which can be such a source of confusion that it constitutes an obstacle, and that is the random factor called mood. Why this factor must be taken into consideration is that a person's mood at a particular time very obviously exists. It is therefore an actual tangible factor, it is something a person is experiencing at a particular time.

Of course if a person is in a happy, comfortable and balanced state of mind or being, or mood, it is easier to do something positive or to think or act in a positive and useful way. But when, as a result of a problem in any one of these areas, the person's mood shifts towards the negative, their reaction to a positive circumstance or a positive situation can be very considerably influenced. In a situation or context which could go one way or another, the mood plays an important role. This is very clear to all of you who are involved in therapy.

What you therefore try to do, both for yourselves and for patients, is what we call a mood focus. "This is a contradiction in terms" you might say, because a focus implies a certain precision, and you have a state of being or a physical or mental condition of mind which is perhaps vague or influenced by different emotions.

There are two ways of dealing with a situation or context which is vague. You can dismiss it by saying "It has no context, value or influence, therefore I will ignore it."

Nevertheless, as you all know, if you are dealing with a patient whose mood includes certain complexes, they will take that as being an attack on them and therefore defend their present state, so that you will then come up against something which is not vague anymore, but very precise indeed to them.

So you use a similar trick on yourself or on a patient. You take one aspect of the mood, and either by yourself or with the patient, you focus on that particular aspect. It is then becoming something which you as an individual, together with the energy of the Tradition, are looking at in order to find a solution. The relationship between yourself and a patient is that this person and you are both looking for and mutually helping each other to find a solution. The way you do it and the skill you use boils down to something I said in the beginning: an attitude.

An attitude which you or a patient might have could also be on a collision course with each other.

So look at this factor both within yourselves and also with your patients. Do not allow it, obviously, to dominate, but don't be dismissive of it. Use a technique to diminish it's influence.

COLOURS

In the Tradition we use a lot of colours and I would like to say a few words about functions of colours and their use. We have a division between prime and pastel colours, and there is a good reason for this: if I am using or suggesting the use of a colour, this colour has a meaning, a quality, a use and a purpose. If I take a prime colour and give it to people, if they are in tune with me and in tune with the Tradition, the effect can sometimes even be shocking.

Let's take a prime colour like blue, which contains a large number of very significant elements. It is possible that by imposing on or giving people this solid blue colour, although it doesn't cause a shock, it may still produce a confusion, a worry or an analysis, because a person looking at and working with that colour gets a feedback.

So what I do when introducing a colour is to start with the

pastel shade of that colour, in the same way that if you are talking to idiots, you talk A - B - C until they can understand the use of a language or a colour. The prime colours relate in a very fundamental and strong way, and the pastel aspects of these colours act in a very subtle, gentle but developmental way by complementing and communicating with each other.

So if one pastel shade provokes a feeling or a thought in a person, another pastel shade of a different colour will produce an answer to that question by producing a harmony with these colours within the individual. In the way we use it, a prime colour in the Tradition represents a colour, a type of energy, a word or a sound. It therefore works together in the same way as a sound or a word when you have a feeling that those things harmonize. In this way the colours harmonize and work together.

Prime colours can also be used to denominate or represent situations. Those of you who work with colours, or who are conscious of the use of colours in therapeutic situations, will have noticed that certain prime colours can influence people and situations.

In some countries and cultures, certain prime colours evoke certain feelings.

Regarding the skill of using colours in therapy situations, and equally, the skill of using colours on and for oneself: the use of these colours depends not only on your understanding of the function of the colours, but on how familiar the colours and their use are to you.

Each colour communicating with the other colour produces a reaction and an energy. The various prime colours represent words, tones and qualities, because since time is not stationary, the same is true of the time factor, as in, supposing an energy passes from the red into the yellow, you have the variation intensity of the tonality.

The choice of the use of colour in a situation or in a context, whether in relation to oneself or in the relationship between a therapist, a patient or a pupil, is subject to modification because firstly, within oneself, certain colours provoke certain reactions.

There is also the mood area which involves likes and dislikes of colour, which provoke certain feelings or reactions.

If you are a car driver, your deep and subjective reaction to red is that it usually means "stop" and green means "go". So in the use of colour you both allow for your own feeling for the colour, and for what the other person might be thinking or reacting to about that colour.

If you are using it on yourself, you are evaluating your own feeling and reaction. If you are using it with another person, you are getting a feedback, using the co-action and feeling how they are reacting. For instance, if you take a colour in the spectrum somewhere between red and orange, this can create a feeling or reaction of: "This represents the sun" i.e., warmth, light and comfort.

When you have different colours on a robe, they are acting and interacting with each other as well as with you because you are wearing the robe, and they will tend to influence or deepen the impact of what you are doing or what you are reading or listening to. You do not control in which order they react, you do not decide that "Today I feel yellow". By a free decision and by a relationship with the robe, you are putting it on and inviting them to react with you.

Certainly, some of the prime colours will always subconsciously be associated with certain things or situations. For instance, the colour red can evoke a reaction of danger, hostility or some form of "stop" on the exterior or reactive level. But it is very difficult for the being of a person to be nervous or hostile to the colour red, because the system and being knows that one's blood is red, so that in a purely anatomical evaluation, red means good and more red means better.

Evaluations like "This person has red eyes, he's drunk", "Green eyes: she is beautiful", "Blue eyes mean clear", and "If you've got yellow eyes, you have jaundice" etc., are automatic, normal and reasonable, and a person reacts to them.

The critical point is that when you are using a robe with colours on it, you are inviting those colours to co-act with you. I repeat, you put yourself in a relationship to the robe or in a relatiuonship to colours by inviting them to co-act with you. And if you are reacting with the different shades or colours on different levels, you can be functioning simultaneously with them all. The critical thing is inviting, allowing, permitting: not forcing.

In many diagrams and activities, we use black. In the Tradition, the colour black represents wisdom. Maybe from the conventional or western point of view you may say that black means mystery, darkness or "the unknown".

For us, black represents wisdom because it means that one arrives at a point where, not everything is coloured black, but you're imagining for instance, something black, and you're not hopefully involving this greatly estimated intellect: "This thing is black" right? If you really want to push it, maybe you can say: "It's light black, dark black, very black, a little black, more black or less black", but there is a limit to the intellectualization of the colour black, just as, on the other side of the balance, the colour white is, in fact, all the colours.

So to pre-empt any question of "Why then do we not have either all-black or all-white robes in the Tradition?": it is because you have to learn to use all the colours between white and black. And using them does not mean just putting them out or painting the rooms of your house in different colours and sitting in the various rooms in order to relate to different colours at different times. You think towards a colour, you visualize a colour, you feel something coming back from that colour. This function of thinking towards, feeling towards and sensing completes the equation.

Certainly, there are some occasions or situations where a colour will not impose itself upon you, but will seem to be present with you. If it is there and significantly perceptible, then, gently and gradually and in a relaxed way, see for yourself what is said about that colour or what that colour represents in the Tradition.

If a colour presents itself or is present, it does not necessarily mean that this colour is telling you to do something or forcing you in any way, for instance to perform some function which relates to that colour. It can be an indication or a proof to you that something has happened or that something is happening. And one's reaction to any identification of a particular colour should be one of a degree of quiet satisfaction.

If you look around in nature, you see that all colours usually co-exist in harmony in a natural and normal way. They complement each other. Take, for instance, a rose. We'll use this particular rose as an example: it is lighter on the outside and it gets gently darker towards the center.

The attraction of the rose is in the center because that is where the perfume is which attracts the bees and insects who will pollenate or use the pollen from the center.

Here again, you have the pastel shades going around and getting towards a more specific colour. Equally, a person may be using many terms of reference, many points of view, many books and other things, but he is nevertheless focusing down towards something in the center.

Certainly, you can look at the total entity of the rose from a distance: you can appreciate its delicacy, its beauty, its form, and then you can optimize further: you smell the perfume. This is not only introducing and using another sense, which is smell, it is also starting a process of co-action with the flower. Details such as the size, form or shape of the flower, how it grows, what it contains, what its essence is, come later.

Using all the variations from the basic colours through the pastel to another basic colour is not just a discipline in the sense of one, two, three, four and so forth, it is recognising that there is a momentum in this, which does not exist in the abstract.

If you are following the pattern of what I have been saying, you will realize that the factor which is added to this process or momentum is the factor of the person.

Now there is an "abstract" connotation: as long as it remains in the abstract, you cannot co-act with it, except to say: "I suppose it does exist in the abstract, but I'm not sure. They say it exists. It's a thing which is very amazing. How do I relate to it or use it?"

The answer is: "A wise man who does not use his knowledge is like a donkey with a load of books".

RELATING TO THE TEACHER

Nasrudin had one characteristic, which I understand without necessarily sharing it with him, and that was optimism. One day he discovered that he had no money, no income, and he was absolutely broke.

He went around and he asked his friends: "What could I do to get some money? How could I develop an income, or a business or some trade or something?" And as usually happens, he was given plenty of advice and little action. Finally he thought: "I will not ask for advice. I will study different situations in the town and make some sort of decision."

So one day he went to a restaurant and he watched people, the next day he went to the tea house and watched people, and after five or six days of this he thought: "I have got the idea. I know what to do to make millions. Everybody in this town eats yoghurt for breakfast or with lunch or supper or at almost any time. Some of them make it at home or else they buy it, but I will establish a monopoly of yoghurt."

This was the idea, but sometimes, as you know, hopes and actual things are slightly different. Anyway, Nasrudin was not seen in the town for two or three weeks after he had made this great discovery.

One day, somebody was walking in the mountains and they saw Nasrudin sitting by the side of an enormous lake, and he had a bowl of yoghurt and he was putting spoonfuls of it into the lake. And the man said: "Nasrudin, how are you? What on earth are you doing?"

"Shsh, I'm making the whole lake into yoghurt" said Nasrudin.

The man said: "There is a normal way of making yoghurt. You get some milk, you put some of the old yoghurt in it and then keep this milk at a certain temperature, and cover it over and then it becomes yoghurt".

Nasrudin said "Yes, yes", and continued putting spoonfuls

of yoghurt into the lake.

So the man said: "Look, Nasrudin, really, how long have you been doing this? How long have you been here?"

"Ten or twelve days" replied Nasrudin, "but don't bother me."

"Look Nasrudin", said the man, "this will not become yoghurt".

And Nasrudin said: "Well, supposing it does."

That is what is called optimism.

There is a factor I would like to talk about which is not directly associated with therapy, but with understanding or attitude.

Yesterday, some people thought they would perhaps see me in a particular place or at a particular time. Some, very kindly, were interested whether I was there or not, or where I was, or what I might be doing.

Now whether I am in a place or not, whether you see me yourself, or whether "He is there" is written up or not, I suggest to you, as I have done for many years: accept me as being present whether you see me or not, whether I'm obviously there or not. In terms of the Sufi Tradition, this is a very real factor. Normally I don't make promises, but this is a promise: if you have a barrier or limitation because of distance, time, or other factors, you are preventing me from working with you.

Any barrier you might think up, such as "He is far away. We haven't seen him for years. I write and he never replies" are conventional barriers. As I have said before, I am as far or as near as you allow me to be.

In order to fully function in the Tradition, it is necessary to have a certain amount of what one might call satisfaction: this is a reasonable and normal and human need. However if it becomes a preoccupation in the sense of "How much have I developed? What is my level of development? Can I check or monitor it?"; what people actually mean is "How can I worry about it?"

Remember that we have a deal: you do the work, you think, and you let me worry. I'm not saying: "Don't think" or "Don't look after details and other things which come up." I don't suspend thought. Although for some of you it is easier than for others.

If you look at the different diagrams and patterns, you see that all of them show movement, momentum, and action. Now any useful action is of a calculated nature, in the sense that if it is balanced and harmonious, it will produce a positive result. If it is action for the sake of action, you get a frenetic situation of "I must be doing something. Am I doing something? Should I be doing something?" So it is important to see and to check one's own attitude.

How one is looking at a context or a situation, how one is acting or feeling in it, may be different to how one is actually analyzing or looking at it. So, as with the Naqshbandi rules, you detach slightly from the situation and, as much as possible, look at it objectively. This is fast, clear and precise, and it should work within you on a deep level.

Observation should be functioning constantly: observation of oneself or of some other person's reaction to one, produces the function. This is because if you are ignoring your own deep feeling or the feedback, in other words the signal from another person or another situation, you get a series of movements but not a fluid motion.

Sometimes I produce or provoke situations which seem to be curious in the sense that perhaps they do not fit with what people imagine I should be doing or they should be doing.

To put it simply: I dance to my own tune, not to anybody else's. If I see that a situation or a person is developing a form of what one might call automatic and non-productive activity, then I break the rhythm and restart it, just as you should do if you are doing an exercise and feel that you are getting into a sort of monotonous or mechanical state. To stop something or break into it is not the same thing as to destroy. When one is looking at oneself and observing, one is not doing it in a highly critical way in order to find fault. You are looking at yourself with the attitude of: "How can I enhance or improve myself or the situation?"

There are several ways of improving or enhancing a situation. You have situations which occur in what one might call one's professional life or in world situations, which you look at, analyse, evaluate and react to according to what is formally required in worldly circumstances.

With your work with yourselves, you may feel or think that you are not able to work as efficiently or as correctly as you would like. You may say: "I find it difficult to do an exercise because my attention wanders" or "I am disturbed by various other factors."

One can stop this worry, distress or anxiety factor by introducing what I think is a positive and useful factor, which is me, in the sense that a person having a problem or an anxiety related to an exercise in the Tradition should understand that when they are starting it and doing it, I am there with them.

So any degree of confusion or worry, and they do exist, should hopefully be cancelled out by simply saying: "It's not just poor little me who is doing this." You can perfectly well say to yourself: "I am doing this activity together with Agha, and he is present to help me to do it."

If you accept and make use of this factor, you have something to start with, something to base your activity on. If you consciously and deeply feel that I am together with you, you establish a very positive rapport with yourself, because whatever reservation or barrier you may put up between you and yourself in the sense of: "I don't understand myself" or "A part of me is negative or hostile" with people dividing themselves into "one me" and "the other me"; well, I neither accept nor believe this attitude, even if it is commonly held.

But if this situation of the "one me" and "the other me", in other words the positive and the negative, does exist, and there is some sort of tug-of-war between the two; if there really is some sort of competition between these two selves or beings, why do you not use me as the referee?

I interfere, I intervene, I involve myself in everything you do. I don't do it aggressively and I don't even ask your permission. In all modesty, if you consider me as a referee and really do accept me, because it's more than just saying: "Yes, why not?", you will find that I can actually be useful within that concept; not so much in the sense that I make unbiased judgements between the one self and the other, because I am totally biased in one direction, and that is in the direction of the positive. If there is any appearance of the negative I will blow the whistle and kick it off the field.

So simply, in any activity which has certain aspects of useful function: use me. After all, in what one might call conventional life or conventional activities, if you have to do something, you choose the most efficient tool, you go for the best instrument to use.

I am a good professional, so that if there is a situation where you need a professional in the context of the Sufi Tradition, use me. I am not a plumber, nor will I repair your car: I mean I could, but it would cost you a fortune.

So when you are in a deep and profound area, you normally look round and see how you can enhance the situation you are in. And if you look around carefully enough and in a relaxed way, and if you are sufficiently harmonious and relaxed within yourself, you will find me in that situation with you.

The more you and I work together and the more you use me in situations, the more you will —either slowly or quickly because it in fact depends on you — discover or perhaps surprise yourselves by finding that whether you are doing an activity or an exercise alone or in a group, I am present there. If you try to stop me for whatever reason or erect a barrier between yourselves and me, I can and I will get over that barrier if you want me to do so.

So there is really no valid reason or valid excuse not to use me in a functional way in a useful context. Of course, this may sound like an invitation to phone me at any time of the day or night or write letters. People do that in any case so that is nothing new.

For a number of years I have tried to educate groups in various ways: I explain, draw diagrams, visit them, talk to them and see them. But there is one problem: for some curious reason, certain groups in the New World, Latin America and other friends, have somehow not been able to make the quantum leap in awareness, which is: what time is it in England now? They more or less know the time wherever they are, which is already something, and a lot of them even know what day it is, but between the two points there is a sort of grey area.

But one day I will make the big breakthrough, which is simpler than you might imagine: I will buy several hundred clocks, set them to English time, and send them everywhere, even unto Manaus, so that people will know what time it is in England.

Count on me, depend on me, use me and put me into your function. This is not a reassurance in the sense "I don't have to do anything because I can always bring Agha in and he will compensate." I will compensate for certain situations or problems and I will always be ready to back you up in positive situations. I will double or treble the amount of useful activity you do.

If I do this, which I can do, you then have the momentum established and that momentum can be maintained. I help you to maintain it, I want you to maintain it, but I must have some, not reassurance for myself, but some feedback which tells me that you understand that. I don't need to be checking you out all the time or receive telephone calls to be told: "I am doing this, that and the other thing." I know more or less what is going on.

So if you accept the fact that, even if it sounds strange, I am enthusiastic about you — I am in fact, like Nasrudin, actually optimistic.

Maybe it's pessimistically optimistic or optimistically pessimistic, I'm not sure.

RELATING TO THE TRADITION

There are certain similarities between myself and Nasrudin. We share certain faculties, certain points of view. One aspect of Nasrudin I do not share, as some of you may have noticed over the years, is his appetite for eating. I'm not saying appetite for eating is a good or bad thing, I'm just saying that he has his way of thinking about eating and I have my way.

It appears that on one occasion he decided he was going to have a real feast. So he went to the bazaar, bought two kilos of meat, took them home, and left the two kilos there while he went out on his business.

After he left, his wife came in. As people can be, she was greedy. She saw the meat, cooked it, and quickly ate it all up.

So he came back home around lunchtime expecting a meal, and she was sitting there happy and full, and he said : "Where is the lunch, where is the food?" and she replied: "Er, the cat ate it."

"Right", he said, and he went and brought in some scales. He put the cat on one side of the scale, and he put a weight of two kilos on the other side of the scale, and it balanced.

So he said: "Well if this is the cat, where is the meat? If this is the meat, where is the cat?"

Now I'm not trying to encourage or discourage you from eating, but what this means is that things can have a structure.

For instance, in a professional situation, in your job or in your work, you most certainly do have a structure. You go there in the morning, you come back in the afternoon, there is a structure.

Similarly, one can say that in the Tradition there is a certain organization, certain things to do and certain ways of doing them: ways of feeling. You are not just sort of "following orders" but understanding the suggestions given to you. These suggested tactics or strategies must be put together with your effort to produce something, otherwise they can just remain in an abstract area of "That is what we should be doing. This is what we should believe in", and there is a distance.

You can very usefully and positively begin to understand what the structure or nature of the Tradition is. You can say "I would like to understand because I can function better if I do understand." You can also say: "Because of my conditioning I need to understand the various aspects of this structure."

Actually, I would prefer if people did not try and "work through" understanding every aspect of the structure. Saying: "Unless we understand it, we cannot function with it" is not correct, just as it is not correct to say: "Unless I understand certain useful aspects I cannot use them".

The relationship which a person has with the Tradition is not dependant upon how they feel or how they analyse. They come in freely, hopefully without any hesitations, and without being given any promises or menaces. It is understandable that they should want to know how this thing called the Sufi Tradition functions.

It is also understandable that, because of conditioning, it's a little difficult for them to say: "Supposing I just get a taste of it and I don't have to understand the whole function" or to say: "I am part of the structure. I am helping to develop my part of this structure".

People say: "How can I construct something if I don't understand it? I would like to know exactly the right thing to do at the right moment in the right way so that I and other friends will benefit. In order to do this usefully, I have to understand the whole structure."

Who said so?

A person can imagine the structure of the Tradition and make it as complicated as they imagine it to be. Or they can look at it and say: "I am in it and want to be in it; I feel with it and Agha will tell me what to do."

There is another possibility somewhere between these two attitudes, which is that a person starts to have a sensation of or a feeling for what this structure called the Tradition is. And throughout the time that they are involving themselves in finding out or working out what the structure is, and throughout the time that they are associating with activities within the Tradition, they are in fact building up a comprehension of the structure, in the sense that they are building up an understanding for instance, of their own responsibility towards themselves and towards other people who are either members of their immediate group or who are in the Tradition in the wider sense.

They are not and should not be frightened of this responsibility. It is or should be a way in which they are focusing better on their function as beings, and when and where they function in one area and when and where they function in another.

The feeling which tells them when and how to function comes from a deep instinct. They do not just follow orders in the sense of : "You will do this or that. Today is this day, you'll do one, two, three".

The energy and quality of the Tradition assists a person if they themselves are drawing it out, asking for it and using it. First and foremost, their responsibility is towards themselves; but they cannot really feel and sustain that responsibility unless they understand what it means, what its quality is.

The term "responsibility" can cover a large number of circumstances: we who teach in the Tradition are responsible for people in the Tradition, but we can only function according to the reasonable efficiency of the people in the Tradition.

We function through the structure of the Tradition, in areas that people can hopefully understand, and if they don't understand precisely and exactly, there are ways, activities and functions by which they are encouraged to think more precisely.

For instance, if one talks about the authority structure in the Tradition; there is a structure. The authority comes from the people who are in the Tradition, singularly and collectively, because they have decided upon and chosen a way of living.

They are looking for nourishment, they are looking for something to feed their being, and they develop a harmony with the Tradition and its activities. By their connection and reasonable enthusiasm, they work in the Tradition and the influences and energies of the Tradition work through them.

In order to make proper use of the energy, a person has to be very much in contact with themselves and in harmony with the circumstance or situation they are in.

Now here is something which is plainly obvious but it does require repetition: the right thing at the right time. "But how do I know what the right thing is? What is the right time?"

Divide the two ideas into time and activity. If you are harmonizing and harmonized with the situation, the time element should be clear.

If you are harmonized within yourself, what you then do, or the tactic or activity which you introduce at that time, will in fact project itself. It will suggest itself and offer itself to you.

Again, this is a fluid action. You should not get into the situation where you know what is happening and then you wait for an idea. In the conventional world, people do not have the time to wait. If somebody comes to you and says: "What would you like to eat?", and you say "I'm thinking" and it takes you three hours to come up with an answer, you will get a cold meal.

You don't think it out in that much detail unless you're a professional: "This aspect of the steak means that it should be done in such and such a way", etc. Even professional eaters have to make a reasonably quick decision because it answers their need, which is that they are hungry.

In the deeper area of the profound being, it does not mean that if you are in a situation, it automatically follows that there is something which you instantaneously do. If you are harmonized and in touch with both your being and the situation, the action will produce itself. But in order for it to manifest itself, for the energy to show itself, it has to have some sort of guarantee, some sort of strong feeling from you that if and when it shows itself, it will be used correctly.

Before you start getting complexes and saying "I'm supposed to guarantee it, and if I do this and it doesn't work, it's going to be the end of the world": not entirely.

Place yourselves in a receptive mood: allow the energy to function or not. You cannot get it and use it uselessly. The energy itself will not control you in the sense that it dominates your entire activity, because in a way you have to signal your availability to use the energy.

You don't do it by filling in an application or in so many words.

You do it, again, by the being-to-being contact which says to the energy: "I can, I want to, I am able and prepared to use it. Perhaps I am not sure in exactly what way, or what form, or to what degree I am capable. Perhaps I am not even sure whether I am capable, but I would like to think that I am."

Unless this availability, unless this openness exists, you cannot work with yourself.

If, because of conditioning or other reasons, there is a breakdown of communication with yourself, you might have to get over this barrier; and it may be a source of conflict and confusion to have to fight "with yourself" as it were.

You do not have to fight with yourself and you should not be doing so.

If you want to fight with anybody, fight with me. Fighting with yourself provokes confusion, anguish and difficulties, and you lose. If you fight with me, it will be quick and sharp and you will still lose, which means I don't really suggest you fight with me, I hope you won't need to, but I really do recommend feeling and making use of the being rather than fighting it.

I assure you that there is really no need for this great "battle with myself".

People can imagine there is this great battle, and society and the western intellect can encourage you to think like this. And of course, this other part of oneself, this obstructive aspect or negative faction can be almost as big as you allow it to be.

But supposing you say: "Right. This aspect, part of, or other me is threatening to dominate me. It's giving me problems" as if it is perceptible and actual and tangible, as, as it were, an alternative you. If there is this alternative being, this additional problem or quality which is disturbing one, then take it out and look at it.

It is not something which is so unimaginable and complex that one cannot focus on it. And if you do take it out, look at it and focus on it, you can start understanding its weakness: not its strength, its weakness.

If you hold up a plant, you can see whether it has roots or not. If it's just sitting on top of the earth, you don't know whether it has roots or not without taking it up and looking at it. This applies equally with a situation or a feeling: if you pick it up and look at its whole context, then you can reasonably analyse perhaps its function, and certainly its strength and power.

If you find that it is so significantly deep within you, then you can use a process based on your knowledge of yourself. Because the skill is in putting together the energy of the Tradition with your knowledge of yourself to make a force.

You are not controlling the energy and you are not being controlled by it. You are establishing a functional co-action.

ANCHORING ONESELF IN THE TRADITION

Because this will be the last more or less formal talk for this congress, it will be useful to go through various points I have talked about. We have talked about co-action, interaction and also the dynamic of the fusion as represented by a graphic design.

The inner circle, represents a concept, the co-action movement. You will notice that I have added other circles to the same diagram because a co-action takes place in a circumstance, in a situation, but it also can and does influence other circumstances which are in the past or in the future.

In a particular co-action circumstance, the aim or target of that co-action is represented by a triangle or a pyramid, which is the focal point of the co-action. In a co-action you are aiming at achieving something, and when you are involved in this co-active situation, it doesn't mean that you are disconnected or un-associated with other circumstances, it is a question of the degree of the co-action.

These circles represent other activities, and there can be many of them happening simultaneously, but in a particular circumstance at a particular time, that is the focal point of the activity. And having co-acted, having focused on this and achieved some measure of success, then the center or the point of focus can be shifted to one of the other circumstances.

So it is a fluid or flowing momentum which you are building up. When you have the interactive situation represented by this diagram, again, the energy and the activity is flowing within that circumstance. Diagramatically, you might think "This is a limitation of a circumstance" and if there is an energy going this way and an energy going that way, will these energies be hitting or pushing against the wall in order to try and get out? No, because within the context, they reach an outer limit of usefulness and they flow. They don't go to infinity and decay.

Now with two concepts or factors, with two diagrams, you put them together to enable them to function and be used better. These are functioning; they are helping and complementing each other's activity.

For instance, one might be a physical situation and the other a mental situation. Then putting them together in an area which is the dynamic, the result of that operation then becomes the fusion of these two, where you have the two actions being used through a tactic, a technique or an activity leading to a fusion and a useful function.

Now part of the concept of the dynamic is the optimizing of the two factors which produced the dynamic. In fact you could say that those two concepts represent the "raw material" and the dynamic and optimization is the purification and cleaning of that raw material, producing the fusion of these two, represented by that diagram, which is the delicate, positive and useful human material.

In the area of the dynamic, the purification or refining, there are problems of psychological conditioning and other different factors which can delay this product. The conditioning and outside impacts people receive all the time cause delay and confusion, as well as complexes.

So if somebody says: "How long could it take to arrive at this fusion situation? Can I lose time, have I lost time? Can I catch up?"; these thoughts in themselves can add to confusion and complexes.

This is not a university course in the sense that you have term one, the second term, the third year, the fourth year leading to some sort of degree or certificate.

The person understands that a situation of fusion can exist, and that in that fusion situation, he or she is becoming more conscious and more able to understand. They have that aim and in different forms, in different circumstances, in different times, the time factor is in minutes or seconds or years.

Regarding the using of these functions to arrive at an

understanding, a feeling, or a degree of consciousness: a person in the Tradition should be using various tactics and various techniques all the time.

When I say that it is possible that the movement or time-factor can be seconds or minutes or years, it is that sometimes this happens, and there is a feeling, a breakthrough, a light. Something happens: "I read something, I did my exercise and at the end I felt happy, I felt good".

One has thus been using the factors and arriving at a certain point of feeling. These feelings are what we call traces of the being. Having made a breakthrough, having made a contact with consciousness and having felt a certain happiness, a warmth, a certain satisfaction: remember it. Remember what it felt like, what the sound or the taste was, what the colour was.

Remember it because it is a very clear demonstration that development does signal itself to you. When you have this feeling, when you get this signal, you remember it so that the next time you put yourself in the situation of reading or listening to something or doing an exercise, try and start from that point of memory.

You have already done it, achieved it and experienced it: if you can use your conscious and unconscious memory to hold on to those feelings, in other words, all these different traces which have occurred to you in different situations and which you have experienced, go towards building something.

If you have built something for the purpose of using it, it would be stupid, inefficient and ridiculous not to use it. When you build a house, paint it and furnish it, you establish a feeling, a rapport, a connection with that house: you do not then abandon the house. You go in it, you live in it, you feel happy in it, you become a part of it.

If you drive a car, you learn how to drive, you learn how to steer and change the gears. The functions of starting the car, changing gear and steering become perfectly normal because you exercise them regularly. You do not suffer the same fear, anguish and worry in the same way every morning as you did the first time you ever drove that car. You know how to use the various instruments and functions of the car, at which point you get a satisfaction or pleasure out of driving it.

You have built up experiences. You originally suffered when learning to drive. Sometimes you drive for pleasure and sometimes the road seems to be full of traffic all the time. Sometimes you are relaxed, sometimes you have time and you drive because you want to, because it feels good and because it's satisfying.

In the same way, if you become familiar with and accustom yourselves to activities in the Tradition, you use them in the way that you have learned to use them.

You might say: "That's obvious. That's why we learn them." But there is also a question of how you use these activities. Each reading, each music, each colour, each exercise, complements something else.

If you say to yourself: "I will do an exercise at a particular time, and start by telling myself why or what I am about to do", you then add to that activity with your attitude, with music, with colour, optimizing on the situation.

During an activity of a positive nature you should not constantly be checking as to whether the "situation is right", "you are harmonious", "you are relaxed": there should be the instinctive inner relaxation or inner satisfaction that this is a useful and good situation.

Nobody can tell you and there is no book which will tell you what a feeling of happiness is. Achieving something should produce a satisfaction, happiness, tranquility: you are relaxed or at ease with yourself.

If you are constantly examining and testing the degree of happiness or satisfaction, you are examining the sensation instead of enjoying it. If you have to ask yourself whether you have achieved a degree of contentment or happiness all the time, you are using the wrong measurements: you are questioning and not feeling.

Satisfaction and happiness with oneself can be achieved.

Factors which interrupt or prevent you from understanding this satisfaction are the tensions and conditioning which western society places upon you. And there are a certain number of measurements or conditionings which you place upon yourselves: "I remember the only time I was happy in my life was such-and-such a time in such-and-such a circumstance in such-and-such a place."

Well, does that mean that one should then wait for exactly the same situation and circumstances in order to say: "Those happy circumstances are now recurring, therefore I am happy"?

It may be possible to recreate these circumstances, and if a person is able to do so then they certainly can feel happy. But if they have set certain conditions to happiness, "Without the presence or existence of this factor and that factor, I cannot be happy", what happens if a lot of these factors are beyond one's control or beyond one's ability to recreate? That would then mean that if it is not possible to create or recreate them, a person will always be looking for and perhaps never finding them.

During these past few days I have introduced some new factors, and perhaps you need a little time to familiarize yourself with the use of these factors.

The main intention of this congress is to study therapeutic activities, but I am sure you will all understand and appreciate that such techniques and dynamics you may use on patients should also be used on yourselves.

If some of you think: "Does that indicate the fact that we all need therapy?"

You need a source of therapy, you need a form of therapy and you do need a therapist. All those factors can, according to the way you feel or think, exist in me.

So until the next congress, I hope and I am sure that you will familiarize yourself with and use these concepts, and monitor your performance, and how you use them on yourselves and others. You should monitor carefully and constantly, because I am also monitoring you and your performance.

FORMULATING A THERAPY

At the first therapy congress, those of you who still survive will remember that I said I would like a therapy in three years. As always, of course, I was optimistic. I said three years because it is a convenient length of time. If I had said ten or twenty years, everybody would relax, take it easy, and do nothing as usual. If I had said three months, everybody would panic and go mad.

We have now had three years and some, and I am sixty percent content with the development of the therapy. There is still a long way to go but the position is encouraging.

You have now got over the big initial problem, which was professional jealousy: "I have secrets, why should I share them with somebody else?" If you do have such marvellous secrets or techniques and you talk about them, you are not sharing them with everybody in the world, you are sharing them within a family.

Our aim is not to put every possible therapy together into one single therapy, because I must be honest with you, as always: when I look at the list of different therapies you use, I am amazed at the human ingenuity involved.

The real secret or technique is to find which therapies are compatible, which ones complement each other, and which can be applied under different circumstances, be they social, cultural or racial.

In this meeting and in future correspondence with you, I will gently suggest that some therapies might be less useful than others. From information I have, some of you, who are more remarkable than others, seem to be simultaneously expert in a very great number of different therapies.

I would suggest to such people that they might concentrate their attention, energy and activity more narrowly, and possibly judge for themselves which one out of a number of different therapies they are studying, they find more harmonious to themselves.

Of course, this might sometimes produce a bit of a problem, since a person might say: "I use such-and-such a therapy, and although the results are generally good, I am personally not entirely happy with it" or else "I do not completely harmonise with that particular therapy."

Nevertheless, there is no problem here because there is no competition between the two. You can use any therapy which produces results. If it happens to be the one which is harmonious to you, it is all the more marvelous. If it happens to be another type of therapy, then you can try and develop it as a parallel therapy.

We are not trying to accept some therapies and reject others. What we are trying to do is to take positive and useful therapeutic elements from any therapies at all, and put them together.

The basic intention of all therapy must be to cure. The techniques or instruments are different, the intensity or length of time may be different, but the basic factor for all therapy is cure.

Let us say you have a therapeutic context, in other words a context and situation for curing. For example, in a surgical situation, you have a pre-operative or pre-surgical period, you have the actual surgical or operative situation, and then you have the post-operative recovery and convalescence period.

The pre-operative stage is to prepare the patient, physically and psychologically. During the period of the operation, the therapists or medical staff involved are the surgeon, the anesthetists, and the nurses. The post-operative situation involves the staff that deals with the convalescence or recovery period.

All these periods are, in fact, equally important. In all three stages of the process, the most important factor and person is the patient as a person. The intention of every individual therapist throughout all three periods is and should be, to assist in the process of curing that person. During these periods, you cannot have competition between individual therapists, otherwise the result can be the death of the patient.

In all disciplines of therapy, the reputation of the therapist is certainly important. After all, it is their profession, and such a person has to earn a living.

It is also important for another reason: if the therapist's intention to cure a person is strong enough, you are transmitting something extra to that person who is sick, nervous, worried or tense. You are not just saying to him: "Yes, I can help you, I will try and cure you." Your intention is that, and if your intention is well enough focused on that, you are passing that factor to the patient as well.

Certainly, the patient expects and hopes you will say: "You will feel better after this treatment"; and I hope all therapists say that in any case. It is a very poor therapist who says "I'll try, but I think you're done for." The person expects you to reassure and comfort them. You must therefore transmit to them on another level, so that they feel you are working for them, and not just on them.

You therefore fix your intention and you transmit that intention.

I already warned you that I would not always be complementary about you, individually and in general, because my function is not to comfort you and hold your hand. I am neither Valium, aspirin, nor benzedrine.

One criticism I have is that, to put it mildly, in some groups being a member of a Hakim group has acquired an element of self-satisfaction. Some have more satisfaction, some less, but please let me not hear of divisions between Hakims and non-Hakims in the Tradition.

As far as I am concerned, some of you are less stupid than others, but I am always optimistic. Mind you, my optimism costs me a lot of effort. You can notice it over the years just by watching the colour of my hair, because I am really quite young; all this is worry.

For those of you who are familiar with the Afghan language I will give you a quote which is quite interesting: "Nim hakim hatere jan, nim mullah hatere iman" which means: "Half a therapist is a danger to life, and half a priest is a threat to the soul." You can explain to each other what significance that has.

During past Congresses, we have had a theme. I don't think there is a particular theme this time, but there is one issue I think it would be useful to study.

I know you normally do look at this aspect but I would like you to study it a little bit more this time, and that is the treatment and therapy which involves elderly people. As you all know, increasingly, because of the improved nourishment, surgical and medical techniques, the world is supporting more and more elderly and old people.

Younger people do certainly have a responsibility to older people. Older people in a society also have another important value for us, which is experience, and they have memory. This is where this value is precise and significant: verbal traditions, stories of their family, their parents and the society of 50, 60, 70 years ago, including poetry, music, habits and legends. If they are encouraged to talk and to remember, many old people produce valuable experience and facts.

As those of you who deal with old people know, it is also a useful therapy for them to talk, not only because they feel wanted insofar as they have somebody who is listening to them, but also because when somebody is interested in what they are saying, they feel useful.

I am going a little bit away from the main question here, but when dealing with old people there are two factors which coincide and come together, and it's a partial answer to other questions I have been asked: beyond what point does one technically and mechanically prolong life?

This can be a question of great moral debate. For reason of advanced age or accident, some people are technically and theoretically brain-dead. What is the professional or moral attitude of a therapist toward that situation?

Also, from the point of view of the Sufi Tradition, at what point is the person no longer actually present? Some people have said: "Do we have the right to switch off the life-support machines?"

From our point of view we are satisfied that with brain death, the person no longer physically exists. Such a decision therefore has to be made by the doctor or therapist in consultation, obviously, with the family.

SYMBOLS

During our conference I want to have a few short talks like this, not necessarily to explain things to you, but to mention some aspects of the Tradition you might talk about among yourselves.

As you know, in the Tradition we have many symbols we use, which are all significant, useful and serve a purpose.

They have a function and they perform this function under the correct circumstances. This function is both selective and qualitative. Some friends have collections of these symbols and they use them and keep them in their homes and offices.

This use is perfectly all right. Their existence or presence in your home or office can be enhanced, firstly by positioning, but more importantly by understanding the particular significance of a particular symbol.

Professional interpreters among you, and by this I don't mean language interpreters but the interpreters of symbolism, will have noticed that the geometric symbols are usually based on the figure 8 or 9, the octagon or the enneagram.

Looking at the figure 8 as it is used, the representation of the figure 8, the actual figure, has a symbolism in the Tradition.

Interestingly, in Roman numerology you have either the VIII, which means 8, or the IIX which also means 8. In both cases of the Roman numerals, the VIII or the IIX, if you count the points you'll find that both add up eight, because if you count two points for the V and six points for the III, it adds up to eight points, and in the other case, when you have two ones and the X, you have four points and then the four points of the cross.

Also, with the points we count in Arabic when you write 786, these points also add up to 8. The figure 8, as it is usually written in Europe, is also represented in a different way in the formula of the Yin and the Yang, and, in the designs of the Tradition it also relates to the point in the middle of the 8 where the two circles meet, which represents the human solar plexus.

What is the 8 and what is the 9? To start with 9 is one more than 8, and actually, it's all you need to know and all I'm going to tell you.

So why did I introduce the subject?

I wish I knew. However I will make a guess, which is that it has some cosmological significance.

Why?

Simply because the cosmos is older than the Tradition, but the people who created and designed the Tradition had to take their inspiration from somewhere.

Naturally, I'm going to disappoint you because I'm not going to tell you where or when, but what I can say now is that the reason and function behind both of these numbers is very specific.

You will see both these numbers in the form of the octagon and the enneagon or enneagram in 75% to 80% of the designs of the Tradition, in permutations of these two numbers.

Tracing or identifying the use of a numeral, either the 8 or the 9, is very interesting and can be also very complicated for those of you who are mathematically inclined. You can perhaps look at a kilim, a carpet, a Moorish ceiling or wall and you will see how the permutation of the 8 is arranged.

The 8 is permuted both downwards and upwards; it is permuted down in fractions of four and two, and it is permuted up by 16, 32, 64, and so on ad infinitum.

The prime numeral 9 is also permuted downwards and upwards, ad infinitum.

This factor or factors, as you will all agree, is mathematically quite straightforward, and with a little experience and study, the 8 permutation or 9 permutation can be identified. However, that is only the beginning of the use of the permutation of the 8 and 9.

Where it becomes complicated is where there is a permutation between the 8 and the 9, if I still have your attention, either as the prime number 8 times 9, or additionally, 8 times 8 and then 9 times 9 to the power of 8 or 9, which is a big number.

Supposing then you look, for example, at a kilim, a tapestry or a carpet which is based on what we call the inter-permutations of the 8 and 9. How do you work out what equation has been used in the formulation of that design?

The answer is you don't, because there is another facet to the equation: if a craftsman working in the Tradition wishes to use one of these inter-permutations, he can do it in a geometrical pattern or through the number of knots per square inch.

So what does it all mean? You have a design which is a surface design that is functioning and working together with the chosen colour for that design. And you have a sub-level of the number of knots per square inch, which is functioning as a multiplicand of the prime design and material, which means you then have a working entity.

That is where we get the phrase "hay varios niveles" from, there are various levels.

In order to permit and help a design to work with you, the understanding of how it is constructed helps the design to help you and harmonise with you.

Therefore the various symbols of the Tradition are certainly not merely of a decorative nature, they can be used to focus the attention.

Another of their functions is to emit certain things.

Some of them are built to have a certain percentage or degree of magnetic field. Some of them function when exposed to the rays of the sun or to moonlight; some function only in the presence of people, and some function only in the absence of people.

There is no place in the Tradition for any superstition connected with the emblems of the Tradition. In the correct context, under the correct circumstances, they function.

Their positioning in a room or in a house can enhance their function. Usually, they are best placed on an access, that is South facing North or North facing South, or West facing East or East facing West. Please note here that I am not, in this case, talking about the placing of the Alif, and I am not talking about Mihrabs because these are quite specific in themselves.

How do you know or how do you find out which is the best orientation of a particular symbol? Simply by placing one of them in a position facing North, South, East or West, and looking at it at different times of the day over a period of four or five days under natural light conditions, and you try and use an inner element of perception to see in which position they appear best.

For instance, if you have four walls and several symbols on each wall or else just one on each wall, there is no clash, no disturbance factor and no problem. Correctly positioned, they create a relationship between each other.

Regarding the actual physical size of an emblem or figure, in some emblems the actual size is important; there should always be a proportion. Very simply, the proper proportion is that a symbol should not be copied from its original site, from the original place it came from, and then made either enormous or very small.

If it is necessary, useful and beneficial to make an enlargement of it or diminish the size of it for a good reason, the same law of proportion should be applied, i.e., 8 times larger or smaller, or else a division down by 4 times, twice the size or a multiplication up or, again, by a proportion of 99, division downwards or upwards.

CONNECTING WITH THE ESSENTIAL BEING

One important factor in the whole area of therapy is confidence. The confidence of the therapist in his technique and the confidence of the patient in the therapist.

As I said, it is certainly all right to reassure a patient. The relationship and communication between therapist and patient must be continuously increased, but of course there is an area you must avoid, which is over-identification with the patient and over-dependence of the patient on the therapist.

I am sure that all of you, especially those who deal with the psychological therapies, have experienced this dependence problem, and there is a very fine and delicate line between confidence and dependence.

Since the relationship between patient and therapist is always different in the sense that all patients really are different and the technical experience of the therapist is hopefully always working upwards, so it is not possible to have a sort of "book of rules" saying at which point you break off a particular relationship.

It is obviously the observation by the therapist of the relationship with the patient which counts the most. Especially in areas of psychological therapy, there are modifications of the relationship with the patient where these variations both of the therapist and of the patient are sometimes quite extreme, so psychological therapists have to depend very much on their feeling of a particular situation.

"How far do I go in this direction? When do I stop?"

Among you, doctors or surgeons have slightly easier decisions. If a surgeon has to operate to remove an appendix, he operates, removes the appendix and sews up the incision. Unless there are complications or infections, that is his surgical function. He doesn't say: "While I've got that patient there under anaesthetic, I think I'll have a look at his liver, heart and lungs"; at least I hope he doesn't.

The psychotherapist, if you want to call it that, who is dealing with all aspects of psychological therapy, knows all of these things I have just been saying, so why am I saying it?

Because if you then add one more factor to your therapeutic technique, which is the factor of the Tradition, this can be a guide, a measure and a defense for you.

It is a defense because one can use it to prevent absorbing negative impulses from a patient. One can use it as a measure by using a traditional feeling; for instance you can use certain techniques of breathing, relaxation and music of the Tradition with that patient.

These techniques will also help the patient not to produce the dependence factor. You don't have to tell them: "Listen to this and it will stop the dependence on me".

It works naturally because it develops and maintains a good and natural harmony between yourself and the patient. As I said before, one important area of therapy is, of course, the question of confidence.

If you are using techniques from the Tradition on yourself and in your therapy, you yourself have to have confidence in such techniques, and again, the confidence you show in the technique is received by the patient, either by your confident tone of voice, or in the confident way that you behave, touch them, manipulate them, massage them or whatever.

You are therefore transmitting high confidence to them by your tone as well as by what you say, as well as by touch, by tactile sensing, by what from their point of view is the efficient way that you move, operate or manipulate instruments.

You establish a different and extra bridge of contact with them. On that level of contact, you are transmitting (subliminally, if you like) the fact that you are interested in their bodily and mental health, and that you are confident and capable in the techniques you are using. And also, that you are interested in them as a person, not just as a number, and that you have something a little bit different by which to help.

By definition, a patient is in an abnormal condition, that is, either physically or psychologically disturbed; and somewhere, either consciously or subconsciously, they are afraid.

Fear produces tension, and tension produces a block between the patient and the therapist.

Some schools of psychological therapy aim to break through that block. This is certainly not always the most efficient way of overcoming it. You can go round this kind of block, over it or under it; once you have penetrated it or gone round, over or under it, you can actually ignore the existence of that block.

You don't say: "I've made contact with the person but the block still exists" and then just stop worrying about the block as well.

True, you have established a certain initial contact with the person and the block is still there. This block is not a threat or menace to you as a therapist, it is simply the result of their tension, neurosis or whatever.

As your treatment and therapy progresses, that block will diminish. You work with and help the patient, both subliminally and subconsciously, to dissolve their block.

You should not necessarily say to a person: "I am sorry, you've got this block and together we are going to break through it" because the block will become more important, more menacing and even more of an obstruction to them.

Tell people only what they need to know, what they can understand and what will help you. Sometimes it is necessary for you not always to tell them the truth; because sometimes they don't want or need the truth at that time.

Here again, we come to the question of your own feeling and judgement about when to tell them what.

Regarding when to introduce techniques or aspects of the Tradition into your therapy; you always introduce aspects or techniques of the Tradition, but only when you yourself are comfortable with them, when you understand them. At that point, they are familiar instruments to you, and subconsciously or subliminally this inspires confidence in your patient.

You can be using techniques from the Tradition at the same time as you are using your particular therapy discipline; by techniques I mean either music, perfumes or other things of the Tradition.

At best, you are communicating on two levels with your patient. One level incorporates the usual senses of sound and vision, and both are complementary to each other. If a person goes to a medical doctor or surgeon and the doctor drops his instruments or blows up a piece of equipment during the examination, this simply does not inspire confidence in the patient.

If the doctor, technician or therapist handle their instruments in a confident and calm way, the initial degree of slight tension: "I am going to a doctor" or "I'm going to a therapist" diminishes, because the person says: "I hope or want to think that he knows what he or she is doing".

You cannot visually show them or demonstrate the Tradition techniques you are using, but they can pick up on the confidence you feel in yourself when using those techniques.

If, within them, within their memory, you are building up, if you like, not a psychological dependence but their psychological confidence in you; if they have conscious tension, doubts or worries, the subconscious confidence will tend to overcome those conscious doubts or tensions.

You should try and get through to what, if you like, is called the essential person or being, because it has an enormous power. All of you, I am sure, have experienced situations or seen patients who have shown just a glimpse of this power.

What you have to do is to establish a deep line of communication to tap into and connect with this essential being, so that you can help them to build this up and increase it. You can also help them to make contact with themselves, with their own essential being, and use it.

Unfortunately, a very large percentage of people do not know how powerful this inner being is. And yet, I am sure you have very often heard people mentioning it. People will say, for instance: "I was in such and such a condition, I was actually done for, and then I did it. I don't know how, but I did it."

If you can establish a real and perceptible line of contact with that being, you can often produce what are conventionally considered to be miraculous events.

I'll give you a banal example: during the Korean War, I had an Afghan sergeant-major under my command. He was very big and tough and shaped like a sort of amiable bell.

He came from a valley near the part of Afghanistan my family comes from, and traditionally and historically, there is a little bit of friendly competition between neighbouring parts of Afghanistan.

Anyway, during that day's combat, which I remember well because it was Christmas day and twenty degrees below zero.

There was very heavy fighting and I was going up towards the front; the medical people were bringing casualties back, and I saw that sergeant-major being carried in on a stretcher, so I said to one of the stretcher- bearers who were carrying plasma and everything:

"How bad is he?"

And the medic repled: "He's taken eighteen bullets".

The sergeant-major was semi-conscious and he came from the valley of Panshir, so I said to him: "You Panshiri are all weaklings" and I walked off, and half an hour later he came up to me, covered with blood and carrying a machine-pistol, and said: "Nobody talks to a Panshiri like that".

That may be a banal example, but I know my people, and I promise you, if I had said to him: "Die in peace", he would have died.

Of course I am not suggesting that you treat people who are exclusively in that condition. What I am suggesting is that you use a technique which you feel, with your own knowledge, and which applies to that person according to the situation.

You can appeal to their courage, to their honour, to their patriotism, but whatever it is, it has to be somehow getting through to something. You may use something real or else some trick: if your intention is to cure, use anything.

Somewhere deep inside every person, however stupid, poor and old, there is a spark, and I am not just talking about the spark of life itself. By definition, a spark can be the source of a fire, and a fire can most certainly destroy; but you can also use fire to cook or to keep warm. Constructive fire is contained.

One of your functions in the Tradition is to blow gently on that spark to produce a flame.

What this means for those of us who teach in the Tradition is that fortunately, for us in our work, there are no frontiers and no limitations. It is not a question of a person's education or culture, because we deal with the being.

Certainly, the being is contained in something called the body. People say things like: "I don't like my body" or "My body is an embarrassment" or "I'm fed up with my body".

For the moment, it so happens that it is the only body you have. If everybody had the body they wanted, every man would look like Tarzan and every woman like Marilyn Monroe, and I think life would probably be very boring, because if you have seen one Tarzan or Marilyn Monroe, you've seen them all.

So in regard to our function, we have aspects of therapy in the Tradition because we deal with both the being and the container of that being, and in a way, there must be a harmony and balance between the two. You don't do something to one that will prejudice the existence of the other.

Any activity in the Tradition, such as what we call an exercise, for instance a zikr which is properly performed, is also physically beneficial.

Certainly, this is the case from the point of view of correct breathing. During a zikr, a person, is hopefully quiet, calm and tranquil, and therefore the whole system does not have to be working, it is in a situation of relaxation.

As in a state of sleep, the physical system checks itself out, repairs certain local damage, and carries out various physiological activities.

So you have the dual functions, with the two functioning together for the mutual benefit of each other.

WASTING EFFORT

My attitude towards certain philosophies is well known. If you like, let me give a comparative example between a technique of zikr we use, and, for example, a Hindu technique.

I am not getting into the area of comparative religion and this sort of thing, because that discussion is endless, but I do give you an example which is capable of being examined on a comparative basis.

You might have a dervish who goes and sits in a tekkia or a mosque and does a zikr, and you might have a Hindu, what they call Fakirs, who for instance, sticks a knife through his cheek or puts his hand on a hot coal. I'm not questioning their dedication, but I am very deeply questioning their technique.

It is certainly possible to subordinate sensation in order to hold a hot coal, but for us in the Tradition it is a waste of a valuable commodity which is energy.

The dedication and discipline is there, the belief is there. The dervish (and I admit to being prejudiced in favor of dervishes) is hopefully using all his energy and being in a productive and developmental way; the Hindu has to divert some of his energy to suppress a natural feeling.

This is a pity and a waste, because certainly, in that man, as among all human beings, there is a spark.

So, try to develop and arrive at a confidence for yourself, and then transmit it to the patient.

To put it simply: get through, establish a communication with that spark, with that being.

That spark exists in everyone, even in you.

THE STRESS FACTOR AND FLEXIBLE RIGIDITY

Before I actually start my discourse or whatever you want to call it, I want to comment on two or three factors.

In the Tradition, we are a family. I want you to understand the meaning of this, and to feel, each one of you, a member of a family.

We are not a cult. We must be careful of this because, unfortunately, the abuse of the word cult is widespread throughout the world. We are not a religion, we are a family of traditionalists.

One aspect I would like to talk to you about this morning is the stress factor in everyday life. As you all know, the industrial revolution, with the increase of factories and their intensive way of working produces stress by itself.

Perhaps the constant sound of machinery, or the vibration and positive ionization produced by electrical machinery in a factory, the pressure or requirement to produce a certain amount of objects (say textiles) per day, per hour or per week; or again, the work itself and the absence of job security, all these are very familiar factors in the buildup of tension in a person and community.

Those of you who are interested in or who studied industrial medicine and therapy know these factors. As therapists, I'm sure you have all seen the results of this stress factor, and, in one way or another, you try and diminish the stress factor in the patient.

You are all familiar with the noise factor, the hurry factor, the production factor, and the dust factor in a factory. Have you noticed the factor I have just mentioned, which is the tremendous production of positive ionization from electrical machinery?

In a work situation, which is an industrial situation of stress and tension, you add to that tension the presence of enormous quantities of positive ionization.

If it produces dust or contamination in some industrial situations, air filters or air purifiers are used. You have a fan which pulls out contaminated air and another fan bringing in fresh air. Those fans themselves are producing positive ionization.

Nowadays, more and more people are using computers and sitting in front of the visual display unit. The VDU screen itself produces positive ionization.

It would be an excellent and beneficial situation if industrial plants and factories installed ionizers. Unfortunately, since factories tend to be enormous in size you would have to have powerful and large ionizers to compensate.

OK, so you have a patient who comes to you for treatment for some condition. Now, certainly you produce case-notes, age, background, this, that, a case profile of the person and you may come to the decision that this condition, perhaps psychosomatic, is stress-related.

By one therapy or another, or a combination of therapies, you can produce a therapy or technique which will help that person. You can say: "This person works in a railway, a factory, or in front of a VDU and there is tension and the impact of noise and hurry is producing a situation and an effect in that person".

With your experience, you can suggest or use a therapy which will help them to withstand noise or extremes of heat or cold; you can work with them and on them and give them medication or massage or suggest relaxation to them. Another additional factor: while you are treating them in your clinic, consulting room or wherever, you should remember that they are very probably saturated with positive ions.

We recommend the presence of an ionizer in a therapy situation. There are additional techniques you can use which, with contact with the patient, can also produce negative ionization. Your intention of seeing, examining, treating the patient is to cure him or her, and also, to help them to help you to help them. So how do you actually consciously produce negative ionization?

Your intention is to cure: in step one you relate with the patient, you create a harmonious ambiance with him or her, you know the need and importance of negative ionization. Those of you who practice any form of therapeutic massage know the beneficial effects of touch. You hear in fact and in legend: "Such-and-such a person has a magic or healing touch." This is true, some people do.

It also includes the transfer of negative ionization. The natural source of an enormous negative ionization is a waterfall, a fountain or a flowing current of fresh water; in other words, the passage and the contact of a natural and organic substance with another natural and organic substance. The result is negative ionization, which means no friction, no heat.

In an electrical or mechanical apparatus, say an electric fan, the contact between the carbon and the coil spinning around it produces friction and heat, which means it is producing positive ionization.

The tactile contact between a therapist and a patient is an organic natural substance contacting another organic natural substance, but the actual contact itself does not produce negative ionization. It is the movement which produces it. Certainly, in terms of contact to contact, there is a certain amount of heat and warmth, but because it is an organic contact, such a friction or heat does not produce positive ionization.

If this form of contact is true, and it is, how easy and familiar can it be for somebody who uses massage to use this technique? Also, it may be difficult for a therapist who does not use massage or physical contact techniques to use it, so how can it be done?

Of course, if doctors and therapists starting generally stroking people, this could be misinterpreted.

But there is a form by which one can use what we call the "harmonious touch" without actual physical stroking contact.

Now saying this to a person is a little bit of a trick. You have their details and everything, you make the examination, and you feel it will be useful to provide them with some negative ionization.

Then, with your intention clear, with your confidence in the value of the ionization itself, you tell them, in a way, to use this stroking technique on themselves.

Now where is the trick?

The trick or element of trick is how you tell them what to do.

For instance, you may say to them: "You have this problem or that problem or this pain or that pain — would you just help me by sort of feeling yourself to see if there is any particular point of pain?" "For clinical purposes and in order to complete my notes, just start here and see if there is any particular point of stress, tension or pain."

By this, you are getting them to produce the ionization through you. And this can last two, three or four minutes and then you say to them: "Right". You get them to produce their own ionization, which really happens, because you give them the impression that they can help you to help them to help themselves, because in any therapy situation the therapist and the patient must work together.

So you see them every day or every week or with whatever frequency you have established, and you say to them for instance: "I can't see you or it is not necessary for me to see you every day and since it is not necessary, I would like you to check yourself once or twice a day, and then, next time we meet, report to me about your findings or feelings".

Or else you say: "I am not asking you to become a doctor or do my work, but check yourself in a normal way once or twice a day, just as you check yourself in the mirror in the morning before you go out."

You are giving them a technique by which they can, through you, produce negative ionization in themselves.

The very great common factor in all psychological or physical illness is that some part of the system is not working at its correct level of efficiency. Sometimes the illness may even be of a genetic nature.

The human body and system is an extraordinary entity, it is a very extraordinary mechanism because it has a capacity and an ability for curing itself. In some people, this capacity may be weak or attenuated, or else it may simply be latent in the person and need to be awakened.

Whatever reason, whatever the cause, it is your function and duty to try and stimulate the body's own system.

There are, obviously, certain self-defense mechanisms in the body; things like the biological time clock, and certain safety systems in the body. When the system tells the person that this is "too much", or "enough" or "you cannot take any more"; it can mean that the physical or mental effort is too much, and the system can collapse, for instance by fainting.

But before getting to that point, if a person is reasonably alert there are signals, and you should explain to people and encourage them to watch for the signal in a calm and casual way, not in a situation of tension and watching out for: "Was that a signal? Is this a signal? Am I going to collapse?"

Once again you explain simply and in quite a relaxed way that this is "your own system". You say to the patient: "Look, you should be friendly towards yourself, so try to understand the signals that are put out by your own system."

You are encouraging them to develop a reasonable level of

perception of themselves; you are in fact teaching them how to help themselves by telling them: "Let you and I make a team together to help this situation in which you find yourself. I am here to help you."

It is not enough just to say: "Do this, this and the other thing and go and do it."

You have got to get back-up and you can do so. Try to gradually and correctly re-establish their confidence in their own system. Try to get them to establish a momentum of positivity.

These are the broad outlines of what you can and should do with a patient. Exactly how you do it, of course, depends on the nature of the illness and the personality of the person involved.

You can be more patient or more persuasive with some people. The various attitudes coming down must be based on the same basic values. And you decide which one you use, according to the particular attitude and the degree of harmonization you have with the patient.

Even if it appears to be a contradiction in terms, this is called a "flexible rigidity".

If I hold this pencil to the table, the point between the table and the pencil is the point of your contact with the Tradition, that is your point of contact with the energy. For the sake of example, we will consider that it is also the line of therapy contact you have with the patient.

If I move this pencil without moving the point of contact between pencil and table, this means a certain degree of flexibility. Because the point of contact between pencil and table has not moved, this is the point of rigidity in your contact with the Tradition and in your belief. It is the point of belief and also the contact with me.

If I raise the pencil off the surface so that it is no longer in contact with the table, the pencil is no longer anchored, which in this example means that you have confusion, uncertainty, and compromise, because there is no longer either any guidance or limitation to the movement of this pencil. This therefore is not flexibility, it is whim.

You establish a contact and a harmony with a patient and every time you meet with and treat that patient, every time you are in a therapy situation with him or her, you increase the levels of contact.

You get a feedback on different levels at different times. You consciously or subconsciously analyze that feedback and you then in turn feed a reply or response back on those levels.

On a very banal level, for instance, you can be talking to a patient, listening to their complaints or moaning, and you may be listening and making notes. Whether you need the notes or not doesn't matter, because therapists and doctors are supposed to make notes, and you may be showing interest and smiling and making notes while thinking to yourself: "This person is so stupid that it is unbelievable."

In fact, between you and me, I have this problem myself.

So I'm not forbidding you to think: "This person is so stupid that I won't be able to do anything with him". Allow yourself the luxury of thinking that kind of thing sometimes. But try this. This is a banal level, but while you are smiling and taking notes, try and think back to such people: "I know you are stupid, I know you are lazy, I know this is all psychosomatic and hysteria, but I really am going to try and help you."

If you think that, they will certainly pick that up as a reaction. They will pick up a very banal current of benevolence and help.

This is specially important with patients who are psychologically disturbed, because a person who may be severely mentally disturbed will often have a lot of deep perception working, and they can and very often do pick up your critical or semi-hostile thoughts and react to them, which means that they withdraw and close up.

Although you may be talking to them, they are actually not listening to your voice, and probably not making sense of your words.

Very often they pick some level of communication on which you might possibly be feeling some exasperation towards them, and they make a subconscious mental decision that: "This is", in some way, "my enemy" because they are "smiling at me while sending out a hostile wave, a hostile energy."

So talk positively to people and think positively towards them. Feel an affection and an identification with them, again, to a degree, but not an over-identification; if you can simply use a third channel of communication with a patient, especially the psychologically disturbed people, they will pick it up.

You are being kind, talking to them, listening to them, comforting them, and thinking to yourself: "I think I understand your problem, I want to help you".

You are transmitting positive thoughts to them, and on another level of your thoughts and memories, you think of something positive and beautiful, say the beauty of a flower; you are also enjoying the thought of the beauty of that flower. You are then transmitting your own feeling of the joy of experiencing the beauty of the flower.

This is a very strong connection, especially in people who are psychologically disturbed, and it has a very strong impact on them.

If you really do conjure up, imagine or visualize something beautiful and positive, something you can really love; you must transmit that beauty and love on that third level.

It is valuable and powerful because the feeling of affection, love and beauty does not make the patient think: "This therapist loves me or is sending out this happiness because of me."

You therefore avoid the danger of over-identification of the patient with the therapist, while simultaneously using as many levels of contact and communication as possible in all sessions of therapy.

Do not try to apply and use all the levels of communication with the patient all the time, in all circumstances. If they do exist, you may use one, two, three or sometimes four of them for either shorter or longer periods, depending on the situation and relationship.

You've got a flexibility; but again, don't forget that it's a rigid flexibility based on the intention of what you are doing. In other words, before you see the patient, always keep in mind what you finally hope or want to achieve with that patient.

You do not set yourself impossible goals. You aim for an improvement of the physical or mental health of that person, stage by stage. You gradually try to approach that aim, and as you feel that you are approaching it, you then move that aim a little bit higher.

This may be a recipe for desperation, because obviously, any technique is as good or as bad as the person who uses it. If you have enough techniques, you can feel and find the one which applies in a given circumstance.

You can go into a therapy situation with the idea of possibly using one, two or three different aspects of the same technique, and during the first few minutes of the therapy you should decide which particular aspect you are going to use at that time.

Your attitude should not be: "I think I'll try this one or maybe that, and then I might switch to that" or "How about this? I don't know"; because you are transmitting with the patient at the same time.

Nevertheless, if during the first few minutes of the therapy you decide to start on a particular aspect, you are not inflexibly committed to that aspect throughout the whole period of therapy, or even for that day.

You have flexibility, so you don't abruptly change an aspect during the therapy, like switching channels on the television set; you phase one out and you phase the other one in, so that there is no point of abruptness in the relationship with the patient during that session.

Each therapeutic session with the patient therefore obviously connects both with the last session and prepares for the next one. You must give out positive; and if you receive anything negative, ground it.

THE GRANADA THERAPY AND THE ESSENTIAL BEING

During the last few days of conference activity you have met and talked about your particular therapies, exchanged ideas and opinions about how you can cooperate with your therapies, and I hope you have kept in mind the intention of all these conferences, which is to establish a therapy we call the Granada Therapy.

Okay, you've had your fun, let's get down to work. As from now and until the end of the conference, you should try and make a significant shift in the emphasis of your conversation. This is the third Conference or Congress and I'm going to suggest to you a total restructuring of your effort.

As from now; in all your discussions you will include an element I have mentioned before, not only in Congresses but in meetings with the friends, and I want you to introduce it in significant proportion.

That factor is what we call the Zhat or essential being. Beginning now, after I have finished, I want you to break up into small groups of different therapeutic disciplines, with distinctive and different disciplines within each small group.

I don't want these groups to be discussing or asking for each other's opinion or interpretation about what I have said each morning.

You are now going to introduce the significant theme of the use and function of your essential being in your own therapeutic discipline.

These are the questions to answer: how do you, in a therapeutic situation, establish a direct and perceptible contact with your essential being? How do you maintain that contact during the therapeutic process and how do you then use that essential being and transmit that contact to your patient?

You all know that you have an essential being: this is now a clear and indisputable point. Do not lose time and effort with anguish or worry about: "How big or small is it? What colour or where is it?"

Suffice it to say it is there, and you are interested in developing it and in developing your own perception of it. You establish conscious contact with it by using your zikr or Sirr, and you maintain this contact by a combination of your zikr and repeating your intention to yourself. Don't forget that it is perfectly possible and efficient to do your zikr quietly, mentally, without necessarily using your tasbee.

So you start off with a firm and confident affirmation to yourself of the existence of your essential being: that is step one. You maintain communication and contact with that being by the mental repetition of your zikr, and your own recognition of the quality of your zikr and the quality of your intention.

It is in that state of awareness that you commence the therapeutic context with your patient. This activity can be performed either at the beginning of the day, at the beginning of your activities and also at intervals during the day between seeing patients. It is an ever-evolutionary state within you.

MENTAL TIDINESS

A lot of people have produced very comprehensive and erudite explanations of various techniques as well as certain ideas on how their techniques can relate to other techniques.

These papers and documents are fine; I encourage and approve of them. They should be translated and widely circulated, and comments on or about them as well as criticism of them should be encouraged and expected. During the periods between the plenary sessions of the Congress you have had three days of expression, explanation, fun and games.

When I say this, I am not being sarcastic about your efforts or the form in which you have made use of the last three days. In my own timetable, I allow three days for the settling down and the harmonization between humans and their thinking. After that time, when I judge it right, I introduce the extra factor.

As I was saying to some friends last night, the introduction of another aspect of this factor of the essential being, could cause some effect.

It may even cause a certain degree of perplexity, tremor or shake, but it really should not. It should not produce perplexity, but rather a movement.

From my very simple observation of you as individuals and as groups, I have noticed that you all, both individually and collectively, have an unnecessarily high degree of intensity.

There are, of course, degrees of intensity. You of course want to establish a reasonable and harmonious degree of intensity in your thoughts, conversations and meetings, which doesn't mean a totally relaxed attitude.

A useful and valuable aspect of intensity in study or conversation is when you establish an aspect of intensity we will call tidiness or neatness.

Now please do not over-interpret or under-interpret what I mean by tidiness and neatness. It doesn't mean you have to dress, think and behave in a nice little neat and tidy way. Some people, by personality, are quite naturally more tidy than others.

Introduce this tidiness and neatness into your thoughts and actions in areas of the Tradition and into areas of your therapy.

Of course, for some people, neatness and tidiness become almost a neurosis. Some people sit down at their table or desk and then arrange and rearrange everything into a sort of pattern they always follow.

Those of you who occasionally watch me may notice that I too arrange things, but I have a reason for arranging these things, and that is because very often, although I'm talking and seem to be conscious, I can also be absent. So if I happen to be absent and also happen to be smoking a cigarette, I want to know exactly where the ashtray is as well. Anyway this is one of my problems and it shouldn't worry you.

Of course, tidiness, neatness and order in thinking reflects on action. If one is taking notes, the arrangement of the notes and the flow and function of the thinking is based on the notes or on what one is reading. Another factor of your use and contact with your essential being is that the polarity of the essential being of an individual in the Tradition has a similar polarity to me.

One more thing or two I would like to mention this morning: when you are socially, professionally or in some significant way doing, producing or creating anything, remember that you are working for people, therapists and civilizations still to come.

Leave something good and useful for them, leave them something which will give them a sense of continuity, something which contains a quality and a stability.

Supposing (and I am not predicting this) there was a world-wide catastrophe with earthquakes and cities destroyed. Whole civilizations would be destroyed and future generations of archaeologists excavating our cities, just like those who now excavate the civilizations of the Nile, would interpret the writings and fragments they find and they would form a picture of the civilization they were looking at in terms of the culture, music, poetry and arts of the civilization of a thousand or two thousand years ago.

If a worldwide catastrophe should take place and civilization was destroyed and cities covered with volcanic dust and debris, will future archaeologists form a picture of the philosophy or religion of this present civilization based on what they find?

Will they come together in an international conference from all parts of America, Asia and Australia to compare their notes, decide on certain findings and then say: "Because we find evidence of it everywhere, graven in stone, in large and small letters, according to our measurements and what we estimate to be the importance of that deity in that particular civilization, our conclusion is that the God these people worshipped was called Coca Cola"?

I am not predicting a worldwide cataclysm, but in a precise area, here and now, this civilization must leave not just vague indications of how we lived or thought for future generations, but precise aspects of our thinking and why and what we aimed for.

Our function and duty, for those of you who are acting as therapists in the context of the Tradition, and also for those of our friends who are in the Tradition but not therapists, is to pass on feelings as well as writings, studies and statistics.

I told you the other day that the function of older or elderly people in the community is that they have memories of local traditions, local music, local poetry and culture. All these aspects are threads in the texture of civilization and culture. Just as the woolen or silk threads in a carpet make the texture of the carpet, a cotton or silk thread has a natural integrity and quality: put together, that integrity is magnified and multiplied into the area of perceptible beauty. The thread does not lose it's own character or personality, it willingly offers itself towards the production of a thing of utility and beauty.

An individual person too has an integrity, a quality of being and an existence. Two people acting in a harmonious and complementary fashion produce an extra factor. A number of people working, thinking, feeling and offering themselves together with each one consciously involving his or her essential being, are capable of producing a thing of amazing beauty.

This is your function and your responsibility.

You must take this responsibility and activity freely upon yourselves with all the joy, humility and hard work that goes with such a responsibility; with the confidence, quiet enthusiasm and assurance that your essential being, awakened and functioning, can and will increase your perception. Through using that perception, you will find an element which is called inspiration.

Inspiration is not a constantly exploding or erupting factor in your consciousness, it comes to you when you need it and when you can use it as a result of the Baraka of the Tradition, and it comes with a supply of the energy of this Baraka to allow you to take advantage of this inspiration.

So this practical use of and harmonization with the essential being should be the theme of your meetings and your discussions during the meeting now.

Between this meeting and the next meeting, do circulate your research papers, and do exchange ideas and invite comment. Increase the correspondence, increase the contact, increase the exchange of ideas. Circulate the result of your experiences or research, and direct them especially towards people whose particular therapeutic discipline is either similar or complementary to your own.

A HERB WOKE ME UP

If I say in passing that this morning at about four minutes past six, I was woken up by a herb, it doesn't mean to say that a bush knocked on my door. If I just said it like that, and left it as is, some of the more romantic or esoterically-minded of you might think that this is actually what happened, but as a matter of formal record, that was the time at which I had my first cup of tea, and during the day, I have been similarly accompanied by a herb.

OBSERVATION

As you may have noticed I don't usually speak from notes. On occasion, and this is one of them, I am going to speak from some notes. This isn't a demonstration of me losing my memory, it is that when I'm talking about some aspects of therapy and the Tradition, I have to use notes to be sure that I don't tell you too much.

Hopefully I will end up by telling it all to you in digestible portions. But if anybody, for instance, finds my notes, it won't really help them because although they are in European script, many of them are actually in a Pushtu dialect.

The conditioned reaction by non-therapists toward therapists is hopefully one that a patient or person who goes to a therapist has an attitude of expectancy that the therapist will help or cure them. As you know, when I use the word therapist I mean all disciplines of therapy.

With such an attitude of hope, optimism and expectancy, there is always the possibility of some nervous anxiety within the patient, especially when the patient has some psychological disorder. Nevertheless one can hope that such an attitude produces a state of openness in the patient.

As I said, the therapist should most certainly impart or transmit a feeling of confidence to the patient. This expectancy, optimism, hope and openness in the patient may be elsewhere than on the conscious level, for instance it may be in the deeper consciousness. Nevertheless, it certainly does exist in the essential being of the person.

One of the skills of the therapist is to take this conscious or unconscious hope, expectation and openness and transform it into something else, into an energy and capacity to help you, as a therapist, help that person to recover.

The usual conditioned western attitude of a patient towards a therapist is a combination of these feelings, just as "This man is a doctor because it says "Doctor" on his door also means: "He's got a sign hanging on the wall that shows he is a doctor, therefore he can help or cure me"; in the same way as you see that a man is a postman and identify the fact that he will deliver the mail; or if he is a policeman, he will direct the traffic and so forth.

If you like, it is the conditioned reaction to the first visual contact that is the initial contact point, and your skill is to increase all these levels of contact. Focus the particular part of your essential being, the Zhat, on that person's essential being.

There can be situations, of course, when the initial or subjective reaction of a person towards another person can be confused or incorrect. It can be based on information they have misunderstood, under-interpreted or over-interpreted.

I will give you an example which involved me and nearly led to a disaster. I was about nineteen years old (which makes it about two years ago), I was travelling in the Middle East representing my father at some function, and in the airplane there was a patient on a stretcher receiving constant blood transfusions.

When the plane landed it was met by an ambulance and a very high-tech surgical and medical team. They took the patient to the ambulance, and I was met by various dignitaries and members of the Royal Protocol and so forth, and, as the patient was being pushed onto a trolley to get into the ambulance, I was talking with these dignitaries, and one of the doctors who was accompanying the patient looked around and said: "The drip is finished, what is the patient's blood group?

During that flight I had been walking up and down the plane and I had passed next to this patient, and I had noticed the blood group on the bottle of plasma. So when I overheard the doctor say that, I broke off talking to the dignitaries and said to him: "I think he was a group A B, RH positive".

Anyway, the ambulance went off, and I went to the Palace. A couple of days passed and the third day in the evening I was having a private supper with the King, and he said to me: "You are a Hashemi and a Prince, you are the son of a great teacher, and I have a daughter".

And I said "Yes", because he had four daughters and twelve sons, and he went on: "I also hear that you have inherited the family intuition, and that you are an intuitive physician."

So I said: "Yes?"

Of course, what I didn't tell him was that in the Military Academy in Afghanistan, junior lieutenants all do a six month part-time course in rudimentary surgery. This is quite a sensible idea because it is usual in combat to be able to check your casualties so as to be able to discover whether they are dead or alive.

This very sophisticated surgical technique involved, you know, things like how to dig bullets out of people quietly and painfully. Painfully doesn't mean sadistically, it was just to encourage them not to get wounded.

I didn't tell him all this, it wasn't relevant, so then he said: "You see, you are the ideal person for this daughter of mine."

"Ah, yes?" I said.

He said: "Because your family, your lineage, your experience, your good looks, personality and so forth is just the thing." And with my usual modesty I replied: "Of course I am all these things, and more."

And he said: "Especially the intuitive and family healing power which you have".

So I said: "Oh, yes?"

And then he said :"You see, my daughter is young and beautiful, but she is a manic depressive with overtones of paranoia. Occasionally she is dangerously violent, but since this is my country and she is my daughter, we have been able to bury the casualties quietly, but I'm sure that you, with your abilities and tactics and techniques, will be able to improve her no end if you marry her."

So this time of course I obviously could not say: "Oh yes", otherwise I would have had it. Also, I couldn't say "Oh no", because he was a King and I was his guest, and it would have been insulting.

So I said to him: "I am all these flattering things you have said about me, and more. And there have been occasions in my life when I have had moments of deep and acute sadness and this is one of them, because I must reluctantly reject this wonderful offer you have made to me, because my mother has already arranged a marriage for me."

As a matter of fact, this was completely untrue, but when you have to survive in the Middle Eastern context this kind of reason is understood as being inflexible and you are not expected to break it for any reason at all.

To make the story very short, I didn't marry her, as you may have noticed, but next evening I was invited by the Queen to have tea with her and she said: "When you go back to Afghanistan I want you to take back some very special presents for your mother".

So I smiled and thought "Oh yes?", and she said: "There will be a short letter between mothers" and "what sort of present could I send her?" and I said: "Well, actually she has everything. Also, if this is a personal letter, there will be a problem because she can only read Pushtu", which wasn't true.

After a few more days trying they gave up. So you see that this is an area where you can get into trouble by simple observation.

In your relationship with patients, I'm sure you have all experienced patients who are in a state of various types of shock, for instance physical shock or trauma, or else psychological shock.

It could be an area which is sometimes less than precisely described as "psychic shock". There certainly is such a thing as psychic shock and there are an enormous number of causes for it. Sometimes a therapist might identify the existence of psychic shock in a patient to his or her own satisfaction.

There is a school of therapy which says: "Let me, the therapist, together with the patient, uncover the cause of this psychic shock", and hopefully the sharing of the discovery and identification of the source of this shock will help in resolving it.

There can be a perfectly valuable technique or series of techniques in order to produce this discovery, if you like. Whatever technique you use, I'm sure you all know by experience that it can be very harassing or difficult and take place over a very long period.

In the Tradition, we hold that the essential being of the person, if the person is suffering from this state of psychic shock, knows the cause, and also why whatever physical, psychological or physiological reason can bring it out into the daylight and look at it.

In relation to patients who may have this type of psychic shock, part of our technique is to establish, reinforce, maintain and then use the contact between the person's and therapist's essential being in order to enable the basic cause or influence of this psychic shock to become much more speedily apparent to the therapist.

When being is talking to being, they have a common language. If the therapist realizes the existence of this phenomenon, they may then be able to say to themselves: "While treating this patient, I had a feeling, a thought, impression, or image". Try and remember what that image was, what its impact was, what that feeling was.

If you can remember, fine, try and remember the circumstances or the topic of conversation which produced that impact. Whether it took place by ambiance, topic of conversation or whatever, try and produce that same thing again. Compare the two and see if they are approximately the same.

If it is a feeling, either during the therapy session or afterwards, try and get a fairly precise idea of what that feeling was. It could be everything from an actual taste in the mouth, sweetness or acidity or something like that. It may be a feeling of fear, embarrassment, hostility, anxiety. It may have been a picture or an image.

If, for instance, it is an actual physical taste feeling, say bitter or sweet, you don't automatically make a decision that this person's condition or the psychic shock is a direct result of some sort of acid situation. Look at the context of acidity. It may be, you see, that you are not completely or totally in correspondence with their essential being.

So their being is giving you some very primitive reactions or signals.

You might then examine the situation from a physical point of view. What gives a sensation, what is associated or what could be reasonably associated with the idea or context of acidity, or, if you are getting a sweet sensation, what could be associated with that?

Try to feel and analyze the signals, don't over-analyze, don't guess: "Oh, I think it might be that." Again, perhaps the next time, create the same ambiance, maybe have the same topic of conversation and try and confirm that feeling. Don't decide in advance that "when we get to a certain point, in a certain ambiance, I will again taste the acid because you then will": after all, you too can have imagination.

The difference between the correct signal, i.e. being to being, and your interpretative imagination can produce considerable variations. So your contact with the essential being is one of the factors you use, together with your observation, knowledge and other measures you make of the patient.

Correct observation should be confirmed just as a blood analysis is taken and then checked. You don't check it over and over again because that turns it into an anxiety and neurosis situation, so during the treatment, during the conversation and talking, you observe and you make your little notes, but don't forget you are the observer and in that context the observation is only as good as the observer.

The value and necessity of confirming an observation was learned painfully by Mulla Nasrudin. Nasrudin was very lazy and liked comfort, luxury, good food and being spoiled, and one day the Emperor sent for him and said: "Nasrudin, you must get a job."

Nasrudin said: "Your Imperial Highness, I'm very old and fat and weak and my leg hurts and I am deaf and have rheumatism and I fall over my beard and everything".

The Emperor, who knew that he would do or say anything to avoid taking on a job, had already prepared an answer, and said: "Yes, Nasrudin, I know you are old and on the edge of the grave, but I sympathize and have prepared a very comfortable and warm job for you".

"You will sit just inside the gates of the Palace, and you will have a very comfortable and warm little room there. You can do your meditation and prayers and nobody will disturb you; all you have to do is to watch in the morning, when the gates are opened, and make sure they open on time; but the servants will be the ones to open the gates, you don't have to touch them, no effort at all. You'll just sit in the doorway of your little room and occasionally a messenger will come from one part of the Empire or another and ask you for the directions to the Palace, and you don't even have to point, you don't bring them here yourself or anything like that. All you have to do is to say to them: 'Go along this street, turn to the right and then left, and there is the Palace'".

"Depending on the weather in the winter, you will be also given a very comfortable fur robe and you will be paid one gold dirham every three months."

The Emperor also explained the other luxuries he would get, like gifts of food and fresh fruit, all sorts of marvelous things. And then he said: "Nasrudin, I know you are a deep thinker and a philosophical man and I know this job is a heavy responsibility and you may require time to think about it. Would you like to go away to think about it and then come back? In fact, don't even come back, it could be too much trouble for you, send a messenger to me.

"So Nasrudin said: "Yes, I am a philosopher and a wise man. I think I have to examine the situation and weigh the different possibilities. When do I start?"

So the Emperor said: "Well, this is lunch time, a good time to start is now".

Nasrudin then installed himself and the weeks passed, and it was just as the Emperor had promised, the job was not demanding, the conditions were comfortable, he had plenty of food and when an occasional messenger came, he was directed to the Palace, and he was settling down happily.

He usually sat in the doorway of his little room half asleep, watching things going by.

One day the Chief Minister of the Emperor came to Nasrudin and said to him: "Today is the birthday of the Prophet, and the Emperor and all the Court are going in glorious costumes in procession to the Mosque to pray." He added "Of course, it takes a long time for the Emperor and all the courtiers to dress themselves in all these robes, and they want to know what the weather is like outside so as to dress accordingly".

"It's raining heavily" said Nasrudin to him.

So the Chief Minister went back and three or four hours later the drums were beating and the Emperor and all his courtiers in procession approached the gates. The whole procession went out towards the Mosque, and there was no wind outside, there was no air; it was hot as hell and they went to the Mosque in their heavy robes and they were cooked.

The procession came back to the Palace and the Chief Minister came to Nasrudin, beat the tar out of him and threw him out of the Palace. Later, the Emperor was sitting on his throne and the Chief Minister came in holding Nasrudin, and said: "This man has been fighting in the Bazaar and in the streets" and the Emperor said "Now look Nasrudin, why did you send us out to get cooked like that, dressed like fools. I mean, didn't you use your observation to see what the weather was like? It is not too difficult."

And Nasrudin said: "I did use my powers of observation, I was sitting in the doorway of my room and a cat passed by very fast and it was completely wet, so obviously it was raining outside."

So the Emperor said: "Well, it really wasn't a very correct observation, but in any case why were you fighting and who have you been fighting with?"

"I was fighting with the butcher next door, who was responsible for this counterfeit observation."

The Emperor said: "This makes no sense, but explain what you mean."

Nasrudin then said: "It's very simple, the man next door to the Palace is a butcher and a cat came into his shop and was trying to steal meat and he threw a bucket of water on the cat. The cat ran past me, so the fault of the entire episode is on the butcher."

What the Emperor did to Nasrudin, I don't know, it is not recounted. He couldn't have strangled him because the stories of Nasrudin go on, but the temptation must have been very great.

So along with all the other techniques, you know this one because I'm sure all of you use the power of observation. Confirm and compare it by seeing whether your feeling, your training, the situation, ambiance and observation correspond.

Before I leave you all to observe each other, I'll tell you another very quick story which also concerns observation.

Some years ago I was in Saudi Arabia when Feisal, Emir Feisal was King of Saudi Arabia. I was sitting at the table and Feisal was sitting in front of me and various Ministers and Princes were sitting at the same table, and sitting next to me was the Oil Minister, Sheikh Yamani.

Like all of us, Feisal had some idiosyncratic personal habits. He ate very little and when he had finished the meal, a servant would bring a dish of apples. Feisal would look at the apples and then he would take one apple, look at it and then feel another one, look at another one, and then he would choose one of them and the servant would take the tray of apples away, and he would take a knife and start peeling the apple.

Every day, at every meal, he would do the same thing: he would look at one, feel the others, and then after taking one he would peel it, put the peel down and cut it into four pieces.

After four or five days, one evening I said to Yamani: "Do you notice that Feisal always goes through the same procedure with the same sort of precision, at the same speed?"

And Yamani replied : "Yes, from the time he chooses the apple until he peels it, puts the peel down and cuts it into four, every time it takes 85 seconds".

And I understood a thing which I had so far only observed subconsciously, that at every meal, when I was sitting next to Yamani, I could hear: "Bip, bip, bip, bip."

Inside the sleeves of his robe, he was stop-watching the King.

That is called observation.

YA SHIFA

Various friends have asked me the exact meaning and perhaps the context in which the phrase "Ya Shifa" should be used. The phrase "Ya Shifa" is composed of two words: Ya and Shifa. In Arabic, "ya" means "oh" and "Shifa" means "The Healer". Shifa is one of the attributes of God.

Now, as with all of the various attributes of God, it is an attribute, in other words both a word and a whole concept.

The different aspects of this attribute are all the elements which compose a healer, one who heals and everything which is used in the context of healing. When you have a total concept and one uses a word which, in this case, is "Shifa", you are making a distinct and deliberate contact with that concept and everything that concept contains.

The word is both the contact and the key to the totality of the concept and to all the specific type of energy contained therein.

The type of energy within the context of Shifa or "healer" is specific in aiding the process of healing.

I have already spoken to you about involving and bringing out the contact with the essential being both of the person under treatment and of the therapist. In this context as well, a therapist can, does and should employ the type of energy which is contained in the context of Shifa.

Understand that the energy and Baraka contained in any word representing an attribute of God is most certainly and indispensably a positive and enormous energy, but if one wants to use it in a specific therapy or healing context, one should try and employ a specific type of energy.

Most of you will know that the attributes of God represent something; each one represents something which is in a context and one or another of them relate to a circumstance a person might find themselves in.

Obviously and necessarily, there are no stronger or weaker, or good or bad attributes, but there are the ones which one can better apply in a particular situation.

Here's an example. The attribute Hadi means the Guide or the One Who Guides. That is the whole concept. A guide, a path, a road, a map, a light, an indication, a courage to go on. So in the context where a person may need guidance of a physical or spiritual nature, it is indicated and recommended that they would use the words or the zikr Ya Hadi.

If, in that context, they were to use the phrase Ya Shifa, it would certainly not be wrong; God is God and the power of God is the power of God, no matter what the context or the attribute.

However, the quality of the energy or Baraka one is seeking, in the case of Ya Shifa, is the quality of the Healer.

It can be used in a evocative sense. Before commencing a therapy situation, one can, for instance, recite the Bismillah, and after that Ya Shifa, and then commence the process. One can also use it as a zikr with or without the tasbee to help a person who is ill in a present or distant situation.

For instance, in a therapy situation one can silently and

mentally repeat this formula of "Ya Shifa" and pass on part of this energy to the patient. This is also helping to focus the essential being of the person on the activity before them, in a nature and in an atmosphere of healing.

CHECKING SOURCES

This afternoon I received a letter from somebody who isn't present here, which could provoke a number of questions, if it were adopted as a point of view or term of reference. It praises me as being the source of all wisdom, and in the same sentence, accuses me of being the foundation of all evil and so on, saying the same thing over and over in different forms.

The letter itself doesn't worry me, it is not the first one I have received and probably won't be the last; so why do I mention it at all?

Because a term of reference or source of information should always be examined as to whether it is a good source of reference, a good opinion.

In your different disciplines, you accept some authorities as being authorities in your own therapy disciplines; and you apply their opinion or technique in your therapy, adding to it or modifying it according to the patient or situation.

So examine your source of reference and terms of reference very carefully, and satisfy yourself as far as you can whether it is true or false, and in what form you can integrate it into and apply it to your technique.

A false term of reference or a false document will at best make you lose time and effort as you go off on a false trace, and at worst, it will have a detrimental effect on the patient, on your relationship with the patient.

An opinion is therefore only as valid as the source of that opinion. I am repeating here an obvious fact, but again, it is an operative term of reference. Of course, for your own comfort or hysteria or whatever, I myself am not the source of all wisdom, but as far as I know, I am not the source of all evil either.

I'm something moderately insignificant, somewhere in the middle, leaning a little more towards wisdom than evil.

OBSERVATION, TOUCH, PRECOGNITION & ANGELS

I come back to a factor of therapy I have stressed and repeated: observation. Every therapist observes a patient, both automatically and by training, but we are also trying to add another dimension to that observation, which is getting, maintaining and deepening a contact with the essential being of the patient.

Obviously, in order for your observation to be fruitful and produce something positive, you must use correct instruments or terms of reference, so that, as far as possible, you are obtaining true, objective and useful observations of the patient. You don't make the Nasrudin mistake of deciding on something as a result of a single observation, as in the case of the wet cat.

In Afghanistan, I once visited a small village in my part of the country and they were very happy to see me. They are very simple people, they don't have all that much excitement, and if I don't go there regularly, they feel it to be an exciting and pleasant experience for them, which means that they look at me to see how I'm dressed and how I look compared with the last time they saw me.

At that time, in that particular village and for the first time, I was using a pair of half-moon reading glasses.

After a couple of days, I was taking a walk in the evening through some mulberry trees, and, as is usual in villages, there were small groups of men sitting beside the trees. They didn't hear or see me coming, and I overheard them talking about me, and they said : "You know, Agha's family has fallen on hard times to the point where, when he needs glasses, he can only afford half-glasses".

At the same time, some children came up and looked at me and said: "Why are your glasses like that?"; so I said: "Well, I read a lot when I was younger, and when I started they were the proper size, but then they gradually wore out."

So, an observation should be made with the correct terms of reference, and when you make a clinical diagnosis, you should be as confident of that diagnosis as possible.

You tune in to the essential being of the person, you transmit this element and feeling of confidence and energy which goes with it, and you stimulate and encourage within them another very important factor; not just the will to survive but the will to live at all the levels that a human being is capable of.

In trying to produce the Granada Therapy, you are not only using the professional technique you have learned and exercised on a patient, you are using and broadcasting these different contacts and therapies to the different levels of their being.

Throughout history and right up to the present day, some people are said to have had a certain quality. People try and determine that quality and they say: "That person had a touch".

Certainly, energy can also communicate between people as a result of a tactile or touch situation, but you do not limit the contact with your patient to the tactile.

People who are said to have had this "touch" which has made them famous or remarkable have either consciously or unconsciously developed the quality of harmonization within themselves, which they can then focus.

In a therapeutic context you should and normally do respect an additional factor in the therapist-patient relationship, and all of you know this, I'm sure: there is a point or line between you and the patient. It is not a barrier, nor is it a wall, it can be a line produced by the therapist or produced by the patient.

Let us examine this line from the point of view of the patient. It is called "the threshold of privacy", which means the threshold of personal private integrity. This threshold or line exists in some people; sometimes it's more distant from them and sometimes it is closer. A therapist who is working in areas of psychological therapy will regularly come up against this threshold.

Some opinions and disciplines of psychological therapy insist or suggest that this threshold or line should be breached for the therapist to be able to function together with the person at a deeper or more subconscious level than their surface consciousness.

This can be a valid attitude which, again, depends on the patient and the degree of their disturbance.

But this disturbance may also be a combination of both persons' personality threshold, so that we can say that there is no single fixed attitude that a therapist should develop towards this line. It is true that it must be broken through, it must indeed be breached. Nevertheless, you usually have to decide how, in what way, under what circumstances this should be done.

As you all know, a patient may have a conscious feeling of this line or threshold's existence, and they may feel that any attempt to breach it is a violation. For them, such an action may be aggressive, threatening or dangerous, so that the defense mechanism comes up and the person withdraws into themselves.

Once you have identified where that threshold or line is, your skill is to decide how important that threshold or line is to the patient. Are they going to stand and die on that line? Or are they prepared to allow the therapist, if they have confidence in him or her, to allow that threshold to be pushed back gradually?

It is obviously your own observation, judgement and assessment that indicate the flexibility of your technique to you, depending on the psychological state of the patient at that moment. The position of this threshold can fluctuate and a therapist may notice this and call it, I don't know, I'm sure there is a more technical term than this, but let's call it "change of mood", in which one is more receptive or less receptive, more hostile or less hostile. If it is fluctuating, of course, there may be actual psychological reasons for this fluctuation. A therapist should not come and go, nor go away and come back according to the fluctuation of this threshold. They should establish broad contact on various levels and gently push, test, and feel out this resistance.

Naturally, the type of threshold involved, because there are different types of thresholds, depends also on whether the therapist is a male and the patient is a woman, because, basically, the threshold of a man towards a woman or that of a woman towards a man will also be different.

Of course, a therapist can and should establish a situation of: "Look, you are a woman and I am a man but you are a patient and I am a therapist."

Confidence in the confidentiality is naturally understood, but since the primitive nature of a man and a woman reacts to the opposite sex on a primitive level, this is a factor which should be taken into consideration. There are aspects of the essential being in each individual which can be called "primitive"; for instance, a surface and physical reaction or else a deep reaction to cold and sound.

Somewhere in the inner being of the person, and in a very primitive part of that being, a feeling of cold is equated with danger and death, because primitive man had to survive, to find shelter when the temperature dropped.

Nowadays, in present day civilization, a person experiences cold and notices snow or clouds and puts on more clothes or switches on the heating, thus benefitting from technology. And the tiny primitive part of that person is satisfied.

The primitive part of the essential being also reacts to sound, both the actual volume of sound and the nature or tenor of that sound. It was essential to the survival of primitive man for him to react immediately to sound.

Primitive man couldn't analyze the quality of a sound. He didn't stop and listen to a trumpeting animal and say: "That is the sound of a mammoth, I wonder if it is black or grey or old or young. I wonder, is it happy?"; because for him, that train of thought would be terminal. Since he knew it, a millisecond after that sound arrived, he was gone.

What we are discussing here is the question of analyzing the volume of the sound, based on survival. Our primitive man also simultaneously received and analyzed the tone or general tenor of that sound. Now he was not analyzing the musicality or general accuacy of tone of the trumpeting mammoth, because it really didn't matter what its musicality was.

What the primitive man and/or therapist needed to use was the analysis of the tone of the conversation between himself and somebody else, and he learned this by experience and by associating it with changes of tone in the voice, thus identifying two basic things, the friendly harmonic or an inharmonious and hostile tone.

Primitive man didn't have a book or any other type of term of reference, he learned by experience and observation of his own experiences, which could be painful or even sometimes terminal, or else by observation of the tone of a situation.

Within himself, in his own being, he did have knowledge of what tone was friendly and positive and what tone was negative and aggressive. To survive, he had to learn very quickly, because if the people you are talking or meeting with were carrying stone clubs, quite apart from the visual recognition, you had to instantaneously identify their tone of voice and act or react appropriately according to it.

These capacities obviously developed more and more over time, because there was more noise, more things to see, more things to analyze and people learned to be able to ignore the background noises and concentrate on the noises, sights or feelings of a limited and effective situation. They learned to judge and they learned to filter. They were receiving an increasing amount of impacts of a tactile, sight and sound nature, and they realized that if a situation had all three impacts, they could learn to recognize such impacts and hence make use of them by focusing on the more prominent and useful ones.

This recognition or cognition can and should be recognized, enhanced, and developed.

There is a state which people in the West call precognition, which exists in everybody. It has always existed. In fact, the secret of existence, the cosmos and the galaxy, and the various secrets of life itself do and have always existed since the birth of humanity.

Before a child is physically born into the world and before it becomes a being independent of its mother, that child knows the secret of life, of existence, of the cosmos and galaxy.

If a child is born with that knowledge, why doesn't everybody born naturally know that secret and be able to recall it, examine it and talk about it?

The answer is everybody has a depression under their nose, because an Angel places his finger on the baby's lip an instant before birth. Which is why the baby doesn't come out, look up at his mother and say: "Look, the secret is..." The baby knows and has the secret, but cannot speak it.

So, now we have another most interesting subject: the existence and function of Angels and Archangels.

"How many Archangels are there? What are their names? Where are they? When are they around so that we can go and ask them questions? What is the hierarchy of Archangels and Angels?"

And as far as therapists are concerned, which Archangel or Angels have a particular energy, power and authority in which you can participate and with which you can harmonise?

Of course, having led up to the question, I'm certainly not going to give you the answer, except to say: "Yes, there are four Archangels and their names are not written down, but different ones out of the four Archangels have the capacity of all the functions, cosmologically and galactically, and yes, one of them has a specific relationship with the healing process through a chain, a network, a hierarchy of other angelic beings."

Now those of you who live in the West are familiar with the following type of thought: "Such and such is the Patron Saint of such and such a profession"; based on some kind of race memory or some historical event or situation.

Some of this kind of selection is fairly accurate and some of it is random. There are those which are based on cosmic realities; others, which have not the same quality are those which have been given to or adopted by a profession.

For instance, you have a group or a society in which there is a new activity, and perhaps it is a very new discipline they are engaged in which is not traditionally associated with a particular

Angel or Saint, so they go through the complicated process of sending a deputation to the Bishop, the Cardinal or the Vatican to be given a Patron Saint. And after what I am sure is adequate consideration, prayer and fasting in the Vatican, they are given a Patron Saint. And one hopes that the Vatican uses terms of reference, points of view, feelings which will provide a harmonious Patron Saint.

If the existence of an Angel or a Patron Saint can be a form of reassurance and a guarantee of contact, fine, why not? There is nothing against it, assuming the relationship is functional and not superstitious.

Actually the mental and theological and tactical gymnastics the Vatican uses in deciding such cases is quite extraordinary. Who is the Patron Saint of Computer Engineers?

There has to be and hopefully usually is some relationship between that profession and some aspects in the quality of the Patron Saint. So if there is a contact in the quality of the Patron Saint or Angel to the discipline, it is then processed through the discipline to the people who are involved or who receive the effects or benefits of that discipline.

In all cosmic and galactic circumstances, and this also applies to the human context, there are harmonies and harmonics. One does not force a harmony. Harmony is established and maintained. If it is obviously and by definition a forced harmony, it does not have a harmonic, because the inner being of that person is constrained into harmonizing with that hostile or forced harmonic, and you have a situation of chaos and anxiety.

If the flow of harmonic and energy is constantly present in a flexible and fluid nature, you have the flexible rigidity situation. Take, use and exercise this energy, this harmonic. In therapy situations this harmonic, this energy passes through you.

Now some of this energy and harmonic remains with you. You are not just a tube or a wire through which something is passing, you are human.

There is also a type of harmonic, of energy you receive which passes through you and out of you to a patient or to another person, either because you do not need that specific and particular type of energy at that moment, or because you have that quantity and quality already, and in that context, yes, you are a wire or a tube. You may therefore pass it to another person, or a patient who will then use it and harmonise with it; and they, in turn, may carry it as a carrier to pass on the benefit to another person.

Every time you function as a therapist in the Tradition, your intention is to help, to benefit, to cure. By using a quality of energy from the Tradition you are also directly benefitting and developing yourself.

So we come back to the harmony you have. Feel comfortable with it; feel it as something you have worked for, which you have earned, and which hopefully you merit.

Feel the confidence that it gives you, and transmit, in turn, that confidence or some aspects of that confidence, to your patients. Focus on their essential being, stimulate their will to live and recover.

The will to live, the will to recover is already there. It may lay very deep, it may be covered over with layers of all sorts of conditioning and other rubbish.

If you accept that it is there, the next step is, as I say, to establish a positive contact.

TOWARDS THE GRANADA THERAPY

I would like to start by giving you one or two of my impressions and observations: you are progressing towards the Granada Therapy. I am relatively satisfied but there are still one or two aspects I think you still have to work on.

Certainly, I did suggest that you explain and, to a certain degree, compare your different disciplines of therapy in order to try and see which aspect of your own therapy could be put into the Granada Therapy, with your different aspects of them complementing other aspects.

These aspects of your disciplines are not in competition with each other and not pulling or working against each other. A therapist is not supposed to learn all the other therapies which exist among you and apply them all in the same situation.

Let us take an example of an inharmonious use of several useful techniques of therapy or diagnosis: it is a situation in a clinic on the planet Coca Cola.

A patient is admitted to the hospital suffering from abdominal pain and the initial testing diagnoses acute appendicitis. So the surgeon consults the necessary X-rays and other tests and then he calculates the horoscope of the patient, makes up his own horoscope and compares the two, and then he consults Tarot cards and then he has a cup of coffee while his assistant massages the patient with aromatic oils.

The surgeon, having finished his coffee, does a half hour zikr, examines his being and then goes into the operating theatre and creates harmony in the operating theatre by singing and playing the guitar. He anesthetizes the patient with a martial arts karate blow, and then he sits in on the post-mortem of the patient to confirm the diagnosis, the cause of death, which was unsurprisingly, peritonitis and associated conditions.

In certain proportions and in certain aspects, all of these things are valuable and useful. A useful thing he did was to do his zikr, and a second useful thing was to have a cup of coffee. This "total therapy" can therefore be terminal for the patient. And in the professional area, it does not enhance the reputation of the surgeon.

What I will therefore encourage you to do is to see what part, what segment of your discipline, you can put into the building up of the Granada Therapy that can be used in a practical and efficient way.

What is the nature of illness? It is actually a physical and organic condition or a psychic condition. It can be lack of balance in the essential being of the person, reflecting into the physical body or with both aspects reflecting into the psychic make up of the person and producing an imbalance or dysfunction of a part of the body or mind. Lack of balance in a system or function produces a surface physical effect.

An aspect of this is called psychosomatic. If you are faced with a patient showing what you diagnose as being psychosomatic symptoms, you most certainly try and use techniques you have learned to analyze, and you treat this condition.

It may very well be that the exterior manifestation of this psychosomatic condition can be handled by the conventional psychotherapy disciplines you have learned, but add another factor, which is the recognition of the existence of the essential being of the person. Do not consider that you cannot make a contact with the essential being of that patient.

However it is true that by conventional means or conventional surgery, you cannot necessarily do this. So you should be developing this deep contact and trying to examine it at the same time as you are perhaps physically examining the person, or else when you are probing or applying psychological tests, try and let your being probe or communicate with their being.

See whether you feel there is a degree of imbalance and then remember that this is an ongoing contact, it's not that you get an impression back and stop with it at that point. If you do this on that level, you can get erroneous or false signs, and you yourself can make a false analysis of true signals.

The essential being of a person can suffer from certain categories of existence. The essential being of a person can be disturbed, or else fatigued or tired in a certain context. The essential being of a person may be suffering from a lack of energy.

As far as you can, you are trying to analyze the person's essential being in very delicate terms. This narrows down the terms of reference, the scanning which you are trying to develop.

You are not trying to look at a person's essential being to see whether it has got a broken leg. In such a case the area of diagnosis of fractures and bone condition is useful, but not on this level. If the patient obviously has a broken leg, you hopefully reach for plasters, splints and a bandage, and not a pack of Tarot cards.

You do not look at your own or another person's essential being with an attitude or approach which could even vaguely be considered hostile or aggressive. You should not give any impression or have any attitude which could be considered in any way embarrassing or demanding in relation to that essential being.

The human system, the human body and its associated psychological mechanisms, if you like, are hungry for balance; it knows it needs balance and it wants to be fit and well. Very often a state of illness will be the absence of the impulsion to help itself. This is natural, because nobody wants to be ill; they would like to be able to summon up their whole being and will to live.

So you connect with this being or will to live, and awaken within the person the taste of a feeling for what it is like to be fit and healthy. They may have lost the way to use themselves, to use their own system in order to maintain this equilibrium; but they have not and do not lose the capacity and ability to help themselves.

Certainly, if they are ill or in a situation where they need surgical intervention, say if they have got a broken bone, then of course they need the technical expertise of a surgeon or somebody to set that bone. Then, the system alerts itself to go into the healing or the cure mode.

Regarding the post-operative phase: this is not only correct nursing, massage and other factors like psychological counseling, gradual exercise, and correct diet, which are all necessary and familiar to you; you are also encouraging them to add the other factor by stimulating their will to live, recover and become healthy.

You are stimulating and encouraging that person's essential being to push that will to live and to exercise it's energy.

To a certain degree and according to their own personality, therapists usually structure their approach or attitude to a patient by experience and practice. They quite naturally react to certain attitudes or emissions from the patient.

They are not controlled or taken over by such emissions from the patient. They structure their attitude and approach to relax the patient, to establish a rapport and they establish a harmonious situation and relationship.

You already know that I keep on repeating the word harmony. You are introducing the contact with the essential being. You can introduce this other factor into this situation, into this context.

For instance, you can introduce or have present in the consulting room or clinic, an emblem or something else from the Tradition. That symbol corresponds with you, corresponds with the situation and is impacting on the patient, whether the patient recognizes it or not.

Don't forget, this condition is a qualitative impact. You can have a symbol, but you shouldn't have all your walls covered with symbols. If you did this, a patient could react in a defensive way or have a confused reaction on a very primitive level, because "These things are alien" and they don't understand them, or else they are "from another culture" and on a primitive level, they can feel tense or uncomfortable.

If, for instance, one is establishing a rapport with a patient and they happen to comment on a symbol, you can tell them something which you think will be useful to their state of mind, as much or as little as you like, depending on their attitude, or in what way or what question they might ask about that particular symbol.

For instance if they say: "What is that?", you hopefully don't reply: "None of your business, stupid!"

You can say, for instance: "I don't know, I bought it or picked it up somewhere, etc.

You can also take it down, turn it to the wall or take it away and continue the conversation.

The presence or absence of that symbol has, again, a flexible energy connection. If you know it is there, you relate to it.

If, because of the horror of the patient, you take it away or turn it to the wall to calm him down, you know it exists, you know it is there, so it hasn't disturbed the rapport between yourself and that symbol, and it's influence or impact on the patient, whether the symbol is absent or present, then comes through you.

This holds equally true for any symbol or object from the Tradition. Whether it's an object, a robe, a tasbee, a kilim on the floor, a piece of material on your desk or anything like that, you do not overdo it, you don't do what is called overkill, even if these things are functional in themselves and generate energy.

The harmonic with the patient is mainly established by you personally and their confidence and hope factor is increased by the reasonably confident attitude you have towards them.

You are transmitting confidence and sympathy on a social level at the same time; for instance, the patient may also be taking note of all the framed diplomas you have on the wall behind you. In fact, they are looking and hoping for a positive attitude on all sorts of levels from you. So you use all possible positive factors which are positive to you and which transmit and create confidence in that patient. You are projecting confidence, contact and positivity both on the surface and on all other levels.

One day Nasrudin was looking for a job and he thought: "What is the successful job or profession which will produce a lot of money without much effort?"

So he walked around town and watched the number of customers at the butcher's and the baker and the fruit merchant, and he looked to see how much money they were taking in, and said: "The butcher makes quite a lot of money but it's a bit of an effort buying the animals and cutting them up. Bakers and fruit-sellers also have problems; they have to get up early, go to the market, buy the produce, and then clean it and arrange it."

"But out of all these people with shops, probably a good one would be to open a carpet shop, because I understand and like carpets, and another thing, if I have loads and piles of carpets, it is very comfortable to lie down and sleep on them."

So he had more or less decided that he would open a carpet shop.

Then he went to a café to have tea with his friends and said: "Well, you know, commerce is wonderful, buying and selling good objects is a good thing, you can get a fine income from it"; and someone said: "Yes, but you know, it's much more socially acceptable and prominent to have a profession like a doctor, lawyer, dentist or architect. People will respect your opinion, listen to you when you talk, and if you are a good professional, you can make quite a good income."

So he went home and thought: "Dr. Nasrudin sounds good."

So he went to town again and visited doctors, lawyers, dentists, architects and other people in the professions and he saw that they had quite a number of clubs, so he set himself up and asked if he could join.

Their reply was: "Yes, that's a perfectly good idea, but there is one considerable problem which we feel does not provoke the necessary confidence in the patient, because in the frame behind you on the wall, unfortunately, there is a painting of your donkey."

Certainly one uses skill, technique to create an ambiance and contact, and you then build on it and deepen it and use it, instilling confidence and contacting the essential being to stimulate the person's will to live.

I advise you to try and chop off certain extraneous aspects of your therapies; try to match the essential part of your therapies to the essential part of the other therapies.

When you go back home from this Congress, read your notes, listen to the tapes and try to take a piece of paper and write down the central aspect, the central value of your own particular discipline. Communicate by letter, by telex, by conversation with other people who hopefully are doing the same, and see how they can be related together.

TERMINAL AND OTHER CONDITIONS

As you may have heard, I will be leaving tomorrow. As far as my timetable is concerned, I have performed my function, and the Conference will continue on as scheduled, depending on your various programs and travel plans.

You will have the opportunity, I hope, of taking your own notes, videos and certain recordings back with you. During the remainder of this Conference, I would recommend that you discuss, compare and examine points of view and ideas which can best be communicated when you are together here, and that you establish a strong basis for exchange of ideas, both individually and group to group. As I have said before, maintain a good and high level of contact.

Conferences like this produce a high degree of togetherness and harmony, but there should not be a complete fall-off between conferences. Establish a degree of contact, and try as best as possible to maintain a high level of exchange and information.

I would like to touch briefly on two or three matters involving aspects of and attitudes in the Tradition, and which also deal with one or two questions I have recently been asked.

Since the reply to some of these questions will be especially valuable to certain people, I have not replied to the person who originally asked me, because I consider that the answer might be valuable and useful for everybody.

The first question concerns the contact, nursing and treatment of patients with terminal conditions.

One can also include in this category people who are psychically or physiologically severely disturbed.

In the area of normal nursing and care, most of you know what to do technically. But how do you handle the situation that it may create within yourselves?

When you leave the clinic or hospital, the patient remains there, but you go away with the feelings and sensations you have had with that contact. It can certainly be difficult and emotionally disturbing, especially if one has established a reasonable bond of contact and sympathy with that individual, and this can happen even if you are trying to maintain a certain distance between yourself and the patient.

Even if it may seem otherwise, the effect of the negative or emotional situation created within the therapist is, however, only a surface effect. It can be very strong and visual, but I am calling it a superficial or surface effect because it doesn't penetrate into the deeper levels of a person's being.

A person has several protections against this emotion or

negativity. One is because they have a contact with the Tradition; they are protected by the energy and influence created by their zikr or Sirr, and, in a very tangible and tactile way, by their tasbee and their crystal.

One of the functions of the tasbee is to remove the negative from a person using it. The negative charge or negative energy does not remain in the tasbee, it is destroyed by contact. The same is true for the crystal. The tasbee or crystal receives it, identifies it and destroys it. One can therefore use it if one is emotionally disturbed by this contact, repeating at the same time, to oneself, the zikr or Sirr.

An even more simple tactic is to ground the negativity through a natural object connected to the earth. Stone, wood, a wall of stone or a wall of wood can be used, and this emotional, nervous, negative charge is absorbed.

Certainly, in the visual or present memory, there are traces of this negativity. These charges or impulses can be greater or less, according to one's relationship with the patient and how much one identifies with that patient.

I am not telling you to abandon or to change your very human feelings of sympathy. I'm not encouraging you to become like stones, I am only telling you about and showing you techniques of how to discharge negativity.

The same techniques hold true if one is dealing with a terminally ill patient or a very severely psychologically disturbed person. Therapists not only can and should discharge a patient's negative energy, but they can and should produce and transmit positivity to the patient.

Such tactics and techniques are not only useful, they should be constantly exercised and used. You should not hesitate or wonder: "Is it right?" or "When?"

It is useful to be in constant contact with the organism. In this sense, I am talking about the cosmic organism.

The cosmic organsim is not an abstract. It is so vast, in that it encompasses all Creation, that most creatures use or recognise only those parts or influences of it which directly impinge upon them.

Such contact, usefully and correctly used, can be developed, albeit with effort.

The Granada therapy, the basic truths of which lie in the Tradition, will be formed by those experienced in all aspects of the healing process. It will call, clearly and unequivocally, for a pact between the patient and the therapist. A pact which forges a positive link between them and through which a positive flow of energy can be passed and focused, by both, on the problem.

The patient must be taught to mobilize the body's natural defenses, considering their mental or physical ailment or imbalance to be THE ENEMY.

Brutal and implacable the enemy may appear, but it can and will be beaten.

EDITOR'S ADDENDUM
CONTRIBUTION TO THT CONGRESS GRANADA 1994

ON BEING CURED

I take the floor here to speak to my friends in the Sufi Tradition about therapy not only because I edited Agha's tapes to turn them into a halfway readable book, thus granting myself the right to spread myself across these subtle and relevant talks like peanut butter, but also because I am totally unencumbered by any knowledge of the subject, which gives me a freedom of opinion which none of you have.

Nevertheless, my knowledge of illness and therapy is the knowledge which I share with almost every man that walks the earth: I have been ill and I have been cured, although I suppose technically that if one considers that the original illness or wound took place at birth, I am only in a state of temporary remission until the inevitable end.

I do think, however, that the experience of illness was a useful one, and so my contribution is offered here from the point view of the patient, because in a congress of dairymen, who listens to the cow?

So here's the story of an illness and the story of a cure, along with a few questions and jokes of a more general nature that I will attempt to draw from my own experience, and which congress attenders may or may not wish to use as part of their discussion.

One day in the late spring of 1985, my wife and I were looking at a television discussion programme of mind-numbing idiocy, in which the star of the show was a French pianist and musical promoter called Eddy Barclay, whose chief claim to fame seems to be that he has been married an amazing number of times, knows a lot of movie stars, and has a very user-friendly approach to the media.

We were in the midst of looking at this amiable and mindless TV pap when Mr.Barclay mentioned he had just recovered from a cancer. In response to the interviewer's question, Barclay said that he had had a sore throat which didn't get better for a long time, and that he had seen a doctor who had diagnosed throat cancer. He had then undergone treatment and was all right at the present time.

My wife and I looked at each other: it was just the symptom I had been complaining about for the past few weeks. The next day, Catherine got the name of a throat specialist from a friend and made an appointment for me. The doctor did the normal thing of prescribing antibiotics, which had no effect. I went back to him two weeks later, he looked down my throat again, asked me to drop by a clinic where he worked, and without saying what it was for, took out an instrument rather like sugar tongs and withdrew a little piece of phlegm from my throat for further perusal.

When he asked me to come to his office the following week to discuss the results of the lab test with me, I was not entirely surprised to find that a "rampant and invasive carcinoma" had lodged itself on my right tonsil. I had just been through a difficult year. Professionally, I had subtitled two feature films, had been cheated out of payment and I had also had a great disappointment in the Tradition, which I mention here because disappointment, anger and the desire for power can take over the best of us and even affect one's body, and the incident is worth mentioning as a cautionary tale. I had proposed to Agha to try and start up a group in New York City, where a number of people who had previous connections to the Tradition were residing, and I had initiated exercises there in the previous autumn. I was appointed responsible and was then relieved of the job less than a month later. Nowadays, I would regard such an event as a blessing, but at the time I took it harder.

So if I look at my situation in the summer of 85, I have a number of parallel personal and professional frustrations in action. My family and interpreting work is going well, but this doesn't really make me happy because I want to be a writer and a big time Sufi Star. Yes, I know that this is a contradiction in terms, but I am a human being too. I feel unloved and unappreciated by my teacher. I am angry and am probably undergoing a classic mid-life crisis.

At the age of forty-five, I look ten years younger, my hair is blond, not white, and I seem to be in the pink. I am an atypical patient insofar as I neither smoke nor drink, and the doctors at the hospital think I have such pretty teeth that I'll go through a whole fluoride bathing process in order to keep them from being yanked out for the radiotherapy. I am being treated in Paris at the Hôpital Pierre et Marie Curie which is specialized in radiotherapy whereas the Villejuif cancer hospital, according to medical scuttlebutt, is more specialized in chemo and surgery. My cancer appears to be in a yet fairly undeveloped state, so radiation appears to be the way to go. I put out of my mind the fact that the Curies' discovery of radium cost them their lives and try to think positively about my treatment.

I phone Agha to give him the news of my cancer. He has already been told about it and the Paris group has already spontaneously convened to do the Ya Shifa exercise to give me strength. Agha does not say very much, but there is one thing he says which I will carry to my grave: "It is your enemy and you want to kill it." In other words, no bullshit about "coming to terms" with whatever. It's a fight to the death; the cancer or me.

While I am under treatment, groups throughout Europe, Spain and South America perform exercises on my behalf. Many people among us today today participated in these exercises, and besides thanking them, there is little I can say beyond the simple fact that I am still with you nine years later. I have absolutely no idea whether or not this effort produced any medical effects, but this I can say: one of the things one drags along behind a difficult and lonely childhood is a feeling of being everlastingly condemned to being unloved and unwanted. When I saw what the possibility of my death meant to the friends all over the world, let alone to my family, this feeling disappeared forever never to return.

Of course, if one wants to look at my illness realistically, the cure rate of throat cancers is between eighty and ninety percent.

Also, at that time, Aids hadn't yet pushed cancer out of the scarecrow's limelight. But as a poet, it suits me to present myself as a man of indomitable courage, my jaw nobly clenched and staring into the middle distance as I face down my own death.

When they were rolling me into the operating theatre for the endoscopic examination to determine that the tumour has not developed elsewhere, somebody puts a card into my hand. I am already fairly heavily drugged with local anesthetic when I look at the card and begin yelling at the top of my voice: "Stop, stop, the wrong instructions have been given!"

Doctors and nurses come pounding down the corridor, saying "You musn't get worked up like that, you're going into an operation, you've got to calm down." I hold up the card, and they all look at it blankly and then look back at me, saying "Yes, so what?"

On the card is written "Remove all teeth".

Just then the dentist who had first examined me comes walking by, whistling, with his hands in his pockets. He bends down over me to see what the fuss is all about, takes the card and tears it up, saying "Honestly, the bloody fools" and ambles on into theatre.

When they wheel me in, the dentist and the head doctor are immersed in a conversation that has begun some time before. They pursue their dialogue as they delicately ram the instrument down my throat for the recording.

"Here at Curie, we're doing work which is just as good as those guys over in Villejuif."

"You betcha" says my dentist.

"But I tell you what, you know why all the funding goes to Villejuif?"

"Why?" says the dentist.

"Because of the media, that's why" says the head honcho.

"Schwarzenberg?" says the dentist.

"Exactly" replies Big Doc, "He's President Mitterrand's blue-eyed boy. He's the top talking head on television, ask him about any medical question, he'll come up with a thirty-second opinion that'll fit in nicely before the commercial break."

"They get the coverage and they get the money" says the dentist sadly. "All we get is the leftovers here. Our radiation machinery is down half the time and the new stuff is being installed in Villejuif" says the head doctor, "But I tell you, what we're doing here at Curie is as good as anything else in the world, and the boys and girls here do it just as good as Schwarzenberg."

"Gotta get more coverage" says the dentist.

They both look at the endoscope for a moment, and the doctor says to the dentist, "Tell him to keep still a minute, will you?"

The dentist leans over me and says: "Do you mind holding still a second, so that we can get another reading?"

Terrified, I make myself stiff as a board.

I hear a whirring and then it stops. The head doctor comes over to me as I lie on the table looking up with the probe still stuffed down my throat. He speaks to me for the first time: "It's all right, there aren't any secondaries" he says.

Back upstairs in the hospital room, the anesthetic is wearing off, and Catherine brings me my mail from home. I open a letter from Brazil: a beautiful and sweet young lady from among the friends is shocked to learn of my illness and wants me to get better. She even knows of a former priest who is specialized in healing cancers, and she will be sending me some herbs from the Amazon basin I should take. The only thing is that in order for this cure to work, I must make sure that I don't submit to any modern technology like chemotherapy or radiation.

When the course of radiation begins at the hospital, I protect myself as much as I can from other patients' emotions by getting there at eight o'clock in the morning and being the first to go under the machine. An added advantage of going in first is that the machinery is still working: breakdowns generally happen later in the day, and the cyclotron or whatever it's called seems to break down at least twice a week.

As I lie on the slab I recite myself the Fatiqa, my zikr and the Ya Shifa. Gazing up at the needle, I think of the ceiling of the chamber of the Two Sisters at the side of the Court of the Lions in the Alhambra. I don't know why I do this. Perhaps because those ceilings reflected in the water below in their infinite metamorphosis, are the most beautiful places I know. The machine above me is similarly relentless.

The head doctor of the department, the media expert referred to above, generally comes to work at about the time I am laid out on the table beneath the machine. I am there every day on the table at eight-thirty, and every morning he walks in, says hello to the attendant, and ignoring me, casually puts his hand on my neck to feel the tumour. At this time of course, my arms and legs are strapped down and I feel quite humiliated at being handled in this casual way without any kind of acknowledgement of my presence at all. I am a throat and I am a tumour, but I am not a person.

Either I am going to give this uncaring idiot a piece of my mind, or else I am going to have to do something else: create some kind of relationship. For reasons of obvious self-interest, I don't want to antagonize the doctor that's treating me, so I pursue the latter course. The opportunity presents itself when he speaks English to me; I congratulate him on his good English, and he tells me how he finished his oncology studies at Harvard Medical School. We get into the habit of speaking to each other in English every day, and he gets a kick out of showing his excellent English off to the other members of his department.

After about three weeks of daily treatment during which I get my daily feel-up in passing, he pauses a moment, and then puts his hand back on my neck one more time, keeping it there for a while. He pauses for reflection, and then asks the nurse to call everybody into the radiation chamber immediately, even if they are with other patients. When the whole department of about twenty people is assembled, he informs them that the placement of the rays for my tumour has been carelessly aligned, that the way to the tumour is blocked by the jawbone and thus not entirely bombarded by radiation and that if things were simply left to take their course, about one-fifth of the tumour in my neck would still be there at the end of the treatment cycle. Since radiation cannot normally be practised twice over in the same place, the patient would be forced into other forms of treatment because the department was too careless to do its job properly.

The doctor's cold fury is quite impressive, and it scares me half out of my wits. After all the minions troop out, he smiles at me and goes back to speaking English again. "Don't worry" he says, "with all the hundreds of tumors we deal with in this place, it's very easy for the doctors to fall into their routines, and I've got to wake them up from time to time."

"I'm using you as an excuse. We'll add on three or four extra radiation sessions, change the angle of the machine, and as far as you're concerned, it won't make any difference."

Anyway, as you know, this story has a happy ending, since I am here to tell it. Suffice it to say that I enjoy good health and my tumour never came back.

But I think this story raises a number of therapeutic considerations that may be worth discussing or at least thinking about. Because I am talking about my own case history here, I feel I know some of the answers, but not all. For instance, I have no idea if it was the radiation, my own prayers, the prayers of the friends, Agha's prayers or the increase in my own self-confidence and self-trust as a result of the attention paid to me that backed me and my immune system up enough to deal with this illness.

The following points can be raised:

1) If I had listened to my sweet and tender friend from Brazil and had foregone high-tech therapy, would I still be alive to tell the tale, or to put it another way, would she have my blood on her hands? After all, the beginning of wisdom is knowing where your knowledge stops, and the relationship between "soft" and "hard" medicine is obviously important. Also, this knowledge should include a clear awareness of possible distortion. The recent example of the mad homeopath cult leader Luc Jouret leading his followers into what can only be called terminal homeopathy is there to show us how dangerous the prestige of medicine can be when divorced from the Hippocratic Oath and turned towards cultist manipulation.

In fact, the knowledge of how cults work is quite a useful tool in dealing with things like hospital intrigues etc. The pyramidal authority structures of medical bodies everywhere encourage cult situations; and an abundant literature shows this to be quite characteristic, for instance, of psychiatric associations over the last century.

Of course, there is no limit to the arrogance of high-tech medicine, as well, because there is so much money involved. How much research money goes into plants or "soft" options? Pharmaceutical companies are heavily committed to new and better molecules to the exclusion of other options, because the former will produce saleable allopathic medicines with a measurable effect. How do you measure a psychiatrist or a homeopath?

Even genetic engineering is undergoing a tremendous funding problem as people find out that the applications aren't going to earn their money back as quickly as was first thought, and the investors are disappearing in droves.

On the other hand, every discipline has its craft. If that arrogant old doctor had not had all that knowledge in his hand, I might not be here to tell the story.

2) What is the difference in therapy between training and craft? At what point does the craft come in, and how is it possible for it to be recognized by those who are not in possession of it?

3) To what extent is it possible to use the "Granada Therapy" as an adjunct to one's training?

4) What are the limits to a therapy based on inner balance and harmony? If I want to throw myself out of the window, do you stop me or stand by and wring your hands?

5) How and when does one move onto "heavier" techniques, and what criteria does one use to do so?

6) Is there a thesis to be written on the curative properties of the Alhambra?

And finally, a few words on the brain and consciousness. Informed opinion in the sixties and seventies seemed to think that the likeliest analogy to the workings of the brain was the computer. This led to a whole raft of articles and books about "cybernetic" awareness, in which the brain was likened to some sort of ultimate calculating machine.

Just as the computer has developed and changed immensely since that time, so-called "informed" thinking about the brain and our perception has changed as well. The analogy for the way the brain works is no longer a finite system of calculation like the computer, but an infinitely variable system of reactive adaptation which more than anything else resembles the body's own immune system.

In other words, physiological analysis itself is now saying our intelligence does not come from the amount of information we acquire, but from the flexibility with which we deploy it, and nowadays we are being told this not by philosophical argumentation but by the latest microbiological research.

By now, most of you who have managed to read this far will have understood the drift of my argument. It is very simply that traditional learning systems, including the Sufi Tradition, have always worked on this basis, i.e. flexibility as opposed to accumulation, adaptation as opposed to construction. We can be pleased or perhaps somewhat bemused that physiological research should at last be catching up with us, but our own problem remains constant, which is the age-old one of integrating this capacity for change into the innermost part of our nature.

Nevertheless, it may be that our way of thinking can make a breach in the fanatical borderline that exists between "hard" and "soft" therapies, and between "hard" and "soft" science. As research hots up in the attempt to find some kind of solution to the HIV virus, most people are still working in terms of some sort of pharmacological barrier, but there are others who are trying to enable the immune system to mutate even faster than the virus. We'll see who wins the race.

Our way of thinking is timeless, but unfortunately, we aren't. Therapist or no therapist, if we can communicate the love in our hearts to the people we come across, we have done something, whether it can be measured or not.

Augy Hayter   Oct. 94

THE SAGA CONTINUES

Less than six months after the above words were written, an unknown hand reached up from within my throat and struck me down again.

At seven in the morning on Saint Valentine's Day, I rose up from my armchair intending to take my morning trip to the toilet, when I felt to my horror that my sphyncter had let it all go, and I had pitched over onto my side and was wriggling around face-down on the carpet, quite unable to get myself upright again. I rolled myself onto my back but it didn't help me because the left side of my body was paralyzed and I couldn't use my left hand, arm or leg.

I never lost consciousness throughout this incident and realized very quickly that I had myself some kind of brain stroke with hemiplegia. When I called to Catherine for help I realized that I wasn't talking too well either. She came in and immediately called the SAMU (French emergency medical service) explaining the symptoms. They were there in fifteen minutes, with a doctor in attendance who was administering a blood thinner a quarter of an hour after my stroke had declared itself.

My memory of that day is somewhat patchy, because a lot of people took care of me, but I remember being taken to the neurological ward in the evening, I remember some very courageous people wiping me clean, and most of all I remember recovering the use of my hand, arm and leg by nightfall. "Il a la baraka, celui-là" said one of the doctors to another outside my door (it should be realized that baraka means good luck in French slang).

So once again, I had danced over towards the edge and had pulled back before going over.

Then came the observation period in hospital and all of the tests and scans and arterial checks to see what happened. A small blood clot had disloged itself from my right carotid artery; both carotid arteries were highly blocked, which was strange insofar as the rest of my arteries were in good shape; I had no high blood pressure and neither smoked nor drank. With the help of the cancer specialist that had worked on my radiation ten years ago, it was finally decided that it was the external radiation I had received for my throat through my neck at that time that had caused a deterioration; I had been irradiated through both carotid arteries, and the buildup of platelets in the artery was situated exactly in the irradiated area.

When I was taken in for surgery, I had still not yet met the surgeon who was going to be wielding the scalpel (a situation which is quite frequent in France where they feel that knowledge is best left to the experts). So when they started to administer the anasthetic, I refused to be taken into the operating room unless I was personallly introduced to the surgeon. This message was relayed on with delight by the nurses, and within a few minutes a very angry-looking man was looking down at me from over his surgical mask.

"What's going on here?" he asked me indignantly, "I have studied your file and I know it backwards."

At that point I relaxed and let them knock me out. I was a file, not a being.

I woke up looking like Robocop or Frankenstein with a very fetching zipper on my throat. The scar took about a month to absorb and doesn't look too bad now. Then I had to go back in and get the right hand artery flushed out and cleaned. The second artery was apparently in a worse state, and had to be wrapped up in a Dacron backing; when I saw this in my medical file, I had a fantasy about having one of those terrible drip-dry shirts from my youth sewn into my neck.

As I write these words I am about three weeks past the second operation: the scar is healing but the nerves around my gullet have been affected, and I can't yet feel myself swallow.

I have seen specialists who say that my cleft palate should normally heal, that my voice will come back in time, and that liquids will eventually stop backing up and pouring out through my nose whenever I try to swallow. Anyway, I make my way through each day with the help of painkillers, and I expect things to get better over time.

To my great shame I have forgotten the name of the young

Brazilian lady who offered to send me herbs from the Amazonian basin, and I hope she forgives me. I am now not far from thinking that she was the one who was right all along the line, and that my own patronizing attitude towards her efforts was just another episode in the endless superiority complex of western technological medicine over its native bretheren. Then again, an Amazonian leaf my be just as efficient a murder weapon as a surgeon's scalpel.

After all, I must pay homage to the talents of the doctors who took care of me. Hi-tech medicine is indeed a most wonderful instrument for dealing with the problems it creates.

Augy Hayter May 95